Dress for SEXcess

Cover illustration comments:

The ScissorMan modifications made on the cover outfit are as follows:

The rear-pocket cutouts on the jeans, with a glimpse of bare butt showing, is from chapter 6, "**Advanced Jeans Modifications**."

The visible side of the front breast showing the vest-pocket cutout, with pocket flap still buttoned up, is from chapter 4, "**How My Imagination Developed More Ideas**."

The large back-of-the-vest heart shaped cutout from waist to shoulders, showing lots of bare back skin, is from chapter 8, "**More Top Modifications**."

There is another jeans modification that does not show in the picture but which will make a Husband **VERY HAPPY.** It is the "**Great Idea**" I discovered in chapter 3, "**Why I Got Started with the Scissors and My First Great Idea**."

The big come-hither smile on her face shows a completely satisfied wife after the way her husband has responded to the new ideas they have both been trying from *Dress for SEXcess*.

Dress for
SEXcess

New Ways to Dress Up and Decorate the
Female Body in Very SEXually Attractive Ways
on a Tight Budget for More Variety, More Fun,
More Sex, and a Happier Marriage

ScissorMan

Master
LOVER
P U B L I S H I N G

© Copyright 2015 Master Lover Publishing
Wyckoff, New Jersey 07481
www.MasterLoverPublishing.com
www.DressForSEXcess.com

ISBN: 978-0-9837189-1-8

I am asking all the readers of my book to please write an honest review of this book and please post it on the page for my book on **Amazon.com** and any other places that you know for readers to post book reviews. At least a few words about it would be appreciated.

Please also post the review on the review page at my book website, **DressForSEXcess.com**

Please also **take the free survey** linked to the **DressForSEXcess.com** review page to register your opinions about what features on a woman a man likes best. The men's version asks guys to rate what visual aspects of a woman's appearance they like best. The woman's version asks the gals to give their opinions of what they think men like best. I think the results of what men like most will be interesting, and I am very interested in what the differences will be from the women's viewpoint.

Acknowledgments
Art work – Felipe VanRompaey
Primary editing help – Joseph Kranak.
Formatting text – Sarco Press
Formatting cover – Hitendra Talaviya

Dedicated to the sweetest, sexiest, most wonderful girl in the world

My wonderful wife.

Disclaimer:

Although the author and publisher have made every effort to ensure that the information in this book was correct at press time, the author and publisher do not assume and hereby disclaim any liability to any party for any loss, damage, or disruption caused by errors or omissions, or for any potentially risky behavior suggested or indicated in this book, whether such errors or omissions result from negligence, accident, bad advice, or any other cause. This book is written strictly for entertainment purposes only and any attempts to implement any ideas mentioned in this book shall be done solely at the risk of the reader. The use of any scissors, sewing machines, or other items suggested in this book should not be permitted by anyone not qualified and properly trained in the appropriate manner to use such equipment. Any injury to any person from the use of any such equipment shall not be the responsibility of the author or publisher. Any damage to any clothing or other possessions of any individual by anyone using the ideas in this book are also not the responsibility of the author or publisher. This book is not intended as a substitute for the medical advice of physicians. No one should attempt any activity suggested in this book without consulting their physician – they should be sure that their heart or other physical requirements are healthy enough for any sexual activity. Readers are solely responsible to follow any proper requirements for safe sex or birth control in any suggested sexual activity that they engage in – to avoid any sexual transmitted diseases or undesired pregnancy. The author and publisher, particularly disclaim any responsibility with respect to any pregnancy caused by following any suggestions in this book. However, if any such pregnancy does occur, because any reader does not follow the proper precautions suggested, or because they purposely ignored the advice in this disclaimer, or for any other reason, we want to offer our warmest congratulations to the new parents.

Contents

INTRODUCTION

What is the *'Dress for SEXcess'* Book About?

N ONE SENTENCE, it is about new ways and ideas to dress up and decorate the female body in a very sexually attractive way to rev up the male libido, resulting in more variety, more fun, more sex, and a better marriage in a long-term married couple's love life.

This book may be aimed at some new ways to spice up the visual stimulation of a husband's libido, but as you read it, you will find that it is a very unusual marriage manual to help couples in many ways. You will also find that it contains a lot about a very unique, true life 'Love Story' – the over 55 year relationship story of my wonderful wife and me. I hope that you enjoy reading our story and discover some useful tips that can improve your own marriages.

All too often, in any marriage, the sex life can get stale. If it is always the *"Same old, Same old"* in your marriage, then you need to try something new. I have read hundreds of books looking for ideas to add spice to my own marital relationship. Most of these books include versions of the same ideas, and after reading the first dozen books or so, I discovered that it is hard to find a book that has even one or two really new ideas that haven't previously been written about numerous times. However, in this unique little book, there are lots of new tricks that you won't find in other books.

Married love should be full of frequent fun, laughter, and great sex. If you would like more of these things in your relationship, try some of the ideas in this book: just for fun, just for the added sex, and for a better marriage.

This book shows some new ways to add more of these benefits to your own marriage in many ways, even on a very limited budget. It is guaranteed that you can get more 'Bang for your Buck' with the ideas in this book than you can get from Victoria's Secret. So if you want to get banged the right way, banged more often, have more fun, and still not break your budget – read on.

There is a lot more in this book about having fun with sex and having a happier marriage than just clothing modifications. There are tips about marriage, about love in general, about understanding your spouse better, and about sex in particular. Some of these I have never seen published anywhere else. Some things are just my different take on common subjects. These tips and ideas are combined with me and my wife's unusual personal story and various clothing suggestions.

I have also quoted selected wisdom from some well-respected experts to show how some of my ideas fit right into the marriage principles that these experts teach. One of the experts that I need to quote right up front at the beginning of this book is my wife. She has insisted that I state early in this book that no matter how good an idea written here may be, no matter how much she likes his modified outfits, no husband should start cutting up any of his wife's existing clothes without asking her first. This quote has real wisdom for you husbands.

This book is for any husband who wants to take an active role in playing more with his wife in any sexual romp, fantasy ideas, role-playing, or having fun with her as they rev up their sex life with some new tricks. Does any of this appeal to you guys? Then invest in this book and a pair of scissors, and see how much fun you can have with some of these ideas

For you wives, it is no secret that the normal guy always notices sexy-looking women. Almost every wife knows her husband was probably first attracted to her because of how she looked. She also knows that, unless she keeps him blindfolded, he will never stop noticing every sexy woman he sees – in person, on TV, in the movies, on the Internet, or in print. My wife knows that I first noticed her when she was sixteen and she walked past me a few times one summer in her cute white short shorts – I really noticed her nice legs. Decades later, her nice legs still always get my full attention. The business of men enjoying looking at sexy women is a multi-billion dollar business, with the fashion industry, the Internet, all forms of pornography, magazines like *Playboy* and *Hustler*, and general advertising. Most wives would also like it if their husband noticed them more, especially if it meant their guy was looking less at other women.

This book explores how a wife can get much more visual attention from her man. I think it will also assure her that the sort of visual attention she gets will lead to a lot more physical attention too. This book gives hundreds of fun ideas to any wife about how to get more attention from her husband and keep him a lot happier at home. It is guaranteed that he will definitely notice her more with some of the ideas in this book – most of these ideas will give him more of her to notice than usual. She should also get lots of hands-on attention. If more attention is what you want from your husband, then get busy with a pair of scissors, and use some of the ideas in this book. If more attention from your husband is not what you want, then you need a lot more than any book can help you with – you need professional marriage counseling, and you will probably soon need a divorce lawyer, or at least will end up in a loveless marriage.

Many professional marriage counselors point out that you wives need to take a more active role in keeping your man attracted to you and to meet his needs, or you might lose him. For example, experienced marriage counselor and author Jimmy Evans, in his very Bible-based book *Marriage on the Rock* (meaning based on the Rock of God), writes a warning:

> "*When a wife rejects her husband's sexual needs, she is rejecting part of the man, because his need for sex is an essential part of his makeup. Therefore, you cannot reject the sexual part of your husband, and not have rejection affect the rest of his being. ....*

> "When you refuse to meet your husband's sexual needs in a proper fashion, it leaves him vulnerable to temptation outside the marriage."

Then he presents the positive way for the wife to behave:

> "... So just as a man should meet his wife's need for love and romance, a woman should meet her husband's **visual** and **physical needs**. A wife needs to **reveal** her body to her husband and to allow full, satisfying body contact as a part of sex. ....
>
> "As she does so in an **aggressive** and **creative** manner, she will be giving a great blessing to her husband and to their relationship." (Added emphasis is mine, tied to the same words used in the paragraph below.)

My goal in this book is to share some of the tricks I have learned from my own great relationship to enable other couples to keep improving their marriage with new ideas to keep sex vibrant, alive, and very enjoyable. I try to do this by providing husbands and wives with more **visual** ideas and to help encourage more **creative** ways to add fun to your sex life. Girls, if this is what you would like to have in your marriage, then get more **aggressive** and use some of these tricks to **reveal** a little more of your charms and satisfy more of your man's **physical needs**. Your marriage will be stronger for it. Guys, you will enjoy playing with your wife and experimenting with ways to highlight the visual aspects that you like the most about her.

Throughout this book, I will quote several such experts, as I did above, even including the world's best source of expert wisdom, *The Holy Bible*. I want to show that my points are not just the ideas of a crazy, oversexed, old guy; they are backed by wisdom from many other sources. Most of these other sources have the formal education and college degrees to make them recognized authorities about matters of love, sex, and marriage. I do not have these degrees to prove that I know what I am writing about.

However, many of the world's recognized experts have had failed marriages and other sexual and marital problems in spite of their educational knowledge. They often talk from personal experience with having problems to explain what they have learned about how to solve these serious problems. In the same way, I speak from my personal experience with having a One-In-A-Million marriage of over 50 years to teach and help others have a better marriage. I have never had the problems that many people have had and do not claim to have any expertise in solving those serious problems. Most of my wisdom is from my personal experience and from reading hundreds of relationship books. This is a relationship that never had any major problems and is still probably hotter sexually than 99% of marriages for couples of any age. I must have been doing something right all these years to have such a wonderful marriage. In addition, although I lack the formal degrees that add letters after my name, I have read hundreds of books while studying relationships. I will leave it up to the reader to decide the value of the wisdom I try to impart in this book.

Every wise husband and wife knows their partner has dozens of hot buttons – from their toes to the back of their neck – and that half the fun is finding out what works and what doesn't. I think that every person is different. Some tips that have been recommended in some books have no effect on my wife, and conversely, there are things I have learned about my wife that have not been included in any material that I have ever read. It is the same thing with experimenting with new clothing modifications – half the fun is just learning what works and what doesn't work. It is disappointing to spend half a day's pay for a Victoria's Secret outfit just to find out that it doesn't look the same on you or your wife as it did in the catalog picture. However, if it was a $2 item that didn't look as good as you had hoped, so what? Laugh it off, or recut it to take something more off, and try again.

When you follow through on my ideas, you`ll learn that by doing it, it shows your spouse that you still care enough about them to make the effort. If you stop doing things, stop trying new ideas, and act like either you don't care anymore or you take them for granted, then you are going to wake up someday and wonder where all the wonderful love you used to have has disappeared to. Love is like any fire – if you stop putting fuel on it, it will eventually die out. Burnout is fatal to the heart of any marriage. My ideas are just a new, inexpensive, fun way to put some fuel on the fire of your love. You should look at this as opening new avenues to explore sexual attraction – treat it as an adventure.

Somewhere I read once that research has found that one of the keys to sexual satisfaction is a sense of sexual adventurousness – that is all I am suggesting, a new way to be sexually adventurous. All you readers know how most girls are attracted to the "bad boy" image. Most guys and gals have learned how this image attracts girls by the time they are in high school. It is the adventurousness that makes bad boys attractive. The bad boys are the ones who act like "real men," not the timid, wimpy guy. A guy does not really have to be bad – he just has to have that attitude of being willing to do more and take more chances than a wimp. Over thousands of generations of evolution, it has always been the tendency of a girl to want a "real man" to want her, to care for her, to be her best protector, and to be the mate to give her real satisfaction in sex, and to be the guy to pass on manly genes to her children. This has been the basic evolutionary "survival of the fittest" biology. It is bred into the genes of every woman. Playing that role to his woman has been bred into the genes of every man.

How many of you husbands reading this have lost all that spirit of adventure after years of marriage? How many of you wives reading this have lost any spirit of adventure in your marriage? Then, no wonder your marriage has lost some of the spark. When you were first together, the adventure was to explore each other sexually, to learn about each other's bodies, and the newness itself was an adventure. What else have you been doing to put more spark back into your relationship? If the answer is, *"There is nothing new,"* then you need something new. If you approach my ideas properly, you can make it an adventure. Treat it like a fun game or a challenge to see how many good ideas you two can come up with. You guys, see how many ways you can invent something a lot more sexy and attractive for your wife to wear. You wives, see what gets your guy's attention and perks up not only his eyes but also his imagination and parts of his anatomy. Make it an adventure, and as I promised on the cover, this can lead to a lot more variety, a lot more fun, a lot more sex, and a happier marriage.

My book is written mainly from a guy's point of view, and I talk about modifying things for the wife. This is what I have done, how I have fun, and what I know works. It is how I learned to do this, so of course, it is the point of view I know best and mostly use in the book. The visual factor is what motivates us guys, so that is what I try to promote. However, I've got suggestions for the women too. Any wife who wants to improve her appeal to her husband can get the main idea of my suggestions and then take it and implement the ideas herself. Most wives are smart enough to know how they can apply any of my ideas to themselves. A smart wife will also appreciate learning a little more about how guys think and what they notice and like. Hopefully, in a short time, no matter who first reads the book, both husband and wife will be reading it and visiting my free website, DressForSEXcess.com, looking for new ideas to try. I even suggest that you both collect pictures of sexy outfits that you want to copy or make notes about ideas that you can go back to and try to copy.

When I explain an item or a modification, I mention what I like, what appeals to me, and why, I am doing it for two main reasons.

First, as a guy, I want to help educate the wives a little about what guys think and what might appeal to them. I think many women believe too much in what images on TV or comedians' jokes tell them about guys. There are too many assumptions about what all men like and how they feel. For example, big breasts – all women think all men like big ones. I am not even sure that I have ever convinced my own wife that I do not like very big breasts. I like a soft, gentle, feminine shape – size A or at most size B breasts are the most attractive to me. I think big breasts are too exaggerated to be really attractive. I may be a minority, but I know that I am not the only guy that thinks like this.

Women often don't have a true understanding of what guys really think or how they feel about stuff. (Many experts agree on this point – see the experts' quotes in chapter 10 from authors J and Dr. Harley).

The second reason for explaining these things is to plant a few seeds in guys' minds about things they may not be noticing about their own wife. We guys are very different than girls are in how we think, but even we guys are not all alike. I suggest that husbands and wives communicate more and discuss their personal tastes about what "looks" they like. No one is a mind reader. However, many spouses seem to think that their mate should know what they are thinking and what they need. Even years of marriage can't teach anyone to read their spouse's mind. Even after 50+ years, I still can't tell what my wife is thinking. Don't assume your spouse knows what you are thinking – talk to each other. At least my thoughts about what I like might get a husband or wife talking about whether or not my tastes are like the husband's tastes. Sharing different opinions can encourage discussion. Talking is good – great sex is even better, and more talking about what turns each other on can lead to more great sex.

Every husband would like a wife who is very attractive. If a guy marries the girl he loves, it is about more than just getting good sex. If they wanted to, most guys in today's society could get enough sex a lot easier and cheaper than by marrying a girl. A guy marries because of a very strong attraction to a particular girl. If she does things to keep attracting him, he loves it. He will not lose interest easily and will be continually attracted to her. A smart husband also lets his wife know what he likes and encourages her to keep pleasing him, but many guys don't easily come up with good ideas. It took me 25 years to start discovering the ideas in this book, when we were in our mid to late 40s. This is when many marriages start to go stale. This is when men and women get their midlife crisis. For us, this was just when the kids started going off to college and out of the house, and it gave us more freedom to experiment and play. This book is full of fun ideas on how to add interest and variety to your sex life.

The female body is very attractive to the average guy. Good, bare-naked sex will never go out of style, but variety is the spice of life, and therefore, all the lingerie makers will never go out of business. A wife only has one birthday suit, and after a while, most husbands know that outfit very well. Every woman, even the thinnest, most beautiful fashion model, thinks she has flaws in her figure that she wants to minimize. She also wants to draw her man's attention to what she thinks are her better features. However, I'd bet that even the best fashion model's husband sometimes disagrees about what her best features are. The vast fashion industry exists mainly to add variety to a girl's appearance and to show her figure off in attractive ways. The Victoria's Secret-type stuff does a pretty good job of making a girl's features look attractive for intimate settings. Cheerleader outfits, French maid costumes, and harem-style clothes will also never fail to make a guy want to take a good, long look. These costumes appeal to guys' mental fantasies.

No guy I know will ever tire of looking, as long as there is lots of variety. Most guys know places where only guys work, like a factory shop or an auto repair place, where there is often a big girlie calendar always hanging up and showing the "pin-up of the month" in a bikini (The Rigid Tools company used to distribute these). Most girls have probably also noticed such places too. I am sure a guy working there regularly checks out the new photos at the beginning of the month. But by the end of the month, he probably won't glance at the calendar unless he is checking a date on the bottom calendar part. He probably almost ignores the girlie picture by then – it is just like a part of the wallpaper after a month. Some wives probably think that their husband treats them just like that, like last years' girlie calendar, that they are just part of the wallpaper and he hardly notices her after a while.

However, if there were a change in the big calendar picture at work every day, he probably would never miss checking out the **pin-up of the day** photo. This is what guys are like – the variety keeps guys always looking. If the girlie of the day were his wife and not just a photo, he would really keep looking at her. With a girlie photo, he can only "mind grope" the girl (mind groping is covered in chapter 2), but with his wife he can really grope the model. This appeal is what keeps guys looking at Internet porn so much and what makes porn so addictive: Variety. It appeals to the way a man's DNA has programmed him from birth to enjoy looking at attractive female figures. I remember thinking how nice girls looked way back when I was in early elementary school – long before I learned about what sex really was.

Evidence of this natural desire for variety goes back centuries. One specific religion even believes that a man dying as a martyr will be rewarded in heaven with 72 virgins, not just one or two virgins – 72 virgins. However, even 72 girls really do not seem like enough to keep variety over a long-term marriage, and certainly not over eternity. A lot of men will have over 72 women in their lives, although I would bet that they are not all virgins. For a fifty-year marriage, which is a target that many young couples might live long enough to reach, there are 2600 weeks, or 600 months. Divide those weeks and months by 72, and each virgin would only cover 36 weeks or over 8 months each. A lot of real relationships don't last that long. A lot of newly married men are already having affairs by their eighth month. Even 72 women would not seem all that fresh after that much time with each of them – forget about variety for eternity with only 72 girls. I also don't know how any one guy could be happy with that many women. I couldn't even keep that many girls straight in my head, and I sure wouldn't be able to please them all. Many guys may have that many girls over time, but I know that they could not possibly please them all. It is hard enough trying to please just one girl all the time, even when I am sure she is the sweetest girl in the world. If those 72 virgins are typical women, I am sure that the martyr will find that at least a couple of them are real bitches.

It is much smarter to have one wife that I can get used to and get to know well, a wife who knows me well, knows what really pleases me, and knows how to vary what she does and what she wears to provide the great variety and spice in my love life. Fifty years is over 18,000 days, and in my marriage, I feel like I have probably had at least 10,000 different women to love over the years – different looks and scenarios – but all with a girl I am 1000% sure loves me and is devoted to me and me alone. She is usually different in many ways, but I can always ask her to repeat a favorite outfit or scenario that I think is special.

You wives are all smart enough to figure out how to take advantage of this concept if you want to keep your man looking at you. You can become your husband's girlie pin-up of the day. But you need more than one or two very sexy outfits to provide that sort of variety. Using my ideas, you can come up with a new outfit every day, if needed, and never break your budget.

If it were his own wife he got to keep looking at, usually in a different sexy outfit, no guy would want to miss the opportunity to also touch, fondle, and probably screw her thoroughly. If his wife looks very desirable and is ready, willing, and able to follow through, he will want to try and take advantage of her regularly. (To understand your man better, girls, you need to be sure to read about Mind Groping in chapter 2.)

A real man will be smart enough to know that if he wants to keep getting great, frequent sex from his wife, he must also see that he keeps her happy too. If you guys want to be treated like a king, you better be sure that you always treat your wife like a queen. I know it is true because this is ALWAYS how I feel every time my wife comes on to me with a new sexy outfit. Even after 50+ years of marriage – she is still my queen, and I love having her be my sex queen. We have a very big supply of sexy outfits. It doesn't matter if I am not feeling well or am tired, or even if we just screwed a few hours ago. The desire is always there – even if I can't always follow through for some reason like time or location. I almost always can follow through if I have the time, and that is what counts for both of us. This is what has kept us usually having daily sex into our 70s – so we must be doing something right.

The fact that there are so many sexy, stylish variations of outfits commercially available shows that there is a nearly endless list of possible ways to show off the female body. This book is full of ways that you have never yet tried to decorate and add sexual interest to your wife's body and to emphasize her feminine features in ways that most guys would find very sexually attractive. I am not a fashion designer, but I do consider myself to be a fashion re-designer. I look at existing items of clothing and look for ways to add raunchy new interest to them way beyond what they were originally designed for. My ideas are not concerned with proper decency that would be acceptable in public – I only want to add blatant sexual interest that appeals to what I like best.

If you shop conventional retail, there is a definite financial barrier to getting these types of outfits at places like Victoria's Secret or Frederick's of Hollywood unless you are a millionaire. These places have great stuff, and their catalogs are full of nice ideas to try, but the items are usually ridiculously expensive. How they can charge so much for so little in the lingerie shops never fails to amaze me. A pair of high-end crotch less panties must cost almost their weight in gold – a small fortune for a fraction of an ounce of fabric.

Why does it cost a hundred times as much to sell such a little item than it does to sell a typical children's pair of underpants, which needs more material and is more complex to make? I'll tell you why. It is just because guys will pay that much to see their wife decorated in those tiny panties. It is mainly because when she has them on for him, he knows he is going to get a chance to stick what he wants up into that crotch-less hole in those panties. What he gets to do to her in those panties is worth the money to him. Guys know that those high-end panties on his wife are still a lot cheaper than a hooker. He worries that he might not get the same chance to get into her pussy without the expensive panties as a gift for her. Maybe he would still get the chance to do the same thing to his wife without the high-priced crotch less panties, but it would not be as much fun doing just old-fashioned bare-naked sex all the time without the variety of new panties. This is why they keep selling so well, in spite of how expensive they are.

A guy probably likes decorations that make his wife look sexier to him even more than she likes feeling more attractive. However, very few couples can afford to enjoy an endless supply of lingerie and factory-made costumes without being concerned about the dent in their budget. Most couples have to balance the expensive fun they like with a realistic limit on their budget. There are other things that happy couples want to stretch their budget to include – date nights, vacations, etc., which are just as important to a great sex life. Doing it yourself also lets you get to emphasize the feminine features that appeal to you most. There is also a pride I take in coming up with ideas and doing them myself that I don't get when I just spend money for lingerie. Making it is part of the fun of also using it.

Personally, I like fancy lingerie just fine, but there is much more variety in using various costumes that can be made from regular clothes with a little imagination. Silk and lace lingerie on bare skin is fine, but I also really like the contrast of tough denim with soft bare skin – I end up modifying a lot of denim items. I also like to make sheer revealing outfits, like the best lingerie, out of things like sheer scarves and by using very open crocheted or knitted items, like mesh vests where the mesh holes are large enough to show lots of very visible, bare skin and let her nipples poke out. Many fashionable things made to be the top of a layered look are extremely revealing when worn without anything underneath them.

This book is my own story about how I got started with clothing modifications – how I became "The Scissor Man" to my wife because of how I cut things up and reinvented them. It is full of many of the fun ideas I have experimented with over many years. For my wife, I would pull out a new modified item, and she would see the holes, laugh, and say, *"Scissor Man strikes again!"* I later adopted her nickname for me, The-Scissor-Man, as an eBay ID. I also got it as a domain name, and the name has stuck.

My comments may be a little crude to some readers, but I think they are right to the point from a guy's point of view. Guys talking among themselves don't usually use words like penis, vagina, and intercourse. I just believe in calling a spade a spade, calling a cock a cock, calling a pussy a pussy, and calling making love – having sex, getting laid, getting lucky, screwing, and that well-known descriptive term, fucking. So I apologize in advance to anyone that this offends when reading this book. Please just overlook any offensive terms and humor and look for the fun ideas and the serious marriage tips that are also included. I do try to keep throwing a little sexual innuendo, and even some direct sexual humor, into my ideas at various points because that is what good married sex should be about – having very intimate and very good fun with sex.

Most of what I write is only for couples who have some private time alone. Maybe the newlyweds are the ones who have time alone before they have any kids. They are enjoying the newness of sex, and they probably don't need my ideas yet. By the time they need some of my ideas, after a few years of marriage, they also often have children that mess up the opportunity to enjoy some of the ideas I have for private time. In this case they must use their imagination to figure out how to get more alone time – I don't try to deal with this problem in this book. Those who can figure out how to get the time away from the kids, who don't have kids, or who have grown kids no longer in the house, are the ones who will get the most out of this book. However, maybe some of my ideas will help motivate some couples to spend more private time together without the kids. Of course, a few of my ideas can be used on outfits you can discretely wear out in public or unobtrusively around the kids, perhaps by wearing something as a layer over or under the blatantly sexy clothes – just let the husband think about what he knows is waiting for him underneath when he gets the wife in private. However, a lot of my wildest ideas are only suited to use just in the bedroom, away from the kids, just like expensive lingerie.

I did not write this book for children or unmarried readers. I hope they do not read it until they are older and ready for it. However, if there are any such young or single readers, just be sure to read the first chapter, which has some lessons on finding the love of your life and some great ideas on how to win her over, the way I did with my wife. The second chapter is about understanding the male mind better, which may be educational to younger people. There is no point in them reading the rest of the book since there is no racy pornography or sexy photos in the book – only ideas for married couples. There should be nothing shameful or dirty about enjoying the greatest gift God gave men and women – sex – in just the way God meant it to be enjoyed – in marriage.

I have no control over the many unmarried people who will read this book to find ideas to use in their shack-up relationships. However, these people probably do not need this book as much as the married couples because they are most likely still in the hot and new stages of their relationship, which does not tend to need much fuel added to feed their sexual fire. I only hope that these unmarried couples having sex someday wise up and see the value of what many millenniums of human history have proved is the best way to have a loving long-term relationship – a committed marriage.

That is what this book is all about – having more fun, doing more sexual decorating of the wife to add variety and spice things up, and doing it all on a shoestring budget.

CHAPTER 1

Who Is ScissorMan?

M Y WIFE AND I BROKE A LOT OF THE RULES that professionals say are necessary to build a good marriage. We also did not follow the actual practices that most teenagers and young adults seem to all do these days. We have an unusual true-love story. We started dating in high school. She was just 16, and I was 17.

We were each other's first real boyfriend/girlfriend. I would walk her home from school, carrying her books and holding her hand. Her hand felt so great in my hand – it was a perfect fit, and I loved to hold it. I have been holding it ever since, and I have found that she is a perfect fit for me in every way. I can't say "*She had me from hello,*" but it is true that she had me hooked from the moment she held my hand for the first time.

We just saw a local stage version of *Bell, Book, and Candle.* I remember it from the old classic 1958 movie starring James Stewart and Kim Novak. The story is about a modern witch who casts a spell on a man to make him suddenly fall in love with her. Looking back on our first date, I think that this is exactly what happened to me in October 1958. My new girlfriend cast a love spell on me – she held my hand, and I was bewitched. I can tell you that it is fun being bewitched that way, and she has been reinforcing the spell daily by always holding my hand. She still has me bewitched.

I calculate that I probably walked her home at least 125 times during my senior year in high school – I was just a naïve, lovesick schoolboy who was head over heels in love with his first real girlfriend. I drove that route recently, and it is 1.7 miles. That adds up to over 200 miles of walking with her, talking to her, holding her hand, and falling deeply in love with her during that school year. We did not do anything physical, other than to kiss and make out during that year – there were just hugs, kisses, and all that hand holding. It was a wonderful way to build a deep, true, lifelong love.

Yes, we dated lots of other people along the way because our parents told us we should do this. We were separated during my college years, and we were forbidden from seeing each other by her mother for a while to try and keep us from getting too serious. (Thanks, Mom! There is nothing like the forbidden to spice up a relationship.) But we never got even mildly serious or interested in anyone else.

We never developed individual lives as adults, the way the experts say you should do to have a mature, independent adult self-image before choosing a mate and settling down. Neither one of us was ever independent and out on our own in the world – we both went from being kids in school and living at home with our parents, or at college, to being married and starting a family. According to statistics, we married way too young – we were both just 21. Statistics say that marriages that young are more likely to end in divorce. We were too immature to have a good chance at a successful marriage, according to the experts. But those statistics don't seem to consider all those miles that we logged holding hands together or the deep love we developed. One of the important factors in developing this love, which has lasted so long, is that we didn't immediately let real sex get in the way of our relationship, and we became best friends long before the cementing effect of actual sex ever entered our relationship. We waited until our wedding night for any sort of sex, just like a fairy tale.

We were told we had to get our education first, so I went away to college for 4 years after my high school senior year when we had that magical first year of dating. By mutual agreement, we both dated many other people while I was away for my first two years at college, but we never found anyone else we cared about and never had a serious relationship with anyone else. We did what our parents told us we had to do to earn their blessings, and that was it. We were too much in love and way too horny to wait any longer – we got married 3 weeks after I graduated college.

We were *both virgins*, and we waited until we were actually married before we ever had any sex (not even any of the oral sex that President "BJ" Clinton has educated today's youth so thoroughly about). On one of our first dates, my sweetheart told me that it was her dream to have the big church wedding and walk down the aisle as a true virgin in her white gown. It was her dream to deserve wearing that beautiful white wedding gown that symbolizes purity. I was soon head over heels in love with her.

Yes, I desperately wanted to have sex with her and learn all about love and sex. I was a typical, very horny, very hormonally driven teenage boy. But I also wanted to prove my love for her, really *prove it* – so I made her dream, my dream, and together we made her dream come true. I was very naive and did not know how to seduce any girl to get the sex I had started out wanting. When she told me her dream, I did not think about it as meaning that I was not going to get the sex I wanted very soon – I thought about it as her telling me how to get exactly what I wanted – how to get lots of sex with her. All I had to do was marry her! It sounded like a good plan to me.

I soon learned that we both wanted each other completely, in every way, but I told her I was willing to do it her way, and I never once pushed her to have sex in any form before we were married. I did not want to ruin her dream. With college, this meant almost 5 years of waiting. I have since learned that it was well worth the wait. I cannot think of anything that could have better proved any guy's love for his girl, for real, than to do what I did to win her love. I have earned her trust so completely, in every way, in a way unequaled by any other scenario that we could have shared. As a result, I have been rewarded way beyond my wildest teenage fantasies with the actual love we have shared for over 50 years of married bliss. By living the role of each other's Princess and Prince Charming, even without realizing at the time that this was what we were doing, we have ended up with the fairy-tale ending of living (and loving) happily ever after.

My bride looked so glowing and radiant as she walked down the aisle in her white wedding gown to meet me as I waited at the altar for her. It meant a lot to both of us that she deserved the symbolism of that pure white gown she wore on her last day as a virgin. It was like a fairy tale come true for us. I had treated her like a princess, just because I loved her so much and because I wanted to make her dreams come true. I hadn't thought about it, but I was acting the role of her Prince Charming. She treated me just like I was her Prince Charming as a result. After those years of treating each other like that, it became a very pleasant habit. It is a habit that has never died out. She is still my princess, and she still treats me like her Prince Charming. She has always treated me like her Prince Charming, and I have always treated her as my wonderful princess – no wonder I love her more and more each day. This does not happen very often these days.

As we were going through these tough years of dating, being hundreds of miles apart because of college, and knowing how quickly most relationships can change, there were many times that I worried about losing my wonderful beloved. I was afraid that my inexperience might lead me to make some stupid mistake that would turn her off. Or perhaps she would just find that our relationship had turned dull and had run its course. And even more, as we spent the two years dating other people, I was very afraid that some other guy would realize how sweet she was and that he would try to steal her away from me. I had many restless nights at college worrying about these risks. However, when I look back to those years, I now know that I never had a thing to worry about. I now realize that no horny new guy could ever win any girl away from the personal Prince Charming that she already had. That first year together in high school had firmly entrenched my role as Prince Charming in her heart. No new guy could compete with this. It was all a result of how I treated her as my Princess in that first year. She was mine just for the asking, just like Cinderella belonged to the Prince and was just waiting to be asked to marry him. Love can mimic the fairy tales if the two lovers both follow the fairy-tale script without trying to take any shortcuts. However, this does not work if lovers try to take the common shortcut of jumping right into bed to start having sex before their relationship can grow strong and deep without the sex. The old-fashioned traditions have been tried and true for millennia, and they should be followed if you want the best results.

As a tip to any guy, married or not, who may be reading this, if you really want to keep the girl in your life, there is one way practically guaranteed to keep her yours. Treat her like your own precious and wonderful princess, and try to become her personal Prince Charming, and you can have her forever – as long as you keep up the role. It will work for a single guy trying to win his girl over or for a husband trying to keep his love life alive with his wife. No woman, no matter what her age, can resist the dream she has had since childhood when she first heard the fairy tales, like Cinderella and Snow White, and longed to have her own Prince Charming find her someday. Every little girl has fantasies like this. I have watched my own granddaughters repeatedly dress up in princess, ballet dancer, and harem costumes from the costume closet we have. They each dream of being a princess some day. Any guy who can play the role of Prince Charming to a girl can usually win her over forever – whether she is 16 or 96.

In addition to being too young and immature when we got married, most young people today would say that we were also too naive and too inexperienced. Today, judging by the movies, TV shows, newspaper and magazine articles, advice columnists, and the lives of most people we see around us, it would seem that we did not get the proper chance to sow our wild oats. Everyone these days would say that we probably were much too sexually inexperienced to know how to have an exciting sex life. However, in the opposite way, we did follow a few old-fashioned rules that we felt are really important in any relationship but which very few people today ever follow anymore.

My dream as a typical horny teenager was a lot of sex. I had never had any sort of sex and I wanted to discover what it was all about. My girlfriend promised me all the sex I could handle. All I had to do was wait until we were married. She told me that she looked forward to having sex. She said that she thought sex was one of the greatest gifts that God gave to humans, but she said she believed God meant it for only between a husband and wife. I made her dream come true with the big church wedding and wearing the white wedding gown as a true virgin, and then she made my dream come true. I have had all the sex I can handle for over 50 years – and I still get more EVERY DAY. You readers may not believe it, but YES, we have sex in our 70s, making real love, normally 6 to 7 times a week. It has never grown old for us. This book explains some of the secrets that have led to this love affair of living and loving happily ever after.

We have never had any sort of relationships outside of marriage. This doesn't provide much variety in a relationship. Many people would think this could only lead to a very dull, boring sex life. However, with us, right from the start of our honeymoon, we proved that there was never going to be any lack of excitement. Statistics and the rules we broke didn't really matter in our case. What matters is that well over 50 years of VERY HAPPILY married life, with a sex relationship where the honeymoon has never ended, has proven that true love can conquer all problems. Fairy tales can come true.

We both have lived a long lifetime without ever experiencing a personal relationship breakup. We never had any sort of breakup between us. Neither one of us has an ex from any relationship with any other boy or girl in our pasts. I have never used a pick-up line. I only recall one time, on an all-day bus ride headed back to college my freshman year, that I ever even asked a new girl I met for a phone number to ask her out after a few hours of conversation with her. Other than that one time, I never even tried to ask out any girl outside of high school and the small college environment where I already knew every girl for quite some time before I asked her out. We don't have any dating horror stories in our past. We never went past simple kissing with anyone else in our dating pasts.

We avoided all the personal baggage that drags individuals down in most relationships and lots of other problems that most couples have because of complex prior relationships. However we still went through most of the same hard times every teenager does – the uncertainty, the indecision, making choices based on false information and schoolyard stories, making lots of mistakes, doing foolish things, strong peer pressure, and LOTS of self-doubt. But somehow we came out of this period without making any really bad mistakes. It was not an easy time in our lives. I would not live through those hard teenage years again for any amount of money because I doubt we could ever again stumble our way through that tumultuous period in our lives and still not make serious mistakes, particularly in today's different environment. It would be a million-to-one chance of us ever again ending up with what we have. But I would also not give up, for any amount of money, either the memories of our courtship, the strength and trust these hard times built in our relationship, or what we ended up with.

I know from experience and lots of reading that many people see other people or couples and they think that others are a lot happier than they are. They envy other people in many ways. I think I am unique because I know that there is no one in the world that I would like to change places with or swap situations with. I have the best, and I know it. The grass is the greenest in my yard, not in someone else's yard. We have our problems, but they are minor compared to anyone else's problems.

I did not start out trying to follow any strict religious rules. At ages 16 to 17, I began to realize that I was missing out on all the sex that some of my guy friends started talking about. I was just a very naive but very horny 17-year-old boy who set out looking for his first sexual conquest. I wanted to find an easy mark to score with, like most teenage boys today want. Instead, with the first girl I picked to try and conquer, I found a very special, very sweet, very old-fashioned 16-year-old girl and fell head over heels into puppy love. She soon told me that she wanted to be a virgin when she got married and dreamed of the big church wedding, and I just did whatever it took to win her and make HER dream come true. I had been brought up to think that this is the way a good girl was supposed to behave. I soon realized I wanted her forever, and no guy looks forward to marrying a tramp. They all want a good girl and a virgin. I had been lucky enough to find this kind of girl and did what I had to do to win her on her terms.

This is a main secret of why our love is so great. I unwittingly, perfectly played the role of her Prince Charming, willing to do whatever it took, to work toward her dream and to win her as my true love. I NEVER pushed her for sex. She told me right up front how I could have all the sex I wanted from her – just marry her. I desperately wanted her, so it sounded like a good plan to me.

She was my virgin princess, the fairest of the fair. It was worth slaying dragons to win her. Each of us loved helping the other reach their dream and was not just being concerned about our own dreams. Our marriage is so TERRIFIC because this kind of love became a habit that we never stopped, even after the wedding. One result is that, ever since the wedding, she has always been willing and eager to provide all the sex I want, with no demands in return. It turns out that the storybook Prince Charming was really onto something good. Do whatever it takes, maybe slay a few dragons, or whatever, to win the princess on HER TERMS, and he gets a lifetime of getting lucky every day. It truly is the stuff fairy tales are made of. It is how to live happily ever after!

I apologize to any readers who may think I am repeating myself too much in some of the above thoughts, some of which are also mentioned again later in this book, about our love story and relating it to the classic fairy tales, but I think that this is part of the essential success of our marriage. It is an important lesson that is worth emphasizing and repeating.

Ours is an extremely rare and unusual history in today's society. A couple can have a most wonderful love relationship when there is no sort of old excess baggage to carry around – never any breakups and no ex-relationships. And also very important, neither of us has any guilt of any sort from cheating in any way or from breaking the rules. We feel that we followed all the rules – all the rules our parents gave us and all the rules God gave us. Now we feel that there are no more rules to worry about. We have the freest love in the world for just the two of us to share.

Another way to point out the true differences in men and women is that wives spell "LOVE" "**H-O-L-D M-E**"; husbands spell "LOVE" "**S-E-X.**"

Never forget this difference if you want a successful marriage. Remember it, and first you should love your spouse in the way they want to be loved – then you will also get more of what you want.

Many marital problems are related to problems with communication. Many divorces have been blamed on poor communication, which is also a favorite item for professional counselors to try and improve. A lot of communication is poor only because the husband and wife are only communicating in their own language, not their spouse's language.

My wife has always communicated her love for me clearly in my language. This means not just letting me have as much sex with her as I can handle but showing me that she really wants it and enjoys all of it. She encourages me and keeps seducing me endlessly, and she lets me know that I am the only one for her. She demonstrates her love in many other ways too. She is what is described in Proverbs 31:10: *"A wife of noble character who can find? She is worth far more than rubies."* Therefore, she is the most wonderful girl in the world to me.

I have learned to communicate my love for her in her language. I cherish her; I adore her; I like to do things for her, and, of course, I hold her dozens of times a day. I hug her a lot, and this means more than just wrapping my arms around her. It means being her knight in shining armor and enfolding her into my protective armor to protect her, provide for her, respect her, and let her know how much I value her in both words and actions.

This relationship is more important than any worldly possessions, money, career, power, or fame. It is as close to living happily ever after as humanly possible. There are a lot of positives to be said for following the traditional rules and keeping the marriage vows. Wilt Chamberlain (with his claimed 20,000 women), Hugh Hefner (with his Playboy Mansion and all those Playmate girls), and Tiger Woods (who is supposed to have had lots of women) will never know the true inner joy I feel or enjoy the kind of great sex I get every day.

Part of working toward my wife's dreams and concentrating on making her happy after the wedding, and as appreciation for the love and sex she willingly gave me so freely, is why I have always tried to make our sex life so much fun, so adventurous, and more interesting for us both – this is part of romancing a wife and is the best way to keep her happy. Remember guys – if she ain't happy, then nobody's happy! This encouraged me to be creative in many ways.

Our love life has been about the freest, most adventuresome, most uninhibited, and most active in the world. It has been way beyond my wildest dreams from my teenage years – way better than anything books, TV, or movies has ever shown me. My wife is everything I ever dreamed of. She is all I ever wanted and more, and time has proven that she is all I ever needed. We know that we share one of the world's greatest love stories.

CHAPTER 2

Understanding the Male Mind Better — "Mind Groping"

TO UNDERSTAND THE REASONS FOR THIS BOOK, to understand why looks and appearance are so important to every man, you women need to understand some things that are hardwired into male DNA. Hopefully, this chapter will also help you men understand yourselves a little better too. Men are much more visually oriented than women are, and if they are not concentrating on something else, they are also usually thinking about sex, in one way or another – at least about every 10 to 30 seconds, if not even more frequently.

It is a common idea, which most men and women are aware of, that the average guy will mentally undress an attractive girl he is looking at. However, sorry girls, I think it is actually worse than that – the guys are actually also thinking about what they would like to do with you after they have you totally undressed mentally. In studying and thinking about how most men seem to act and how I personally feel, I don't think that this concept of mentally undressing is as accurate as thinking about it as the guy trying to mentally grope ("mind grope") an attractive girl who is the center of his attention for the moment. Most men are thinking about more than just the nude image of an attractive female they are looking at. They are thinking about how she would feel to touch and fondle, and possibly even more. Seeing enough to get his attention makes him check her out and wonder what the parts that he can't see are like – not just to look at but also to touch and fondle.

This idea will probably disgust many women, even more than just thinking about how a guy is mentally undressing the girl he is looking at – particularly when some guy is staring at her - but I think it is true nevertheless. Those people brainwashed by the Feminist Movement will condemn this male mental activity as something evil that men should stop. However, no matter how much anyone objects to it, it is the way God designed men. It is not bad; it is normal, and no amount of feminist objections can change the way God made us men. I don't think God makes any mistakes. Women should learn to accept it and live with it, not try to change their man or get angry with him about the way God designed him.

I think that any woman feeling upset about this when a man is noticing her should change her way of thinking and just be pleased that a guy still notices her. Sooner or later, the day will come, if she lives long enough, when she will regret that no guy ever seems to notice her anymore. Enjoy it while you still have it, girls. At any age, you don't have to be an exhibitionist and show a lot to everyone, but you should show enough to be sure that the guys definitely know that you are an attractive woman. Most women do have something attractive to draw men's attention.

I saw a wonderful *Zits* comic that made this mind-groping concept very clear. The Sunday, June 10, 2012, cartoon sparked some thoughts and helped me realize that "mind groping" a girl is more accurate than just "mentally undressing" her. An attractive high-school-age girl and her boyfriend were sitting back to back as they each held phones or tablets they were studying. The girl had on a skimpy top, bare midriff, and short shorts. The cartoon showed the boy had the top of his head opened like a clamshell, and two very long cartoon arms came out of his head as he just sat there innocently holding the phone in his real hands. The two very long cartoon hands and arms wrapped around the girl like snakes, and she had an annoyed expression on her face. The hands were obviously feeling her up very intimately – wrapped around her legs and her body. The girl said, "*Stop mind-groping me, Jeremy!*" The boy said, "*Like I have a choice,*" but he had a big smile on his face. You can see this comic online at:

http://zitscomics.com/comics/june-10-2012/

This is what really happens whenever a horny male is around an attractive girl. A guy doesn't even have to be looking at the girl to mind grope her in his fantasy. After just a quick look, he has that vision firmly planted in his head. Even as a senior citizen, I often see just a fleeting image on TV of something that really attracts me, maybe just a split-second glimpse of a girl in a commercial. That quick image sticks in my mind for a few moments. Sometimes, if I am alone at home, I will stop the show or recording and back up a little to see that girl again and freeze the brief image on the screen. I'll think to myself, *"that looks HOT!"*, and I really appreciate that feminine image I am looking at. You can rest assured that I mind grope that girl for a few very pleasant moments. Then I resume the TV program, but that image is still being mind groped in my head for a few minutes longer. Personally, that makes me horny and makes me think about when I can get to really grope my wonderful wife again soon.

In the cartoon, of course, the boy had been looking at her just moments before they sat down back-to-back, and he was finding it hard to read or study his phone because he was still only thinking about her – her cute figure, her great legs and all the charms she had under her skimpy clothing. I am sure the touching of being back to back with the object of his desire was making it difficult to think about anything else. In an innocent cartoon series like this, there have never been any hints that the boy and his girlfriend ever had sex; it is presumed that they are both virgins, like my wife and I were when we were dating in school. I can totally understand how horny the boy is and what he must be wishing for. The only unbelievable part of the cartoon was that the girl realized that her boyfriend was mind groping her – most girls don't know how guys think and behave. If a normal boy and girl were sitting exactly like the couple in the cartoon, the girl could be studying, but I guarantee that a boy in that situation would have a lot of difficulty studying. Those mind-groping hands would be invisible, but they would be hard at work in his brain – guys are made like that. Most girls would be totally unaware of the mind-groping effect that they had on any boy in that situation.

I remember back to when I was in high school and I was dating the sixteen-year-old high school sweetheart I later married. I had an unusual tandem bicycle that we would ride together. Both the front and back handlebars moved together, and the bike could be steered from either the front or back seat. The front seat had no upper crossbar; it was like a girl's bike. My girlfriend rode on the front seat, and I rode on the rear seat. We were both sexually inexperienced virgins, and I was horny as hell every time we went for a ride.

I rode for hours on our several rides with my hands on the rear handlebar and her sitting in front of me. The image of her wearing her white short shorts for our summer bike rides and sitting just inches in front of me is still burned into my memory from those hours of bicycling. I loved watching her shapely bare legs just pumping up and down as she pedaled right in front of me. She sure was HOT looking to me – she was the most desirable thing in my whole world. If you visualize this position, you will realize that her pretty white ass was perched right in front of me and her shorts were stretched tightly across her pretty butt while it flexed as she pedaled. I usually didn't ride with my hands on the handgrips on the ends of the rear handlebar – I kept them near the center of the handle bar right behind that delightful piece of ass. The knuckles on my hands on the handlebars right behind her seat were probably less than half an inch away from that very desirable pretty butt the whole time that we rode together. On sharper turns, my knuckles would even innocently bump against that pretty ass as the handlebar turned – WOW!

Yes, there was A LOT of mind groping going on in my mind on those rides – it was going on in my head nonstop and at warp speed. Anyone looking at us could probably see the top of my head open up and see my mind-groping hands reaching out to feel her all over – just like the cartoon. I felt like it must have been that obvious. She could not see me sitting behind her, and I don't think that I worried at all about trying to hide what I was looking at or what I was thinking, regardless of what we might have been innocently talking about as we rode. It was both wonderfully lovely and terribly agonizing at the same time. For an hour or more each ride, I could sit there almost touching that pretty piece of ass I desperately desired as I watched it flex so sexily. I loved watching her sexy body endlessly while she could not see how much I was ogling her. That sexy piece of ass and her pretty bare legs were wonderful to watch as she pedaled. Even the feminine shape of her back and her hair blowing in the breeze looked very sexy to a horny teenage boy. Yet, I know she had no idea of the effect she was having on me; we were just having innocent fun on a bike ride together.

I think most guys realize that a girl looks even sexier than any pin-up picture when you can see her body flexing and working her muscles as she does things. She was right there in front of me to enjoy looking at whatever I wanted to as much as I wanted. She was right there so close where I could touch her if I wanted. That was so delightful! However, I knew that I could not touch her or even let her know how much I was watching her and thinking very sexy thoughts about her looks. It was like seeing the Promised Land just inches away – but not being able to go there at all. It was so frustrating to have to endlessly resist doing any more than mind groping that sexy, young, beautiful, sweet teenage girl I wanted so much. My mind wanted to do a lot more than just look, but my reason told me, "*Just look, but you must not touch!*"

I think that the biggest sex organ in any man is his brain. The more his wife learns to take advantage of this knowledge, the stronger their marriage will be. The key is to use that extremely strong male imagination. I know there are many examples of how letting the imagination work creates a stronger image mentally than seeing a physical image would. I remember as a kid listening to a drama program on the radio, and it seemed so real to hear it. (I guess reminiscing about radio dramas must show my age.) A year or so later, they put the same great story on TV. I looked forward to seeing it because it had been so good on the radio. However, although the story was exactly the same, it was not nearly as exciting to watch as it had been to listen to. I had been free to imagine what was happening much more on the radio, and that was better than just seeing it on TV. Mental visions can often be stronger than seeing the real thing.

In the same way, leaving some things to a man's imagination is a stronger draw than just clearly showing it. In thinking back to those bicycle rides on that tandem, I think the effect of seeing a naked girl would not have been as attractive to me as watching my girl in her sexy short shorts. Letting a guy mind grope is a great way for a wife to keep his attention. Dressing in normal clothes may make a guy mind grope his own wife a little bit, but to increase his interest, and to insure more mind groping, a smart wife will frequently change her wardrobe with some of my ideas to get more of his attention than if she paraded around for him naked.

Think about something like the Dallas Cowboys Cheerleaders in their cute, skimpy outfits. Better yet, Google them or try:

http://www.dallascowboys.com/cheerleaders/home

and look at a few photos of them. Try to imagine the exact same girls stark naked. Maybe you can find a full-frontal photo online of some naked girls to compare the cheerleaders to. Which do you think is sexier or more attractive? Surely, the cheerleaders would look great in just their birthday suits, but I think that there is something more attractive and intriguing about them in their outfits.

The website photos of the cheerleaders' high-kicking, shows the little narrow band of white material of their shorts that covers that genital area between their legs. I know that every guy looking at a photo likes to focus hard at that barely covered area. Every guy knows exactly what is underneath that strip of fabric. Every young teenage boy has seen at least pictures of a lot of female genitals, but he is still fascinated by what that particular girl would look like under that material. At least the fantasy runs through his thoughts of doing more, maybe much more. Every guy is mind groping under those white cheerleaders' short shorts of that girl he is looking at. The imagination of what that little strip of material hides is more exciting in a guy's imagination than a clear look at her pussy would be. Even a cheerleader's husband, who has a lot of experience both seeing and using exactly what she has left slightly covered, is turned on by his own imagination. Maybe I am not like the typical guy, but that is at least how I feel about it when my wife of many years, with whom I've had lots of sex and even three kids, teases me with barely covering up her charms to get my imagination going about what I can't see. I always feel more like exploring what she is teasingly hiding from me than I feel about actually having her show me the targets I am interested in taking advantage of again.

A man's imagination is the biggest and most powerful attraction tool for any girl to use. This same thing is known to apply to any sort of advertising. And isn't every wife trying to sell herself to her husband? She should be if she wants to keep him happy and if she wants to keep him as her husband at all. For every red-blooded male, there are a lot of other women who are trying to sell to him based on their attractive assets. The wife has to make her charms attractive to him. She may not still have the assets that one of those Dallas Cheerleaders has, but she should try to make the best out of what she does have. I don't think that it is too hard for the average wife to look more desirable than the picture of the average stark-naked woman.

There is something special about a woman who not only looks attractive but also has that mental attitude that lets a man know that what she has is available to him if he treats her right. She is not going to just flaunt her bare charms. She is going to expose hints of what she has, but she expects that her man is going to have to be willing to earn the right to investigate her charms and discover what she has by loving exploration.

A naked girl doing a high kick and fully exposing her pussy seems like an exhibitionist display and may come across as a little lewd. The girl in the cheerleader shorts may be flaunting her assets, but she is leaving at least something to the imagination, even if it is being left to the imagination of her husband who has made frequent use out of what she is hiding.

It is the same feeling about wanting to do anything and everything to the pretty piece of ass that I liked to look at while we rode that tandem bike and that first encouraged me to start my first modification of a pair of jeans. I wanted to enjoy the view and still do more, all at the same time. I found out how to do just that. It was like having my cake (enjoying looking at how cute she looked in her tight jeans) and eating it too (screwing her sweet pussy) – both seeing it that cute way and screwing it at the same time – WOW!

Once we were married, I had a full license to physically grope, enter, and fully enjoy the Promised Land that I had only been able to look at and just mind grope when we were dating. I took full advantage of that permission to completely enjoy her pretty butt. Being married and frequently making good use of that delightful piece of ass never reduced my desire to enjoy it over and over again in every way. That desire is hardwired into a guy's thinking. Just because you breathe a lot, does not make you want to breathe any less. The reaction to a sexy female, at least mentally, is just as hardwired for a guy as breathing is to everyone.

Most men are really mind groping when they look at a pretty girl – not just mentally undressing her to visualize her naked. They are visualizing touching, feeling, and enjoying everything about what they see. They think about enjoying how smooth her skin would feel, enjoying how soft and warm she would be, fantasizing that she would respond nicely if they touched her. They would imagine how soft, warm, moist, and sensitive her intimate area would be as they leisurely feel her up and have her squirm sexily in their arms in response. A guy would like to feel her curves and her feminine shape and to explore the charms of a beautiful body. Most guys do exactly this in their head when they mind grope a pretty girl.

A recent, free, five-minute video lesson at PragerUniversity.com titled "*He Wants You*" attempted to educate wives on how the way men notice females is built into the male DNA, but it also explains that it should not matter to wives if they treat their man right. It quoted *The Daily Mail*, a major British newspaper, which listed the top ten problems experienced by couples on vacation together. Topping the list was: "*The man looking at other women in bikinis on the beach.*" This really bothers most wives and girlfriends, but every guy does it, unless he is blind. I'd bet that even gay guys really notice the girls in bikinis, just as much as they notice the good-looking guys. The video lesson's summary message to wives is: this natural attraction does not mean that your man is comparing you to those other girls, that by noticing them, he is not in any way becoming dissatisfied with you, and that he certainly will not be thinking of them later. You are the one he is with, and you are the one that he wants. I recommend all my readers check out this video and the many other great videos at:

http://www.prageruniversity.com/Life-Studies/He-Wants-You.html#.Vay8vfm8538

The videos there are very educational, and like this book, they often are about unusual topics.

However, the Prager University video lesson does not go as far as I am going to go in this book. I want to give you ideas to counter the attention that your husband may give to any other female he notices by showing you how to increase his interest in you. The best defense in your fight to be the center of your husband's attention is a good offense. I promise that you wives will find some unique tactics to help you plan a "sexy offense" to capture your man's attention.

Just like the back-to-back touching in the mind-groping cartoon, any prolonged physical contact can fire up a guy's mental activity. Riding behind my girlfriend on the tandem bike before we were married kept my libido fired up super high. Now, after 50+ years of marriage, my wife can still fire up my libido and my mind-groping imagination just the same way. Sometimes, when we are sitting next to each other – it could be in a church pew, in the grandstands watching one of the grandchildren's sports game, or wherever – my wife will slide her hand between the seat and my thigh and just keep her fingers there for a while. She may even wiggle them a little once in a while. No one else can see or notice, but I really notice. It is enough contact that I am aware of her being there constantly, and it keeps my imagination fired up on high. When we often go out to a play or movie in anything but very cold weather, my wife knows how I like her to wear a skirt (in public, she does not wear miniskirts like she'll wear for me to play intimate games; she wears knee-length skirts, which are as short as she feels are appropriate at her age – and she still has legs that look great) and her dressy, high, black boots. This leaves just her knees bare. During the show, I will at least try to have my hand on her bare knee as we sit next to each other. When there is no one who could notice, I might use my fingertips to slowly stroke the inside of her thigh a little bit higher too. It keeps us both turned on and simmering.

For many wives, this sort of action would just be teasing her husband – of course it is basically teasing. However, my wife is never just a frustrating tease to me; she will actually deliver the goods whenever I want to respond to her teasing in any way. I know that she wants me to respond. When a wife acts like this and wants me to respond with some real sex, I don't consider it teasing at all – I call it foreplay, and so does she.

After many years of marriage, mind groping my wife has taken on a life of its own. There is a difference between what I did before we were married or what runs through my mind when I notice some pretty girl, and what runs through my mind about my wife now. My imagination mind gropes my wife like a well-oiled machine. It is like a very pleasant, well-rehearsed play. It turns itself on at the slightest sexy thought or glimpse of any of her sweet charms, and it runs on autopilot through my mind. As I mentioned earlier, men are almost always thinking about sex. My wife knows this, and she is an expert at making herself the target of my sexual thinking. She still likes to turn me on – she turns me on high most of the time. However, it is no longer just based on imagination – now it is based on memory. I have many years with literally millions of memories to draw from that enhance the reality of my mind groping her. It is much better now based on these wonderful memories than when it was just based on teenage imagination. I have found that good experience can enhance imagination.

The way my wife teases me so often, with the little things like the fingers on the seat under my leg or wearing outfits with bare knees to let me touch her when we sit together, is a delightful way that she uses to take advantage of my imagination. This is another lesson that every wife should learn – turn her man on and keep him on simmer all the time; if it quickly turns into foreplay, so much the better. It keeps the guy's imagination centered on the wife, not on any other girl he may notice or be around at work or someplace else in public. For example, seated at a school sports game watching the grandchildren play, there are always plenty of young girls around in cute outfits – sometimes even team cheerleaders prancing around. They all tend to encourage any guy's mind groping, but I can't mind grope even sexy cheerleaders very much when my wife is teasing me with what I know is foreplay for when we are alone later. Hell yes! I notice girls like the cheerleaders, and my wife can't help but see that I do notice other females, but she knows that I notice her little teasing (foreplay) even more than noticing any cute girls around. A good wife should also be ready to deliver everything her husband wants whenever he needs her; otherwise she is just being a frustrating tease.

Teasing in any way is a turn-on for a guy. If the wife is attractive to look at, she may already be turning her guy on all the time and may just not realize it. Some of my ideas may just increase the strength of his feelings – they might go from simmer to high. Any guy who is turned on would like to have a chance to follow through on his sexual feelings. If his wife is not willing to let him follow through, then she is only encouraging him to keep noticing other pretty girls and fantasizing and doing even more mind groping of these other girls. When a man is frustrated, his mind groping may wander farther and get into fantasizing about having sex with the girls he is thinking about. He might dream about following through with one of these other attractive girls, and he eventually may do that if his wife is leaving him frustrated. The wife who is always available to follow through when she creates sexy thoughts in her husband's mind can be sure that she is getting all of her husband's business.

I find that noticing lots of cute girls does affect me, particularly crowds of young bikini-clad girls at the beach – they do make me feel more sexual and more turned on mentally. We guys are wired that way. I think that being exposed to all that female attraction makes me want sex more than usual. However, there is nothing wrong with that when I have the best wife to do a lot more than just have sex with me to satisfy my sexual desires; she does more than have sex with me – she makes love with me. Sharing sex with her is a lot more satisfying than any sex could be with even the most attractive of those bikini babes. Yes, sex with some other beautiful girl would have the attraction of being new and providing variety, but it could never have the deep meaningful feeling of becoming one with the most wonderful girl that I have ever known.

The Holy Bible describes the sex act, done in the right way as, *"The two shall become one flesh,"* and that beats just having sex. Making love beats having sex every time. A smart wife wants her man to have enough lovemaking that he never needs to think about just having sex.

Even now, every night, whether it is after just making love or not, when we go to sleep together, my wife curls up close enough that we touch – bare skin to bare skin. It could be just her hand touching me somewhere or her knee touching my leg. Whatever it is, it fires up my imagination about actually touching the sweetest girl in the world, who is all mine. I don't have to actually be seeing her. Just like the cartoon, I am always remembering what I have seen and touched in even the most casual way, which is reinforcing my mental images. That little skin-to-skin contact is like touching a live wire. I feel the love connection buzzing between us. I usually count all the charms and all the wonderful sexy memories about her as I go to sleep. I never count sheep – mind groping her is much more effective.

Frequently, parts of the lyrics and tune of the old Neil Diamond song, "Sweet Caroline," run through my head as I mind grope my wife. Her name is not Caroline, so I substitute her name in it, but I am always thinking of her as I hum it:

> *"Hands, touchin' hands,*
>
> *Reachin' out, touchin' me, touchin' you.*
>
> *Sweet Caroline,*
>
> *Good times never seemed so good.*
>
> *Warm, touchin' warm,*
>
> *Reachin' out, touchin' me, touchin' you.*
>
> *Sweet Caroline,*
>
> *Good times never seemed so good.*

I often change the one line about *"warm, touchin' warm"* to *"skin, touchin' skin"* as it runs through my mind.

What I like about being married is that it is much better than just mind groping other attractive females – it gives me permission to actually grope what I see, actually grope with my real hands. I have a wife who does not mind me groping her - she does not mind me mind groping her and does not mind me really physically groping her. She is smart enough to know how a guy is wired and smart enough to know that her guy would prefer really groping her whenever and wherever he can, rather than just mind groping some other girl. If circumstances prevent physical groping, then she encourages me mind groping her, and she knows that I do it a lot. She does not mind my really groping her because she wants me to like groping her rather than being distracted by mind groping whoever else I see. My wife wants all the groping business that she can get from me – physical groping or just mind groping. She is a smart woman, and she makes me a very happy guy.

I often comment out loud to her what I am thinking when I notice her as sexually attractive to me in some way, such as something like "*cute ass!*" when she is bending over for some reason. I might do this a dozen times a day. Most wives would probably respond with, "*Is that all you ever think about?*" in a negative tone, but my wife knows that, yes, that is what most men think about all the time. My wife always responds with a big smile and an "*I love you.*" She appreciates that I still notice her and still like how she looks and still find her very desirable.

I want to tell every wife reading this one important rule to follow: never respond to any of your husband's comments about your looks with that common reply, "*Is sex all you ever think about?*" or anything like that. Understand that your husband does always think about sex and just be glad that he still sees you sexy. Respond with something positive to encourage him to keep thinking that way about you.

You husbands should try to open up and communicate more about what you are thinking – women want you to communicate better. Tell your wife more often what you are thinking when you think something sexy about her – women like to be noticed and appreciated by their husbands. If she ever responds negatively, give her this book and tell her to read this "Mind Groping" chapter 2.

This is a lesson that any woman readers should try to learn and practice in their own marriage. There could be a lot more happy husbands and a lot fewer divorces if a lot more wives knew and practiced encouraging their husband to grope them both mentally and physically.

CHAPTER 3
Why I Got Started with the Scissors and My First Great Idea

B Y EXPLAINING MY BACKGROUND in the previous chapter, I think any reader can understand that I do not intend to be explaining how to spice things up for any lovers who are not married or not really ready for sex yet, for anyone to use with their live-in or shack-up honey, for any illicit affairs, or for any pros in the sex trade. I am only writing this for married couples who want to improve their love life, in long-term, committed relationships.

As you read this, you will see that this is for committed couples who do not have a lot of hang-ups about their own or their partner's body or about sex. Long-term, married, monogamous couples should have a true, intimate familiarity with each other in most all aspects of their lives. If you don't have this sort of sincere, honest, open relationship with your spouse after a few years of marriage, then you definitely need to work on it before you lose them. If that is the case, you need a lot more help than my book can provide – you need professional counseling.

Short-term lovers – new lovers, honeymooners, affairs, shack-up weekends, and sex-for-hire situations – have all the arousal factors that they need to keep things spiced up without my ideas. They don't need what I have to say about bringing new or renewed fun into a long-term love life to prevent boredom from setting in.

To fully appreciate some of the experiences I share, you must be able to look at the fun side of sex. You must be open-minded to have this kind of sexual fun. You will get the most out of the ideas if you talk and joke about them with each other, both before and after each experiment, while modifying something. Discuss what turns you on and why. Build on each other's thoughts and work together to use some of the ideas and improve them to suit yourselves.

Every guy likes a little variety in his love life to keep things spiced up. This desire for variety has been the cause of countless infidelities in the world. Many men don't have the imagination to find the desired variety in any way except by searching for variety by changing partners when they start to feel bored. The grass nearly always looks greener in someone else's yard. In my case, this desire and my situation eventually led me to use my vivid imagination to develop my variety in other ways, and this eventually encouraged my talent with the scissors. I've always worked to fertilize and improve the grass in my own yard. This has worked out very well for us both, and it avoids all the horror stories many couples have experienced with infidelity.

I have read the stories of Wilt Chamberlain's claims of 20,000 women, some more recent movie star's claims of over 10,000 women, and even the problems Tiger Woods got into for just about a dozen girls. There is no real understanding of any of these women by these guys, who are more into numbers than into depth in a relationship. These types of womanizers are narcissistic men, only concerned about getting their own pleasure, and are never going to be satisfied, never going to get enough sex, and never going to get any added enjoyment from enjoying the pleasure their wife gets.

I have found that it is a lifetime achievement to just understand and keep one good woman truly happy. It is both a full-time occupation and a lifetime of enjoyment. Being the "Master Lover" is a title my wife has adoringly given me. I value that respect and opinion by her more than any other title anyone could ever have. I have been rewarded with a love life that is great, and we still enjoy great daily sex – even after all these years and in spite of being too young, too immature, and too inexperienced when we got married. No man can have more than the complete love and trust of one wonderful woman who adores him and is head over heels in love with him. There is nothing in the world that is as satisfying to a guy who has this unusual pleasure.

When you really unite with your wife and learn to make sex enjoyable for her, a guy can enjoy sex a lot more than just getting off with a sexual orgasm with a female partner. I compare it to the way guys get addicted to video games. They endlessly want to play the games and get enjoyment from developing their skills at them. I think video games are dull and senseless compared to making love to a loving, responsive woman who enjoys what I do and lets me play with all her switches and erogenous zones to pleasure her. There is no numeric scoreboard, but I can read my score in her reactions – her face, her eyes, and her body, plus the way she treats me every day. It is more addictive to me than any artificial game could be – it is as real as it gets.

In many video games, as the player gets better, the player gets to move on to more advanced levels of play. In making love to one woman, once you get to know her better – her erotic zones, what she likes, and what she doesn't like, where she wants to be touched and how she wants to be held – you also get to move on to sharing love at a higher level. She will get to know you better too. No guy or gal in a short-term affair or a one-night stand can ever get to know their partner this well. But until you do know your partner this well, you will never maximize your enjoyment by making love at these higher levels. There is no shortcut in the video games to reach all the higher levels, and there is no shortcut in lovemaking to reach these higher levels. (The good Lord designed lovemaking and provides the highest level of enjoyment to those who follow his rules of the game – see his instruction manual, *The Holy Bible*.)

This is something that cannot happen without a long time to learn her body and her reactions. It is also something that cannot happen without taking years of loving to earn the complete and total respect and trust of a wife. By definition, this level of respect can never develop without the commitment of a marriage. My wife's approval of my skill as a Master Lover is my world championship award. Most guys never get this far with any woman – they don't even know what they are missing. However, most guys never put in the effort to try and really satisfy their woman – they are too concerned about their own satisfaction. Hopefully, some guys who read this will make more effort to put their wife's satisfaction first. Hopefully, some wives reading this will realize that it is up to them to encourage this sort of effort from their husband. Many wives just don't respect their husband enough to encourage this. I realize that I have only gotten to this level of being a lover because she makes it possible and enjoyable. The fun we have with the ideas I share in this book about sexy clothes is just one way that we both work on building this level of loving.

The variety in our love has occurred in many different ways, and doing it together rather than with many different partners is a MUCH SMARTER way to go. From the first few days on our honeymoon – out on a deserted beach on a warm night – things were full of variety. The variety has included all 50 states and some foreign countries, hundreds of different beaches over the years (day and night), and thousands of outdoor spots: picnic tables, blankets on the ground, playground equipment, boats, inside and on top of cars, on logs, in or near scenic rivers, lakes and pools, in forests, in deserts, while winter camping in an open lean-to in a snow storm, in historic spots, at famous movie sites or other improvised locations, in the bright sunlight, during many beautiful sunsets, in the dark, under the moonlight, during rain, even outside once in the middle of a hurricane one wild afternoon, in a deserted public park, under an open sided large picnic pavilion.

Our variety in lovemaking sites has ranged from literally in the middle of several major highways and high mountaintops to way below sea level a few times and many of the most romantic picture postcard settings in the world, and even on the exact settings of some famous movie scenes. Sometimes we were totally alone and at very isolated locations. Other times we were just barely out of sight at very busy locations where we could see or hear lots of other people, but they either couldn't see us or they couldn't know what we were doing.

One new marriage tip is to copy something I just started doing. I am making a list of the most memorable times that we have made love and what made them memorable. For your list, you could include locations, costumes, event celebrations, results (maybe like being discovered in the middle of doing it or maybe becoming pregnant), or whatever made you think it was a very special time. Just a good normal romp in bed may be lots of fun, but it would need some other significant factor to make the list, like being the first time in a new city, state, or country. Any different outdoor or significantly new or unusual location might qualify. For every item listed in the previous paragraph, I can think of from one time (the hurricane), to a couple of hundred times (the picnic tables), that are going onto my list. It is fun to remember, and it is going to be fun as you share a time that you want to add to your list. Also, make a wish list of what you both agree you want to do having sex – like on a moving train, as a sultan with a harem girl, joining the mile high club, doing it in the middle of Times Square, NYC, or whatever it might be that you want to do that turns both of you on.

It is not always possible to have the sort of location variety we have experienced, so we have learned to enjoy a variety of role-playing games and costumes. It started many years ago for us with Halloween costumes and store-purchased stuff like the typical French maid outfit and a Playboy bunny set of ears, tail, collar, and cuffs. These things work great, but a couple tires of these ideas too fast – they need follow-up ideas.

There are many self-help relationship books that suggest these ideas, and there is a huge market for these types of costumes. This use of costumes for variety and role-playing must be something that many couples are using to attempt to spice up their love lives. Hitting garage sales with clothing for sale, I find many of the French maid costumes. I guess that they have either gotten tired of the costume or they like it so much that they have an extra one of them. The costumes never seem to be worn out. At least it shows the basic idea is popular.

All I have tried to do with this book is to expand this use of costumes that many couples already use into a much wider way to get more variety and at bargain prices compared to the usual commercial prices of costumes and high-priced lingerie. I hope my ideas can put more imagination and more fun into many couple's personal love lives. There are definitely lots of ideas that are not available in any store-bought form.

Every normal heterosexual male always notices all attractive females. There is something about the female figure that is very attractive to guys. Men are much more visually oriented with sex than girls are. How a girl looks and what she wears is very significant in his attraction to her. Often it is what he sees that make him use his imagination to visualize what he cannot see. A tight, shapely sweater or blouse makes him imagine what is underneath. It can make a guy fantasize or mind grope what it would be like to slide his hands up under the tight top and feel the hidden charms as he makes her respond passionately to his touch; the same for a nice shapely rear. Sometimes the imagination about what can't be seen is a stronger turn-on than just a naked girl would be. Girls have always used peek-a-boo looks to attract guys.

There is nothing new about gals trying to use their assets to attract guys. A little while ago, I was on a college campus in the late winter. It had been bitterly cold for weeks, and this was the first day to suddenly get up into the mid 40s, temperature-wise. It felt like the first day of early spring after all that cold weather, but it was still chilly. However, I saw a coed out walking on campus in her short shorts. She had totally bare legs, except I'd bet they were covered in goosebumps due to the temperature. It just shows how desperate many girls are to flaunt what they have in order to attract guys. Cute white short shorts on my future wife at age 16 worked to get my attention, but that was in midsummer. She was just out to visit a girlfriend a few houses away on their dead-end lane, and there were no other people around that would see her. She did not even know ahead of time that anyone was around to notice her.

Some of my wife's sexiest outfits are things that she also can wear out in public worn in a different way and/or worn with something that she would NOT wear out of the house. Her attitude and how she wears things can make a big difference in the sex appeal of the outfit. This is one of the lessons that I hope you female readers will pick up. Something like a nice warm turtleneck sweater could be a nice part of an outfit that would look nice in public worn with long slacks in cool weather, but worn with nothing underneath the sweater, and with the tiniest immodest little skirt that doesn't really hide anything, along with some high boots, that same sweater will create a different look with all those bare thighs showing and a little jiggle in the breasts as she moves. As part of an outfit that screams "*Come and get ME!*" the modest sweater can look more like an invitation to cuddle up to her and slip your hands under the sweater or to lift the sweater and let her breasts out for some attention.

After a fun session of enjoying sex while wearing a sweater like this, there will be sexy memories recalled every time she wears that sweater again. The next time she wears the sweater out again in public, she may look the same to people she meets, but we both know that we are both thinking back to the way she looked and the sex we shared when she wore the sweater as part of a different outfit. As another example, the most expensive piece of apparel my wife has is a white fur coat. She looks stunning in it every time she goes out in it in the winter. However, every time she wears it – to church or anywhere – I always think about how she has looked when she wears absolutely nothing but the white fur coat, some white fur boots, her wedding ring, and a smile – just for me!

Hopefully, some of my stories and ideas will spark some things that will someday give you readers something to smile about in a similar way, by taking some apparel you already have and wearing it in a new way. You wives should discuss some of your current wardrobe items with your husbands and see what he thinks is sexy. It could be turtlenecks, bare shoulders, big broad belts, tight jeans, bare thighs, high boots, chokers, armbands, etc. Find out what features he likes about your figure for you to emphasize – round ass, big boobs, or maybe small boobs (not all guys like bigger breasts; I like small breasts), bare middle, bare boobs, bare arms, bare legs, or maybe just bare thighs with boots or high socks.

You wives need to discover how your husband thinks – guys can be very different in what they like. In particular, ask him for ideas about clothes you already have that you can wear in a more sexual way as the simplest way to get started with some of my ideas. Even ask him to point out any picture he sees that has some feature that he thinks is sexy, or even point out in private something he sees someone wearing that he would like to see you copy.

You guys need to suggest things to your wife. Tell her about something she has that you would love for her to wear in a different way or as part of a sexy outfit combination – or perhaps tell her what you want her to leave off to make her look more desirable, more available, or just plain sexier. Point out to her things that you see that you would like her to try wearing. It can be as simple as having the wife wear an outfit that she often wears out or at home but with nothing underneath. This lets the guy think about how vulnerable his wife suddenly is in that common outfit and fantasize about what he is going to do to get into that outfit and then enjoy doing exactly that – getting into the outfit and into his wife.

A smart wife encourages her husband to comment on anything that turns him on, even if it is something about another attractive woman. Learn to like listening and learning what he thinks, and never get upset that he has noticed some pretty girl. Every guy will notice such girls. It is in our DNA. You can't stop this, and neither can we. Your husband will appreciate that he does not have to feel that he is walking around on eggshells when he is with you and sees other attractive women. I like that my wife is self-assured enough to know she is my one and only and does not feel threatened when I notice other attractive girls or make an occasional comment about one – she wants to learn what I think and what I like. Building up the level of trust that our almost 5 years of courtship created has proven to my wife that she does not have to worry about my actions in any situation – but very few men have bothered to build up that level of trust.

My Scissor Man experience started when I was thinking about how good my wife looked in her tight blue jeans. I think every guy notices a nice round piece of feminine ass shaped by tight jeans or pants – especially when the girl bends over and points that nice ass right at them. Once in a while in public, I watch all the guys staring at the girl instead of joining them to watch some attractive girl walking by in tight jeans or bending over. Well, with my own wife, I have often thought how much I like screwing that nice piece of ass when she bends it over like that for me to notice.

For example, when we are just at home in the kitchen and she is fixing dinner, cleaning up, or doing anything, she is frequently bending over – to get into a bottom cabinet for something, to reach into the bottom refrigerator drawer, to pick up something on the floor, etc. This flashes her nice butt at me often as she bends over each time. I usually comment, "*You have such a nice looking ass when you do that.*" But seeing those jeans stretched so tight over that cute, desirable ass that I like to enjoy so often, also makes me mind grope her and think about how much I would like to screw that sweet piece of ass again.

Most of you wives have a husband who never mentions it when he notices you this way. To mention it would prompt the typical wife to reply, "*Is that all you think about?*" in a very negative tone. However, I can guarantee that your husband does notice your butt when you bend over where he can see it. That is all he thinks about when you flash a tight, cute ass at him. Unless he is half-dead, he notices, but he just doesn't comment on it.

At first, I always wanted her to do it again for me with nothing on – and she frequently accommodated me that way. She was glad I still noticed and wanted her that much. The next time she bent over like that in her jeans, it was a simple step to instantly wanting to screw that cute ass again, right in those tight jeans.

I took an old pair of tight fitting jeans and made a simple modification with some scissors – I cut out a 4- or 5-inch piece from the center seam in the middle of the crotch area and had her try the jeans on again without any panties. They now were crotchless jeans. It was just a 30-second job to cut out that key, central crotch seam, but WOW, what a result. I had her put on a brief top with no bra, to go with the jeans. Her lower torso was entirely covered, except for the tiny part that the teeniest G-string would cover up, but of course, that is just the part I was most interested in – interested in getting IN!

I want to repeat – guys, never cut up any of your wife's favorite clothes without her approval.

I made several discoveries at this point and soon realized that this was my first great idea with the scissors. It hooked me into thinking up more ideas. First, I saw how good she still looked in the jeans and how extremely desirable she was. I noticed how the crotch modification was almost impossible to spot as she walked around normally. Next I asked her to face away from me and bend over – then I could notice the modification very clearly. Her pussy area was popping right out of the jeans, pointing her cute pussy lips at me invitingly. It was not just exposed from the cut in her crotch. It was very obviously pushing way out through the small slit in the jeans.

I have since analyzed it, and I realize that, when any outfit is tight, it squeezes the body. The flesh tries to pop out wherever it can. You all know how too-tight jeans will give the wearer a slimmer ass but push out a roll of fat above the waistband. Well, in the same way, when there is an opening in the genital area of a girl's tight pants – the flesh pushes out there too. When she bends over, the jeans push even tighter on the crotch, and her intimate flesh pushes out from the cutout even more from the higher pressure. Her pussy area just presses invitingly right out of the little slit over it in her jeans. On my wife, it is sure to get my undivided attention.

See Illustration 3-1. Tight jeans with just a crotch-cut.

Even the best crotchless panties can never emphasize a pussy like that and make it pop right out at you. Only something tight over the whole belly, thighs, and ass can put that pressure on the pussy to give it that look. I had discovered something that Victoria's Secret had never shown me. It takes a tight pair of modified jeans to make the pussy pop out the most. Loose jeans with a cutout still make the pussy area fully accessible, but it won't pop out like that without the pressure of a tight fit.

This is a sample of the ideas I share in this book that I have never read or heard about anywhere else. I'm offering a $100 cash prize to anyone who can point out any book printed prior to mine with this idea and the popping-out-pussy effect mentioned – the prize is available to first person to reach me with the information. If such a book exists, I want to get a copy and see what other great new ideas I might find in that book – I am always looking for new ideas to use.

Speaking of pressure, when she first tried these jeans on and I noticed both how good she looked with her cute ass in those tight jeans and the way her pussy pushed out of the cutout, I realized that I also felt a lot of pressure. The front of my pants suddenly was very tight – this is a frequent hard problem with me when she comes on to me in such an obvious way. I had to unzip my fly, and my flesh popped right out too. With all that flesh popping out, it didn't take long for the Biblical prophecy to reoccur again: *"And the two shall become one flesh"*!

WOW!! We both liked that result. I also made two more discoveries while we were pressing the flesh together that way.

When a girl's pussy is pressed out a narrow opening, it holds the pussy lips more firmly together than usual. The guy has to press his way in and pry her pussy open more – nothing is gaping open even if she spreads her legs as wide as she can. You may need some extra lube, but it feels tighter – which is nice for both the guy and the girl.

Another benefit is that when you screw her through the small denim cutout, the jeans provide very good handles. Nature may provide fleshy love handles on some girls, but a guy can't really get a very good grip on these, and no girl likes you to grab a handful of her flesh firmly and use it to hold her tight or yank her around. However, you can grab the waistband or pockets of the jeans as you screw her and pull or push as hard as you can, and it won't hurt a normal girl while grabbing or yanking her around. You can yank, push, pull, or shake her ass around as hard as you can, or at least as much as she can take it from your cock beating around up inside her. All the force is distributed all over by the jeans and never concentrated on just the spot you are grabbing her. With tough jeans for handles, it will be the cock banging around inside her pussy that will determine how hard you can shake her ass – not the ability to get a good grip or to hold onto her as you screw her and shake her ass around. Shaking her ass a lot lets you really hit all of her inside buttons firmly and repeatedly with your cock. It would be a shame for a husband to keep missing any of his wife's internal fuck buttons. I like it. I recommend every husband try to be sure he hits all of these inside buttons in his wife.

With one of the first outfits I modified, I did realize a limitation to how hard I can shake – I tore the rear pockets right out of a cute pair of shorts. For damage control, I often have her wear a strong belt with her sex outfits to give me a handle that can take it as hard as I can shake it. Many jeans and shorts are stretch fabric too, and you need the belt in that case. You also need a belt if only a zipper holds the waist closed on any outfit after being modified – if you pull too hard on the fabric, the zipper will open up. Even if the waistband and belt loops have been cut away, a series of belt-width vertical slits in the material just below the top edge will let you feed a belt in and out of the slits to hold the belt in place.

As an example of how I have some ideas that are both cheaper and better than what is available commercially, lately, I have seen a product sold on adult toy websites and catalogs. For about $14.95 to $18.95, plus shipping, you can get a "Doggie Style Enhancing Strap," which is supposed to be used in doggie-style rear-entry sex. It is just a short but wide strap with handles on the ends for the guy to put the strap under the girl's belly as she kneels in front of him, and it lets him pull up on the handles and use his arms to pull her up and toward him as he screws her from the rear. He has to always keep holding the strap handles, or it drops to the bed or floor, and he has to pull way up with his arms to make the strap work. The illustrations I have seen make it look unnatural the way the guy has to pull up to make it work. This is spending too much money to do this the hard way.

Almost any crotch-cut item will work better than the "enhancing strap." Any old pair of jeans, a skirt, or a pair of shorts can be modified or even entirely cut away to leave just the top 4 inches or so of the waistband, and then it can be worn by the girl. This works the same way as the enhancing strap, but it stays in place all the time by itself. The guy can use his hands to feel her or do anything else and not worry about dropping the strap. It is easier to grab the denim item anywhere around her waist when he desires to move her ass, and the hands on the hips is a more natural arm position to grab and push, pull, or shake. The cost ranges from free to a couple dollars to buy the cheapest item to cut – this is better and cheaper than an enhancing strap. The very best and strongest grip is a pair of very short shorts or a short skirt where the guy can grab the sides with a hand on each side of her hips and grip each side from waistband to bottom.

I think a small bit of tough denim on lots of bare skin is an attractive look – better than a strap. And better yet, it works just as well in any face-up position, or any position at all, as well as the doggie-style position, which is the only position where the enhancing strap is useful. The enhancing strap would not stay in place in one of my favorite positions, with the wife on her back on the edge of a bed and with her legs up on my shoulders – it would slide off under her butt if pulled toward me. Grabbing her miniskirt or crotch-cut short shorts to pull or shake her while I can look at her face is a real turn-on. My system works better and is cheaper than the Doggie Style Enhancing Strap.

If you play some fast dance music while you screw this way, it adds a new meaning to the phrase, "Go girl, go! Shake that ass!"

However, if you need to use a condom for birth control, don't push into her pussy too hard without lots of lube because of the tighter pressure when using just a narrow crotch-cut where she pops out, like I have described, and don't use the jeans to shake her pretty butt too roughly. These things could make a condom break.

Warning! Accidents cause people!

CHAPTER 4

How My Imagination Developed More Ideas

ANOTHER FAVORITE MODIFICATION that just came along as a natural progression was a modified denim vest. My wife had a nice denim vest with pockets on each side over her breasts – the pockets had flaps that buttoned closed. She looked good in it and wore it while we played around in the modified jeans outfits. The denim top and bottom went nicely together as a denim set. As the fun at our sex sessions progressed, I would unbutton the front of the vest for better top access, of course.

Then, for the next time, I modified the vest to cut the chest pocket sides and under the top flap of the breast pockets, but not the bottom of the pocket. The pocket was still intact and held at just the bottom edge, but only the pocket button held the front of the pocket up in place. The sides of her breasts peeked out very alluringly on each side of the pocket front. She was covered on the nipples and center of the breasts but exposed on the sides. I find the peek-a-boo look very attractive. When the pocket flap button was unbuttoned, the front of the pocket fell down, and her entire breast would pop out of the pocket-sized hole cut in the vest.

See Illustration 4-1, which shows a vest with one pocket buttoned up and one unbuttoned. The front cover illustration also shows a slight side view of the pocket cutout, as well as a large heart shaped cutout in the back.

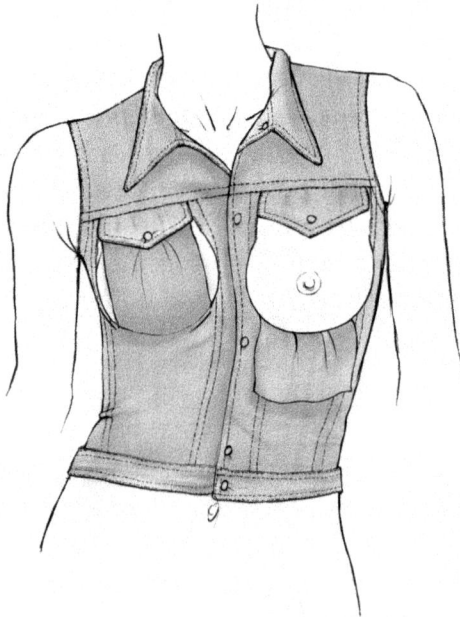

With the proper pocket-cut positioning, the vest becomes like a shelf bra that just holds her breasts up and in a perky, firm position. How far down you cut the pocket sides changes this fit – check your measurements of her and the vest, and plan the cutting carefully. Cut less than you think you need and have a fitting as you cut. Fitting and checking the merchandise can be fun too. You can always cut a little farther, but it is difficult to undo a cut. How much you cut also depends on the size of the wife's breasts; the opening must be larger if she is big busted. It always works for my wife's breast size.

The pocket flap can be called by another name too: the "automatic condom dispenser pocket." Since the pocket is functional, you can put something in it, and it will stay put while it is buttoned up. When the pocket is opened and it falls down upside down, anything in it can fall out. Place a condom in the pocket, and it will automatically be dispensed at just the right time – when the sex gets serious, the pocket is unbuttoned and falls upside down, and as the breast falls out, so does the condom. This dispenser technique can be used for any joke item too – a mini vibrator, a candy kiss, or the "key to her heart" (or her chastity belt, handcuffs, etc., if this is your thing).

Unbuttoned, the firm toughness of the denim vest makes a tantalizing contrast to the soft warm flesh of her breasts framed like an open bra in the vest pocket cutouts. The vest, even with the pockets unbuttoned and the breasts out, still covers everything that would be exposed on her upper torso in a bikini swimsuit top and exposes just her parts that the bikini top would cover up – a very intriguing look.

There is a nice side effect of wearing the open pocket cutout vest. Usually, when a woman lies down on her back bare breasted, her breasts sort of fall off to her sides. Her nipples will be much farther apart lying down that way than when she is standing bare breasted, and if she has a bra on, the nipples are probably even closer together and facing forward even more. The stiff denim vest is even stronger than a regular open bra or a shelf bra. When her breasts are popping out of the cutout vest pockets, they do not fall off to the side, and even if she is standing, they do not sag at all. The vest cutouts hold the breasts right in the position of the pockets from the outer edge of the pocket, but they do not cover the breasts at all – each breast pokes straight forward, just as if someone was holding it in place with a hand. When I hug my wife in the vest with the pockets open, her breasts are a little firmer against me, and they do not squash out as flat on her chest when I press my chest against hers. If I move a little against her, the breasts don't move as much, and I can feel the perky little nipples rub on my chest more. I like that, and so does she.

The briefest thong bikini set exposes everything but around the nipple areas on her breasts and her pussy. In a minimal bikini, everything is exposed except for the barest minimum needed to be covered on a public beach. Other than her head, hands, arms, and feet – a set of crotch-cut jeans and a flap-pocket-cut vest cover up everything on her torso and limbs except the breasts and nipple area and the pussy area. What cannot be exposed on the public beach is the only thing that is exposed by the jeans and vest combo – what can be exposed in public is all covered up. I find it a very interesting exposure reversal on my wife, and it highlights the sensitive erotic areas – and makes her most intimate features totally exposed and available for my enjoyment. I would label it an "exposure reversal outfit."

The open look highlights the more sensitive and more attractive features of the girl's chest and is a very strong come-on, showing that the girl wants more – offering just what the guy is looking for. I can tell you from personal experience, when she unbuttons the pocket buttons on the vest to let her boobs hang out, it seriously means the girl wants sex. 100% of the times when my wife has given me that look, I have promptly gotten laid!

I think many women believe too much in what the TV images or comedian jokes tell them about guys. For example, Jay Leno used jokes about "*Valentine's Day being the only day many married men get any sex.*" He also joked, "*The best birth control system is marriage. Once a guy gets married, his active sex life is almost over – he rarely gets it anymore.*" Also, at a recent comedy show the comedian said, "*You old married guys probably only get it twice a year now – on Valentine's Day and on your anniversary.*" I think that this is totally wrong.

I agreed with the comedian to some degree, from what I read, many wives would be satisfied with this situation of twice a year, but not the happy wives. In my case, it applies only because EVERY day seems like Valentine's Day to us, and often Valentine's Day has even come TWICE A DAY for us. I find twice a day makes both husband and wife happier than just twice a year – and I'm an old, long-time married, guy.

To check if the comedian was right for most couples, I'd like to check birth statistics to see if births peak around November 14th each year (nine months after Valentine's Day). I wonder if this time period is always a peak birth period, the way it happens nine months after certain events like widespread big power blackouts. Those of you born around mid-November may have never realized why you were conceived – Valentine's Day. I have been told that late September has always been a traditional high birth period – nine months after the Christmas and New Year's holidays. For those readers who knew they were normal birth weight and pregnancy time, you should check back to what was special about nine months earlier when you were created.

With this attitude, I naturally like to make every day special. Since the crotch-cut jeans and the vest ideas really worked to make some great fun sex sessions, it encouraged me to keep right on dreaming up more modifications. If something works, keep doing it, and try to do it even better.

CHAPTER 5
Hidden Modifications

WAS HAVING SO MUCH FUN cutting stuff up to enhance my wife's sexual attraction, that I kept doing more and more of it. I started making minor modifications in some clothes on items that she would wear around the house and even wear out in public. Some of the changes were just so I knew about them, and they never showed publicly.

This would be stuff like cutting out the bottom of the front pockets on some of her shorts or jeans, or just slitting the inner layer of the back pockets on her jeans right below the pocket top. When she wore them, they looked perfectly normal, but I knew that if I could slip my hand into her front pocket, I would be inside her jeans or shorts, and I could feel her up good anytime I had the chance to catch her unobtrusively. When I would hold her face to face and hug her, I could slip my hands down into her back jeans pockets and I would put my four fingers in through the inner pocket slit, and that is the right height to get my fingers down inside the top of her panties, if she was wearing any. I would be right down to the bare skin of that pretty ass I liked to look at, feel, and screw.

It has always been fun for us to go for a walk together – ever since I used to walk her home from school and carry her books with one hand and hold her hand with the other as we walked and talked. I learned it became more fun to take a walk with her in jeans with the rear pockets modified inside. Instead of just holding hands, I would slip my arm around her waist and we would walk with our arms around each other's waist. Then I'd work my hand down into her back pocket. To any observer it just looks like I have innocently slipped four fingers of my hand into her back jeans pocket, but I am actually rubbing my fingertips on the bare skin of her ass inside the jeans as we walk and talk through town. No one realizes that my fingers are right on the skin of her bare ass. It really raises the sexual tension between both of us. We may still be talking as we walk along, but no matter what we are discussing, there is something else building up in the back of both our minds if my fingertips are caressing the skin of her bare ass.

I have always liked to walk behind a girl with a nice shape in a tight outfit and watch the way she moves. I discovered it is even better to have my fingertips pressed hard up against the bare skin of her ass by the tight fit of her jeans and feel the muscles in her ass flex as she walks. Feeling beats looking!

I learned that if you have a nice outfit that looks good on your girl, you can modify the crotch with a small cutout, and she can still wear it out. If it is not tight the way snug-fitting jeans are, then the opening is still there to use, but the flesh does not press the pussy out. With most looser crotch-cut shorts, panties, or pants, the opening is not visible unless you look up at the spot, like when the girl bends over – just like commercial crotchless panties. To be sure that it is not obvious to anyone else, she just needs to wear panties that are the same color as the outfit.

My wife wore a cute white top and a skort (a skirt with sewn-in shorts underneath) all day while the two of us were out on a trip and were out sightseeing on a vacation. It was modified with the crotch cut out of the undershorts, under the short miniskirt. She teased me nonstop about what I was thinking all day long. The skort undershorts were white, and she had on thin, white cotton panties to be sure no one got even an accidental look at her pussy. A couple of times I got the chance to sneak a quick feel in her crotch, and I could feel how thin her panties were through the crotch-cut. I am sure that she could feel me very well through the thin panties too. Then near the end of the day, after teasing me endlessly about it, she became more daring, and she visited the restroom and came back without even the panties. I got very hot thinking about how exposed she almost was right out in public in front of lots of strangers. Just by bending over in the slightest or moving in certain ways that would spread her legs, she would flash the world with her pussy. But only I knew how very vulnerable and ready for instant sex she was, even though apparently fully dressed. Several times when I could get her where no one was able to see us for a moment, I would be able to slip my hand between her legs and put my fingers right up into her sweet pink pussy and feel how soft and moist it was. I couldn't wait to get back to our room that night, and I found a dark deserted spot in a park along the way back where I could just bend her over a picnic table and knock off the quickie that I had been thinking about all day while she had been teasing me about her outfit.

The sexual tension from knowing the special hidden features of an outfit, like this skort outfit she wore all day, can be terrific. The best aphrodisiac I know is a guy's vivid imagination when a girl takes advantage of it properly. Physical exercise keeps a person's physical body healthier. Well, exercising a guys' imagination keeps it strong too. My wife sees that I get plenty of exercise for my imagination, which also leads to plenty of good healthy physical exercise too, for both of us – usually via very enthusiastic sex.

There is a comment I want to pass on to you about some things I learned farther along in my experience. There may be situations where the woman wants to wear panties and later take them off to make herself available. For a skirt, there is no problem pulling off any panties. For jeans or shorts, this can be done by visiting a restroom, like my wife did in this prior story, but it can also be done by wearing panties with string ties on the sides. These can be removed by just reaching down the side of her jeans, untying the strings, and then pulling the panties up and off without removing or even loosening her jeans. When I know my wife has these panties on, I have the pleasure of first hugging her and sliding my fingers down to untie the sides and then pulling the panties out as I hold and kiss her. Try practicing it, guys, just like you practice unhooking a bra in the back with one hand. I just love the way she reacts after I have untied the sides and slowly pull the panties out up the **front** of her tight jeans. I realize what and where the panties are rubbing as I pull them up.

To see if know what I am talking about in pulling out the panties, try this at home, get a long, narrow silk scarf, and have your girl put it between her legs with one end at her belly button, and then pull on her tight jeans over the scarf with the long end hanging out over the middle of the back of her waistband like a tail. This can be under any clothes or just using a belt to put the scarf on like a loincloth. Then grab the front end and slowly pull the scarf out as you make out with her. You can experiment with putting the scarf on with no panties, or if the rubbing is too much, try it again with the scarf over a pair of panties to reduce the actual friction in her most sensitive spot. The friction also depends a lot on how slick the scarf is. Some scarves do not slip well at all, but a very slippery-feeling silk or nylon scarf can drive a girl crazy as it rubs on her pussy. Try it again with the short end at her ass crack and pull it out the back – see which way she likes it best. Try a long, steady pull, and then try random quick, little jerks to surprise her and keep her guessing. While wearing a scarf between her legs, try standing together as you hug and kiss to make out a little bit like horny teenagers, and just occasionally tug on the scarf one way or the other. This will add a unique sexual addition to making out like you used to do before you started having sex, if there ever was such a time in your relationship. Like everything I write about – just have fun, experiment, laugh at what doesn't work well for you, and really enjoy what does work. In a lifelong love affair, you have plenty of time to try things and experiment and enjoy.

I like to have my wife change into something sexy when we are home alone for the evening or for any time of the day when we are both home (our kids are all grown and gone). She likes to attract and tempt me all day or all evening, and I like to be boldly seduced by her. This is where outrageous modifications are fun. This means modifications and exposure that she would never wear in public but which makes her look good to me. This means things that could be considered complete exhibitionism or a display of any or all of her feminine assets and which, at the very least, allow me full or easy access to all her important charms. It is more fun to screw her while she is actually wearing her sexy outfits than to just have her seduce me and then fully strip for sex.

There is nothing wrong with bare-naked sex. We enjoy it often, but the sexy outfits offer lots of variety in many ways. She only has one birthday suit to seduce me with but countless different "ready, willing, and available: come and GET ME!" outfits that rev up my libido.

CHAPTER 6
Advanced Jeans Modifications

C LOTHING MODIFICATIONS CAN RANGE from hidden (like just inside of pockets), to just for sex (like the crotch seam cut open), to more outrageous. This can be just peek-a-boo cutouts that show some skin – things that would be indecent to wear in public in most people's opinion but don't show the areas a little bikini swimsuit would cover. Or it can be modifications that show more intimate areas than a bikini would show – anything and everything she's got in a tantalizing way for your eyes only. This is using the clothing just as decoration to enhance the charms of a desirable, attractive female body for whatever the situation you want.

Think about how good a shapely ass looks in a pair of snug jeans, and think about how the area of those normal rear pockets grabs your attention – part of that nice, round, firm, shapely, fully packed look with attractive pocket patterns and even nice-looking decorative stitching. I have tried several modifications on pockets. I have cut out the entire sides and bottom of the back pockets just around the stitching on the outside edge of the pockets. This leaves the pockets entirely intact and usable but just hanging from the top like a flap. Two pieces of her cute bare ass are exposed under the pockets peek-a-boo style. This always makes me want to enjoy all the charms of her nice ass, particularly if I know there is also a crotch-cut to allow immediate gratification.

Another approach is to cut out the entire two layers of the back pocket just inside the pocket stitching and straight across at the top just ¼ inch below the pocket top. This just makes a complete hole where the pocket was. This leaves just the pocket outer seam and stitching in place and makes the pocket cutout just a totally exposed piece of bare butt outlined by the pocket-shaped hole surrounded by the denim and stitching. This is more brazenly sexy and not as much of a peek-a-boo look, but it still shows a nice piece of bare ass that will make any red-blooded guy think about wanting to get his own piece of that nice ass.

See front cover illustration of jeans rear pockets cut out entirely.

One tip for getting the best piece-of-bare-ass look when cutting pockets totally out, the jeans should fit snugly to the girl's rear over the entire pocket area but not too tightly – maybe even just one size larger than she usually wears. If they are too loose and baggy, the cutout area will not be pressed right up against her ass. If they are too tight and are too form fitting to shape her rear, the flesh of her ass will bulge out in the cutout area, and the overall look of her ass will seem lumpy rather than keeping that nice, natural, firm, rounded look. You all know how tight jeans will squeeze a muffin top over the waistband and how I found that it makes a pussy pop right out with a crotch-cut, but you don't want the popping out look on the rear pockets; it is not flattering. This is a good reason why it won't do to just cut out the pockets on a pair of her favorite jeans, because they are probably tight to help shape her butt firmly – you want gently snug but not tight. My preference is also for smaller pockets higher up on the rear – little pockets are more of a tease with this look. A little higher is also a better, a tauter area of skin to peek out from a girl's ass, and when she walks, it may show a little more underneath muscle movement up where the natural butt padding is the least.

A regular pair of most jeans or denim shorts has some other ways to cut out sections to add bare skin for interest. In the front, the area above the usual pockets looks good when removed. The goal is to entirely cut out just the backside of the front pockets from below the waistband and just leave the outer front pocket edges up against her bare skin on both sides. Just cut out the entire front pocket and trim the backside of the pocket from just below the waistband to the front edge of the side seam and then down the side seam into the pocket. This leaves the front side of the hips showing just below the waistband and belt – I like the peek-a-boo look this gives. Some girls have a little tattoo on the front of the lower hip that may show with this cut out. Sometimes I have put little heart and rose decal tattoos on my wife there to peek out from the cutouts at me when she wears this modification.

See Illustration 6-1 for cutoff shorts with these front pockets cut out.

On the backside, many denim jeans have a yoke panel just below the waistband that forms a denim pattern, with another seam sloped from about an inch below the waistband on the sides to about two inches at the center seam. Every area of flat, single-layer denim inside these various seams can be cut out to make a peek-a-boo area on the lower back on each side, just below the waistband and belt. I like to cut out both sides of this entire section. I only cut just above the lower yoke seam from the center vertical seam to the side seams. I don't remove any of these vertical or horizontal seams – just the fabric in between seams in the section. Then I cut next to both the center and side vertical seams and along the waistband seams right below the belt loops. This leaves nice peek-a-boo glimpses of the girl's lower back. However, DON'T cut the center vertical seam out, or it may cause the center rear area of the garment to sag and lose its shape.

Sometimes shorts or jeans have the branded leather patch that hangs down past the waistband. I cut all the fabric away from the bottom of the leather patch, but I do not cut the patch – I leave it hanging down a little over her bare skin there. Also, there are often belt loops in the middle of each side that are sometimes attached to that piece of material of the yoke – you can cut around those spots to keep the belt loop or cut straight across to disconnect the bottom of the belt loop and then cut off the top of the belt loop from the waistband to remove it. The yoke looks OK either way – those side belt loops are not needed even if she wears a belt with the outfit. Always leave the center belt loop.

See Illustration 6-2 for cut off shorts with these rear panels cut out.

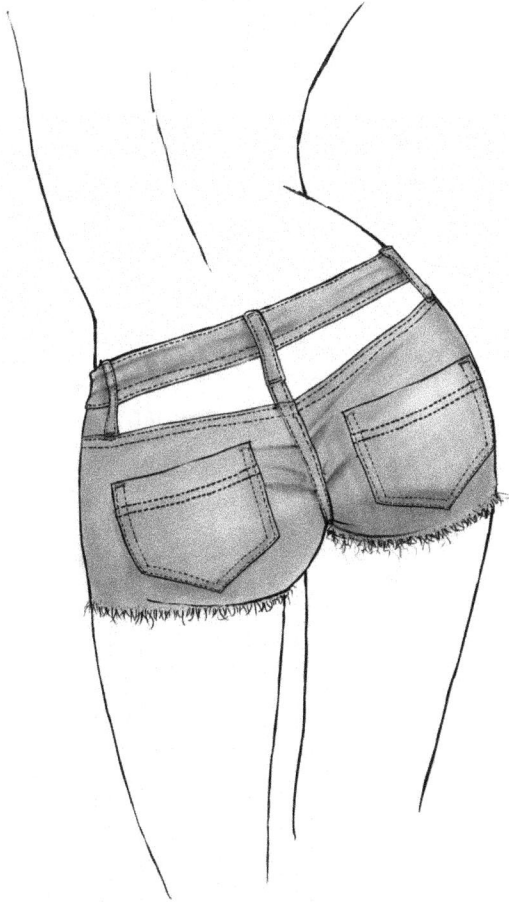

Done front and back, these two cutouts make a tantalizing peek-a-boo combination to show a little usually hidden skin both coming and going. It is definitely very sexy, but it is not indecent – this looks good in jeans or shorts or even some denim skirts that have the same front pockets and rear yoke like most jeans do. I think it probably looks the best for wearing privately as very, very short cutoff shorts. This gives 100% of her bare legs, lots of bare middle above the shorts, and even patches of skin usually covered by shorts. You can combine it with cutout pockets too if you want, but I only use either the pockets or yoke cutouts on the back of shorts or jeans – doing both seems like too much. Of course, I also put a crotch-cut in almost all of the shorts or jeans that I have made any peek-a-boo cutouts in. My wife never wears the peek-a-boo cutouts in public, just in private for me, so I usually want her to be fully available too. I seem to have a very low resistance to her charms when she is trying to seduce me. I think it is from lack of trying to resist her at all for so many years.

Many girls these days have real tattoos, and one of the more common places for a tattoo seems to be the lower back area, just below the natural waistline – the "tramp stamp" tattoo. I think that this area is very sexy on a girl – it is that spot that gives her back the feminine hourglass figure shape as her back flairs out as her hips widen. It is also a sensitive area on my wife – a light touch there makes her quiver. I love to hug her and hold her and press firmly right in that lower back spot, both because it feels so good to me, particularly if I am feeling bare skin there, and because that is where I push most to get that total hug feling of a firm full-body hug. This is where we are pressed firmly together from thighs to chest and lips, and by pressing firmly in the small of her back, I press her pelvis firmly against mine. Many of the outfits I make are just to show off that nicely shaped area for the enjoyment of seeing where her little waist starts to flare out to her hips. I always think of the old *South Pacific* show tune, "*There Is Nothing Like a Dame!*" and the line in it, "*Where she's narrow, she's as narrow as an arrow, and she's broad where a broad should be broad!*" I like slim waists and nice hips and that curvy area in the lower back where many girls get the tramp stamp tattoo.

These tattooed girls seem to like to wear the low-rise jeans, skirts, or anything that shows off this area and their tattoo there. If they have it, they like to flaunt it. The rear yoke cutouts are perfect to show off more of that area and display the somewhat-hidden tattoo in garments that would otherwise hide the tattoo. This gives a girl a much wider selection of clothing to show off her tattoo if she makes this simple modification in higher-rise garments. This is one cut area in jeans that does not tend to have the flesh pop out from very tight jeans – it will work well for a girl who wants to show off a tattoo and still have the tight jeans fit that make her butt look slimmer and is daring enough to wear the cutout jeans in public. The cutouts are not indecent, but they have a bit of a daring image to be worn in public, My wife only wears this sort of stuff around the house just for me, but many younger girls with a tramp stamp tattoo might like this slightly daring, added, peek-a-boo glimpse of their tattoo even in public. Even a temporary henna, drawn-on, or glued-on decal tattoo could spice up a look for a girl who does not have a real tattoo there but might like to try one for a while.

Any girl who likes a real tattoo must like some version of the slightly bad-girl image, or at least like to be uniquely different in some ways, like the tattoo. An unusual, but not indecent, peek-a-boo cutout like this can be worn in public to show off the tattoo and should fit in very nicely with this sort of bad-girl image for the girl.

When my wife and I have been out on the road a while in warm weather and away from anyone we know, this lower-back area is where we like to get a long-lasting tramp stamp type henna tattoo on her. I just like the skin in that nice area, with or without a tattoo. So I like to have a tattoo peeking out at me there. It gives my squeaky clean, good-girl wife, who wants only me, a little of that bad-girl image toward me for a while as a nice variation, even if in public. The henna tattoos last a lot longer than a drawn-on, magic marker tattoo. I like to use a colorful decal tattoo there too, but it can wear off in day if her clothes rub on it. When we do get a henna tattoo, I refresh it frequently with a felt-tip magic marker to make it last days longer and sometimes brighten it up with coloring in the areas between the lines with colored magic markers.

Most of what I write about for jeans also applies to shorts or cutoffs. I like nice legs and I think my wife has nice legs, and therefore, I do more shorts and cutoffs than long jeans. For my liking, just for private wearing, the shorter, the better; the more bare leg, the better. I often make them so short that I not only see ALL of her legs, but she says it is also showing a lot of her ass too, not just her legs. If she says this, I just let her know that I think she has a nice ass as well as nice legs. Some of my cutoffs are cut in the back right up to the bottoms of the rear pockets – of course, the bottom of her pretty ass is showing – all the better! I like the look, and she likes that I like to look at her. Of course, she won't wear these very-high-cut shorts out in public.

There is one advantage to doing the peek-a-boo cutouts on jeans rather than shorts or a skirt. I like to cut the jeans into cutoff shorts, remove the thigh area of the jeans, and then put the lower pants legs back on as leggings. This look leaves only the thighs bare and emphasizes the bare thighs. I really like that look. I love to both look at and caress her bare thighs. I cover doing this and how to do it in a later chapter.

However, another variation for radical modification is only for long pants or jeans. Any long pants can be cut into chaps. Find any picture of regular chaps, and modify the pants to match, or go a little more extreme in what you remove. Regular chaps removes the entire crotch area and just leaves the legs attached to the waistband at the side. I have found cheap, thrift-store, black, vinyl, faux-leather pants that made great chaps. These look more like real leather chaps than denim does. Chaps really emphasize a girl's lower belly, ass, and bare pussy if she does not wear anything under the chaps. If the girl does not want to be totally open, then she can wear them with any shorts or underwear to show off only what she wants in bits of bare belly and inner thigh. To both cover up a little bit and still allow having sex without having to take off the chaps to remove the shorts or panties, you can have her wear side-tie panties, or even a string bikini bottom would work. The side strings will be hidden under the hip section of the chaps. It would only take a few seconds to reach the string ties, remove the bottom, and be totally exposed for sex. You could even modify a pair of cutoff shorts to totally cut away the two side seams and use a belt or some sort of tie to hold them on before putting on the chaps. Take off the belt in the shorts, and they can just be pulled off by grabbing the crotch and pulling. I made a pair of short shorts just like that on a pair of shorts that were a little too small for my wife; I just cut away the side seams, and the outside two inches of her hips were bare except for the belt. Of course, for the chaps, you can use denim shorts or jeans that just have the crotch-cut hole and screw away while the wife looks fully dressed cowgirl style. In any event, I recommend the cowgirl or reverse cowgirl sex positions for the girl to ride the guy if she is going to dress up cowgirl style.

The best items to cut for chaps are pants without back pockets, which are easier to cut to match the pattern of real chaps (the pocket looks bad if half cut.) If there are rear pockets, just cut out the entire pocket area. One important factor in making chaps is that the original pants size practically doesn't matter. The one key measurement you need when shopping for possible chaps is the maximum thigh measurement of your wife. Tape the largest part of the thigh or measure the leg of tight-fitting pants. For example, a thigh that is 16 inches around equals an 8-inch flat pants' leg measurement.

With this measurement, you will find that you can make chaps out of pants that are many sizes smaller than pants that will fit. You can cut out the entire front crotch through the waistband, just leave the back waistband intact, and then use a belt. Or even cut out the center in the back too, and just have two leggings that you can hang from a belt and wear as chaps. The waist and hips do not have to fit at all when the item is separated into two sides – only the pants legs must be large enough for the wife to get her thighs into them. Kids' sizes made into leggings will ride with a lower belt level on the hips or else you must cut away a little of the inner top of the leg so it can be hoisted up to a higher belt level. The legs will be a little shorter too.

I have even found a pair of small, children's jeans that had a very decorative band with a fringe up the outside seam. When cut into leggings and hung from a belt, what were loose pants legs for the child were just very snug, sexy leggings on my wife. They were worn with the belt very low on her hips, and she wore cowboy boots over the bottom of the snug chaps, so the short child's length was not noticeable at all.

Matched with cowboy boots, a cowboy hat, and a sexy revealing cowboy vest as a top, it was a nice cowgirl look. The look makes a guy want to shout *"Yaaa hooooo!! Ride'er cowboy! Ride'er long, Ride'er often, and ride'er HARD! "* As a matter of fact – the harder the better. Just don't forget to leave your own cowboy hat and cowboy boots on when you screw your wife in an outfit like this – it is the cowboy way to screw a pretty young heifer. You can make a set of chaps for yourself too, you know. Chaps on a guy never get in the way of what guys like to do most with a sexy wife.

This brings up a marriage tip for all you wives reading this. Dressing to look sexually appealing can work both ways. If it appeals to you wives, make suggestions about what you want your husband to wear, or make him something yourself. If you want him to wear something completely outrageous to appeal to you or just to make him feel as outlandishly ridiculous as you think you feel in some of these outfits – go for it. Any guy who wants his wife to look totally ridiculous to exhibit her charms for him has to be man enough to still feel macho no matter what she wants him to wear. For example, get a football players outfit – shoulder pads, team jersey top, and maybe pants too – then cut out the essential part of the pants and screw the heck out of your cheerleader wife. How many of you guys have played sports and have a uniform or even a full football outfit, pads and all, and yet you have never bothered to fuck your wife in the outfit to let her fantasize about getting screwed by the team? Just a little modification to let your cock out is all it would take. Fun and laughter is supposed to be part of a good marital relationship. From experience, I can tell you that you can still have great sex at the same time that you are both laughing your heads off. If the attraction and desire is there, laughter doesn't kill a good erection – guys, just remember to keep stroking while you laugh.

CHAPTER 7

Expanding on One Idea for Even More Fun

A S AN EXAMPLE of how anyone can take just one of these ideas and expand it in a dozen ways to have fun with it and add a lot of variety to their sex life, I will go over several possible ways to have fun with just the jeans rear pocket cutouts described earlier in the previous chapter – total removal of the rear pockets, just leaving the pocket seam and outside stitching. (This is just like the jeans on the cover model.)

One thing to try with the full-pocket cutout jeans is to find a felt-tip magic marker as closely matched to the jean's contrasting thread color as possible. Then have your wife try on the jeans and use the felt-tip marker to duplicate the original stitched pattern from the removed pocket on the bare skin right where the pocket panel was cut out. Just draw the outline in tiny dashes to duplicate the desired stitch pattern. You can copy the original pattern of stitching or use the pattern from any other jeans that looks attractive. Or you can use any design that you want that looks like a jeans pocket design. You can put shamrocks for St. Patrick's Day, hearts for Valentine's Day, appropriate flags to celebrate anything like the 4th of July, Cinco de Mayo, Texas Independence Day, etc. For a complete pocket-stitching look, you need to let the ink dry and then pull the jeans down and widen the design on her ass a little. Extend the markings out about an inch in each direction because, when you are screwing her vigorously, the jeans move a little on her ass. The pattern on the skin needs to be a little larger than the hole cutout in the jeans if you are trying to make it look like pocket stitching so that, as the pocket cutout moves a little on her ass as you screw her, it doesn't move beyond the end of the pattern on her ass.

For the next day or two, the result will also mean that she will still be displaying a reminder of the cutout pocket look, even when her ass is butt naked – she will just have the stitching pattern drawn on her bare ass until the marker wears off. Since it will only be the stitch pattern, you can add interest by using a denim blue marker to draw a pocket around the stitching pattern on her ass. This will make her look like she has pockets on her bare ass when she has nothing on. I have often bent my wife over the edge of the bed bare assed and enjoyed the look of painted-on rear pockets on her pretty little ass as I screw her. You can see how one idea can be expanded and explored in several directions if you are willing to experiment and just have fun together. Don't forget that the wife can do body art on her husband too. I imagine that, after some wives read this, some guy will be walking around with the pockets cut out of a pair of his jeans and with some artwork painted on his bare butt. Let's all just hope that he has a nice-looking, tight butt if he walks past us. My flabby old butt would not look very good exposed that way.

Even permanent markers will wash off of skin fairly easily, or they will wear off in a few days. A little alcohol on a paper towel will remove markers quickly. Test a small spot of the markers on her skin first if you are concerned. On the other hand, if parts of your artwork tend to wash or wear off sooner than you would like, you can always trace over it again with the marker to brighten it up. We have had some boardwalk-type souvenir shops do real, longer-term, but still temporary, henna tattoos on my wife. By using black magic markers, I have enjoyed retracing the designs numerous times to keep the look fresh for several extra weeks because I liked the way it looked so much. My wife has a special spot that I like, and in the warmer weather, I frequently use a black marker to draw a little heart there, and I color it in with red. Every few days, I freshen it up again, and she may have it there for a month or more. It is normally hidden, but sometimes she wears a blouse or a swimsuit, and it looks like she has a little tattoo. If something is a turn-on – DO IT!! As long as it is not illegal, immoral, or fattening, just DO IT!! (And even fattening things are sometimes worth it – ideas with fresh fruit, chocolate syrup, strawberry jam, whip cream, and sometimes sweet cordials, hard liquor, champagne, etc. may be worth having to diet it off.) But I don't recommend anything illegal or immoral.

I want to add a warning about using magic markers to put on tattoos. The marker color can rub off onto clothing and other material a little. Particularly when the coloring is fresh, some of the color rubs off. This may stain a bra, panties, sheets, a blouse, or anything else that the tattoo color contacts. This rubbed-off color may wash out of the other material but not always. Just know the possible risk of this if the person will put on nice expensive item after getting a magic marker tattoo painted on. I don't want anyone angry at with me for not letting them know this slight risk. A little color rubbed off on some of the outfits we use is never a problem, but sometimes my wife removes the tattoo with alcohol before putting on any light colored item that she wants to protect.

The little kids like face painting – us big kids like the same things, only we like to paint some more adult areas and use more adult themes. Try it. You'll like it. This can open up a whole lot of variations on any of my ideas.

To really expand the appeal of the decorated ass, after the pocket pattern is done, have her take the jeans off and bend over or lie down naked on a table or bed face down. Restrain yourself now guys, and don't do the first thing that comes to mind when she lays her bare backside down for you to work on right in front of you – just feel her up if you like, and then get the felt-tip marker again. Use the pocket cutout pattern already done on her skin as the start of a lot of free-hand drawing with the markers to cover her entire ass and anywhere else you would like. Draw on some sexy shorts or whatever else turns you on.

Hey, on second thought guys, I realize that I would go ahead and do the first thing on my mind when my wife assumed the suggested position lying down naked in front of me for me to draw on her. I would do the additional drawing after I was finished with the first thing. I would use the logic that I feel more artistic when I am a very satiated, happy, and mellow fellow.

Try drawing on just the stitching pattern of an entire pair of jean shorts – front, back, crotch, waistband, and seams. That look would be like skin-colored jeans, with just the stitching for effect. This way you can enjoy a bare-naked butt screw with the jeans just drawn on.

I have tried doing this with my wife. I matched the stitching pattern and drew the outline only of a set of shorts on my wife. I drew the stitching as dots to do the several rows of stitching of the waistbands, two rows up and down to make every seam and the cuffs. The entire pockets and decoration, the rear yoke, and the zipper seams were all drawn on. She just had on the skin-colored shorts. Use a darker marker to make the outline show up more.

This is body painting her, just like the kids' face painting. This way she looks good in the pocket cutout jeans and out of them for up to several days if you try not to wear it off or wash it off. This is not exactly modifying any clothing. It is just bare-naked sex, but it doesn't look like being bare-naked. My ideas never stop at just actual clothing modifications, and I am including some of these extra ideas for your enjoyment.

With a little blue body paint, you can even draw and paint on the whole pair of shorts. I have seen pictures of stuff, like one of the *Sports Illustrated* swimsuit editions that had nude models with absolutely nothing on except body painted clothes and swimsuits. It was astoundingly realistic – even small wrinkles in the fabric and string ties were just painted on. Of course, *Sports Illustrated* never showed the full-frontal shots of the crotch area, so I don't know how that looked, but the rest of it was amazingly realistic. I have seen one or two full frontal shots of a painted-on bikini, and the model was totally shaved and painted in her pubic area, and it still looked very real, like a bikini bottom. I think the full rear view would show the ass crack too clearly to look real. The reality of the pictures was because of the angles and areas photographed.

I do think that a girl could get away with going topless on almost any public beach for awhile if she wore a real bikini bottom and one of those very real-looking painted-on bikini tops. The idea is fascinating to think about, but I would only really try it with my wife if we ever go to a nude beach somewhere. If this idea prompts any reader to try a painted-on top on a regular public beach or on a nude beach, please visit my free website, **DressForSEXcess.com**, and post the experience there to let me and the site visitors know about it. Tell us what happened – how crowded it was, how many people seemed to notice, how long you were there, if you went into the water or just sat on the beach, whether you eventually had to cover up to avoid unwanted attention, and any end result. A safe approach would be to have a real swimsuit top to match the bottom and then paint on a top that looks the same but is a smaller size. That way, if you decide to cover up, you put on an identical-looking top that is larger and covers up the painted on top. Only the painted-on strings would show once the wife put on the matching real top – it might look like she had on double strings. I suggest you put the real top on first and mark where the painted strings should be as close as possible to where the real strings would be.

While you are at the website, there are more suggestions for body painting. Look under "More Body Painting Ideas" to find more ideas from me or from other website visitors who have posted stuff there. Post your own new suggestions at the site too.

Well, you can screw your own wife with a painted-on pair of shorts, if you like the jeans look on her and are willing to go to the trouble of doing the decoration. *Sports Illustrated* said it took hours to do even a bikini paint job. However, I can think of worse ways to spend my time than painting a pair of shorts on my wife. The biggest problems would be concentrating on it enough to finish it and waiting for the paint to dry before I smear the paint with my body against hers.

If you can do a good job of painting on just pockets that are a close match to real denim and stitching and if a girl is daring and a little bit of an exhibitionist, she could wear the cutout pocket outfit in public over the painted pockets on her butt. You can expect lots of guys really starting at her ass but not sure of what they are seeing – what is real and what is not? Again, if any readers try this in public, visit the website and post the experience please.

With any of these ideas, the result is only temporary artwork. You will always have the memory of the fun you had. However, you can have more than just memories if you plan ahead and have a camera to record your artwork. For years, we used Polaroid cameras and videotape to capture our totally private fun. Now digital cameras and omnipresent cell phone cameras make it so much easier and cheaper to take pictures for your own private enjoyment to remember the fun, and you still never need to let some photo darkroom people see your private pictures. With a little effort, you can collect a portfolio of sexy pictures that would emphasize the nice features of your wife and minimize the possible flaws, and they can be as tame and sophisticated as any glamour art collection or as raunchy as you dare to photograph. Look at some artistic photo books or some fashion magazines to get some glamour ideas and poses to copy. Believe me, someday, ten or twenty or fifty years from now, it will be nice to be able to look back at these photos to remember how good your wife looked way back then. Maybe even someday after you are gone, some adult grandchild may discover some of these pictures and say, "*WOW! That was Grandma. What a doll. She was a real beauty.*" When you are gray and wrinkled, it will be nice to look back

If your wife already has some tattoo design on her ass – the cutouts can be very exotic to let them show a little. One thing I tried was different too. At the shore one summer, I saw lots of girls' cotton short shorts for sale at the boardwalk shops that had names printed on the butt area of the shorts – like "Tom's Ass", "Joe's Ass", "Jim's Ass", etc. – and they would customize them for any names they didn't already have. For the next several days, my wife had my name on her left cheek and "ASS" on her right cheek. I repeatedly bent her bare butt over so I could read it and check if it was still labeled as mine, and then I exercised my ownership privileges again each time. I haven't done it yet, but I will have to try writing this ass ownership again, centering the words on the pocket area of her butt under her pocket cutout jeans the next time she wears them. As I write about subjects like this, I find my imagination keeps working, and I even think up more nice ideas that I haven't even tried yet and new ways to combine various ideas. Imagination is the key to having fun this way – exercise your imagination.

Of course, there is also the use of temporary decal tattoos. I have found that they do not last very long in places where clothing rubs on the skin very much. They are best on arms and shoulders when she has them bare in summer outfits or on areas of the breast that don't rub on her bra, etc. I did use these decal tattoos in at least the front pocket cutout areas of my wife's lower hip, and they lasted fairly long. There was very little pressure there on her clothes that wore the tattoo off, just some occasional rubbing against my pelvis. On my wife's butt, these wear off very fast when she puts on regular clothes after we play games – they are just for one-time use there.

A pair of outrageous panties looks good under the cutouts sometimes too – like a pair my wife has of full-cut, white, satin panties covered with life-size red kiss lip prints. This look doesn't show any skin in the cutouts, but the display of the sexy panties through the cutouts looks hot. But just a glimpse of bare butt skin sure looks great too. If a girl is the real brazen type, I guess she could wear some of these cutouts out in public since they are only peek-a-boo and not illegally indecent, but we just like them around the house for intimate fun play for just the two of us. I like the look of her being outrageously provocative to be just for me, but I don't want to share this with the whole world.

If you have a crotch-cut in the jeans that you want to use and she is wearing panties to show through the pocket cutouts – you can do the same crotch-cut in the panties so that they don't get in your way. I have a few dozen crotch-cut panties for my wife in different colors and styles that I have picked up and modified over time. This way, I have a quick choice of some panties ready to match any outfit I have in mind for her. Sometimes they look better under a micro miniskirt or with some outfits than going bare bottomed. Some of my skirts are so short that they don't even attempt to hide all her sexy merchandise. A pair of crotch-cut panties has the same accessibility to her intimate charms but makes her look more covered and less obvious. Also, some skirts and such tend to ride up higher on her than I want them to – I like them to ride low on her hips. Some things look better worn around the hips rather than the natural waist, but elastic waistbands tend to want to ride up higher. A set of panties that are cut at the right height can be worn, and a few safety pins or a minute with needle and thread can attach the panties' top to the item's waistband, and then the item will not ride up any more. Having different colors and assorted styles of panties ahead of time helps.

There are plenty of skorts available too. These are ideal to use to keep a miniskirt down on the proper place on the hips rather than riding up too high on the waist. Look for larger girls' sizes of these – the skirt layer tends to be shorter and more revealing in the smaller sizes, and they tend to have shorter shorts underneath to keep the waistband top lower on the hips. They are also usually cheaper to buy as children's clothing rather than as women's sizes, no matter where you are getting them. Just be sure that they will stretch wide enough to fit over the wife's hips, regardless of the original intended size shown. I have found that most preteen girls' skirts, shorts, and skorts with elastic waistbands can easily be stretched to fit an adult woman's figure in many cases. A simple crotch-cut in the undershorts makes them great for having sex with them on.

Any one thing I suggest probably has a lot of variations that you can use and expand on to have more fun, like the rear pocket cutouts. Exercise your imaginations and put different ideas together to have more personalized fun. A lot of the fun I have is in the fact that I modified the outfit and did it all myself. First, I found the item to use. Next, I put the ideas together, and I made her look attractive in it in just the way I wanted. And then I get to enjoy all her charms in the way I wanted too. My wife is smart enough to realize that if she wants a HAPPY husband and more great sex, then it helps to encourage me in any way that works. She wants me to want her, and I REALLY DO want her, and I know that there is no one who could make me happier than she does. She seems to love being my grown-up XXX-rated Barbie doll – I love giving her all my business. I know my mother told me that I played with dolls as a child – I do remember some of this. I find it is much more fun to play with a grown-up, real-live doll, than any kids' doll. A kids' Barbie doll is not as nice as having a real, fully responsive Barbie doll to dress, undress, and play with in EVERY way.

CHAPTER 8

More Top Modifications

THERE ARE MANY MORE WAYS to modify tops. I found that the breast pocket cutouts on the denim vests made the front look good, and I found ways to make the back look sexier too. I have found that many denim vests have a similar look in the back, with a yoke across the top formed by a horizontal seam across the top of the back and then a vertical seam down each side to the bottom hem. This forms an almost rectangular panel covering most of the back. I like to cut that entire panel out, leaving just a one- or two-inch band at the bottom edge to hold the vest together. This gives a totally open bareback look from the rear.

I like any look with lots of bare back on a girl. Of course, I like to see nice, smooth female skin anywhere. Also, I can stare at the back of any girl without her noticing that I am looking at her. Bare skin anywhere on a girl's torso and a nice-shaped feminine figure are a turn-on for most guys. I also like a little drawn-on tattoo on a bare back. I often am looking at the back of an outfit. For example, when my wife is working in the kitchen at the counter, if I am sitting at the kitchen table, I am looking at her back; I like to see her pretty bare back and usually bare thighs rather than just the back of some regular outfit.

With my imagination, when I see that much bare skin from top to bottom, I always realize that she could not be wearing any bra (no strap), and that makes me think about the naturally shaped, soft-breast look I will see from the front. It is a male imagination stimulant to know that there is just one layer over her shapely breasts and to think about how soft and nice and natural it would feel if I just slid my hands under that one layer. With the open back, I can stand behind her, slide a hand around her under each side, and fondle a breast in each hand as she quivers in my arms in response to my touch, with her pretty body held tight against mine as I press her breasts to press her up against me. This is just more mind groping, but I know that, if I did it, my wife would probably lean back up against me, and I would start to kiss her neck as I fondled her until we move on to something more. With my wife, I often follow up on that thought whenever possible, always to our mutual delight. I like to touch often, and she likes to be caressed by me, and then she knows that I am noticing how she dresses to please and encourage me.

A marriage tip for all husbands – if your wife tries to please you, always let her know that you notice and appreciate it. Let her know what you like so she will learn what turns you on better. Wives are not mind readers – tell her what you like, and show appreciation when she responds positively.

Another very important marriage tip is that you should touch your wife often when you are together. Touching her lovingly is one of the best ways to express your appreciation for anything. Touching a lot is an essential ingredient in a happy love life – touching of any sort is good, but any skin-to-skin touching is better, and skin-to-skin contact involving your partner's sensitive areas is best. When you are home together all day, like on a weekend or holiday for most couples, you should learn to touch her two or three dozen times a day. Many professionals say that a relationship without a lot of touching will eventually deteriorate. I can state positively from my experience that a LOT of touching is essential to a strong loving relationship for us.

Many wives think that their husband never touches them unless they want sex. Every wife remembers being the little girl who loved to play dress up, dreamed about being a princess, and wanted to be pursued and sought after by her Prince Charming. Every time you purposely touch your wife, you are telling her that you want her, want to be close to her, appreciate being with her, and still love her. This is how you become her Prince Charming, and once she feels that way about you, you'll never want her to change. Guys, action speaks much louder than just words. However, words help too. When you touch her often and tell her why – things like, *"I just like the way that your skin feels so soft and smooth"* or *"Your hand feels so nice in my hand"* – it will soon melt her heart when she realizes that you are sincere about liking her and wanting to please her and are not just looking for sex.

I don't know how any guy can not like touching and feeling any part of a female body rather than looking at any girlie picture if he has a choice. Real groping is always much better than just mind groping whenever you have the opportunity. Once you understand each other, a gentle caress of your wife's arm combined with a loving glance will have a world of deep meaning. Many things can be done even with the kids or other adults around. A gentle caress or a playful pat on the rear is almost always appropriate between a married couple.

Your kids learn more from your actions than from your words. They will learn that a loving touch is an important part of a loving marriage. I remember reading somewhere recently that a study revealed that it is very important for kids to know that their parents love each other. This makes perfect sense when you realize how this reassures the kids about the security of being part of a real family. All the kids today see many of their friends who suffer through the insecurity of having divorced parents. Seeing that this is not very likely to happen to them and to their family is very important to them. It also shows them how a happy married couple shares their love to teach them how to have a happy marriage of their own someday, with lots of touching. When the kids reach puberty, they will have an increased interest in touching the opposite sex, and they should know what a nice sign of affection touching is.

In private, a hand slipped under a blouse or used for any other quick feel can show that you really appreciate your wife. I often give her a hug with a kiss or a quick feel or caress and say, *"Thanks, that was for me. I needed that! Would you like one too?"* And then I get to do it again because she always wants another. That's how love works when you get it right. No, not every touching event should be a request to have sex again. The touching should be so often that no one could ever have sex that often. It should be touching because you love each other and only as a way to keep each other on simmer, gradually leading up to your next lovemaking session.

Now to get back to the subject of modifying a denim vest: One nice variation is to not cut out the entire panel but to cut a maximum-sized heart shape out of the back panel of a vest. My cover illustration shows a nice, large, heart-shaped cutout on the denim vest. It shows lots of bare skin and lets everyone see that she does not have any bra strap on. The heart shape says something about her attitude for dressing that way and so does her smile. This works regardless of the original pattern of the back of the vest. Just as with the shoulder-to-waist cutout that shows there are no bra straps underneath, it offers the same invitation to slide my hands around under the front, and it may show a little less skin than cutting out the full panel, but it is a romantic symbol that lets me know that she is wearing the bare look as a heart because she is in love with ME.

On one vest where the horizontal back seam was low – across her shoulder blades – I used the larger-than-normal back panel over the shoulders to cut out a five-pointed star pattern about 3–4 inches across, centered on the back of each shoulder. This is another way that it helps to be flexible and creative and figure out the best way to modify an item based on the original design of the item. I also have done a vest with a star high on one shoulder and a crescent moon in the other shoulder. I tell my wife that she is "the moon and stars" to me. I also joke about how I promised her the "moon and stars" before we were married – well, this is just one more case where I have delivered on my promise.

If you just cut the back and don't do the front pockets, it is a nice vest she can wear out in warm weather, looks normal from the front, and is just a knockout surprise from the rear. I think the bare-back look is best when her hair is long enough to hang down over the vest top section across her shoulders and brushes over her bare skin in the cutout section. This is just my personal preference, but it is also a tip to any husband whose wife has long hair and who likes that look of long hair brushing bare skin. Because I like the look, sometimes my wife wears an almost waist-length fake ponytail hair extension nicely blended in with her own hair. She is always a knockout to me with that look. A back cutout can be worn in public if the wife is a little daring – it doesn't show anything indecent.

A tip to every wife – most men like the look of long hair. I think it makes a woman look much more feminine. If my wife wears it up sometimes, I love the ability to undo it and let her hair down later when we are alone. Her hair does not have to be carefully styled to please me. Of course, she is a woman and is always concerned about how good her hair looks and often spends a lot of time on it, but I like it worn any way. If it is nicely styled, I think about how much fun it will be to tousle her hair when we make love later. After we make love, I like her to leave it all tousled and see how it lets me enjoy the well-loved look of her hair with the well-loved smile on her face. You wives should definitely find out what you husband likes – then do what you can to please him. This is one more way that you show how much you love him.

Today I see that most teenage girls wear their hair very long. I think that they realize that this is more attractive to the boys, and almost every teenage girl is at least subconsciously trying to attract boys – for many of them, this is almost all that they think about. I think that most boys find that long hair very attractive and very feminine looking – I sure do. As a question for the wives, why do you stop trying to look attractive for your husband once you get married? Don't you want to keep him? What about all the long-haired, slightly younger girls he sees at work, around town, or even at church? Do you want to give away an attractive advantage? Find out what your husband really thinks. Don't just ask him, "*Do you like the way I wear my hair?*" That kind of question is like asking, "*Do these jeans make my butt look too fat?*" No intelligent guy would dare give the wrong answer to those questions. Try something like, "*I saw an old picture of myself when I was in school. I had long hair back then. I was thinking of letting it grow long again. It was a little more work back then, but I thought that it looked more feminine. What do you think?*"

Another way is to get a long-haired wig to see how it looks. Perhaps go to a wig shop with him, or try one of the places at many flea markets that sell wigs. Try a few on and see what he thinks about the length, and you will even get to see his reaction to some different colors. You can also get wigs at eBay or many other online stores. You can even buy a long, fake ponytail that matches your hair color, wear it for him, and see his reaction. If he promptly makes a pass at you, I think it is a fair assumption that he prefers the long-haired look. It will at least prove that I am right about how every guy likes some variety and how it perks up his interest in you to have a different look for him once in a while.

A favorite thing I do to make a super-sexy-looking top is to shorten the top or cut peek-a-boo holes. Any tee shirt or knit top can be cut up in many different ways. I can usually get many tee shirts at various rummage sales, thrift shops, or garage sales for about one dollar or less. I will buy quite a few when I find these sales – to get an inventory of stuff to cut up. Size or color or printing or designs are not very important. Sometimes the printing on the top will suggest an outfit or entire fun role-playing scenario. Being too small is not always a problem – I like to have some things very tight and formfitting, and even so tight I have to cut it to make it fit at all.

One tip is trying to make a very small top fit comfortably enough for the wife to wear it a short time. Be sure it stretches enough to fit her bust size. If it still seems too small it means it is too tight under the armpits for the wife. Cut out the bottom side seam on each side to let it split out under the arm, right where it is too tight. This will give it a few extra inches to be pulled up by enlarging the armhole opening at the bottom. Cut all the way from a few inches below the bottom of the sleeve up past the sleeve seam to the sleeve opening on a short-sleeve shirt. This will let the arms be comfortable even if the top is a kids' size that has to really stretch to fit over her bust. A nice side effect of cutting the underarm area of a too-small shirt is that the husband can easily side his hands under the shirt from the sides. From the rear, he can slide his hands around his wife through the underarm cuts to cup his hands on her breasts as he hugs her. From the front, he can hug her with his hands on her bare back under her shirt. I love the feel either way.

If it is not quite large enough to fit around the bust size properly, it can be given a couple extra inches by a vertical slit made up the center of the back. This adds to the front most of the width that it expands by stretching open the back hole.

These tricks often let you take a very little girls shirt with a printed message or picture and let your sexy wife give it a new meaning. Things like "Daddy's Girl," "Angel," "Heart Throb," "Heart Breaker," or heart symbols take a little more risqué meaning when it is a little girl's shirt stretched over a sexy, full-busted woman who wants to be very available. Next I mention adding words to the message or emblem. For example, I like taking a Hello Kitty emblem and adding something like "Warm and Willing Pussy."

One simple modification to any item, and particularly a tee shirt, is to just use a marker instead of scissors and write a sexy message. Anything provocative that you can think up will work. For example, we were teasing each other about a "Think" sign we saw up on a wall somewhere. I joked that, every time I try and think, all I think about is how sexy she is. Somehow that talk led to a plain tee shirt on which I wrote, "The 'Good Word' for the day is "LEGS." Spread the Good Word!" I kept telling her to "spread the good word!" It finally worked well enough when we played around and she lay down, spread the word, and got royally laid. Then all day for several days, I would tell her, "Spread the good word!" and reach in to check how wide she was spreading her legs, and then I'd say "Wider! Wider!" This is now of those standard jokes between us now – I will often ask her, "What is the good word for the day? Is it still 'legs'?" And we both have a good laugh, and I try to get a good quick feel. Of course, it may be even more fun to use both the marker and scissors on any item you want to use – add a sexy message and cut it indecently short too.

One modification that I have used once or twice when an item would seem just a little too tight a stretch for her bust is to use it for an open-bust outfit. I cut the chest area to let her boobs hang out in the open.

Sometimes this open-bust look is because that is the look the item suggested. One item I bought was a bright red tee shirt that said "I

LOVE" on one line on the upper chest, and underneath it said "NASCAR" right over the bust area. I just made a horizontal oval cut about 2 inches high across the front to remove the "NASCAR" wording. When she put it on, it just said "I LOVE" right above her naked boobs hanging loose. I sure loved that look, and I did a lot of touching. You could do exactly the same thing on any plain tee shirt and just use a marker to write on the shirt anything you want. For example, "Best BOOBS in the World Award" or "We NEED A Massage!" would be nice with a totally bare-bust look.

For more ideas on suggestions for an open-bust cutout or more slogans to use with these cutouts, go to my free **DressForSEXcess.com** website and look under "More 'Open Bust' Cutout Ideas" to find more ideas from me or from other website visitors who have posted stuff there. Post your own new slogan ideas there too.

Another way to use the open-bust look is to use two individual, round cutouts for the two breasts and make them look like two big letter **O**'s or zeros. I found a kids' Superman tee shirt with the Superman S on the upper chest area. I cut out the two boob holes and used a marker to draw a circle around them to make big letter **O**'s out of the holes and then wrote big letter B's on each side of the **O**'s around under the arms on the tee shirt. It read "Super B**OO**B." I called her Super B**OO**Bs all that day and have referred back to that nickname frequently since then. There are so many Superman tee shirts available that anyone can duplicate this for a girl who does have super boobs. Any double-**O** word or phrase could be done with the two boob-cutout holes. "WH**OO**?" "w**O**w- w**O**w," "w**O**w-m**O**m," "L**OO**K," "B**OO**K," "G**OO**D," "**OO**h," "s**OO**," "m**OO**re," "M**OO**!," would all be able to be put into a tee shirt word or phrase – like "L**OO**K at these Beauties!" "What are you L**OO**King at?" "Seeing D**OO**uble," "L**OO**King For Trouble," (with these you should add some crotch-cut panties that say "Trouble Is down Here), "Do you want m**OO**re?" or "$1,00**O,O**00,000 Baby" written as a wraparound all the way around her chest and back.

The double-**O** boob cutouts work well as the eyes on any big face you want to place on a tee shirt. A happy face with his wife's boobs for eyes and a foot-wide smile drawn across her belly on a tight, bright-yellow tee shirt would make a lot of husbands very happy. Any husband might have a foot-wide smile when he sees her in that shirt. The breast eyes can be full-size breast cutouts, with the breasts left plain and natural, or this look can be combined with the idea of body painting, the breasts being decorated – maybe paint them all white with black eye pupils where the nipples are.

Another example of how to expand on an idea, add a pair of crotch-cut yellow panties and write your own slogan on them, front and back – something like an arrow pointing to the crotch and the words, "Please INSERT Mr. Happy Here" or "Smiles Refreshed While You Wait." Have fun.

There are also a few ways to use one breast exposed and one covered. On the upper chest area, write a big "A Perfect," and then, centered over the right breast, write a big 1. Then make a single boob cutout hole on the left side, and it turns the number into "A Perfect "1O." The variations are endless and are all a lot of fun.

All of these different breast cutout ideas should give a guy all the touching opportunities that he could need for quite a while. However, if you need more ideas go to the free **DressForSEXcess.com** website and look under "More 'OO' Boob Cutout Ideas" to find more ideas from me or from other website visitors who have posted stuff there. Post your own new ideas too.

I also like to use the scissors for very small breast holes – just 3/8-inch nipple holes. To do this right, your wife must first try on the tee shirt and jiggle around to get it to settle on her body and breasts in the natural position in the shirt. Then use a marker and put a dot right on each nipple. Cut a tiny nipple-size hole at each mark, and then have her put it back on and work the nipple tip out each hole. You can try to get the shirt to stay in place with the nipples poking out with a little rubber cement around the breasts close to the nipples, like you would use on pasties. I love to see just the perky nipple tips sticking out and to gently caress or kiss just the tips of the nipples. It also seems to drive my wife wild.

What I also like to use on these little nipple holes is what is sold as a "titillizer" in many sex toy catalogs and stores. When the girl moves, the breasts tend to jiggle and the rubber cement does not always keep the nipples in the holes. This titillizer is a decorative little chain or cord with two tiny slipknot loops on the ends. The slipknots are to fasten over the nipple and tighten just enough to hold the loop end and a lightweight chain in place hanging on the nipple without hurting. I have them available for sale at the cheapest price I have seen them for on my free **DressForSEXcess.com** website. They are sold as a bare-breast decoration but work over a tee shirt with nipple holes just the same.

I like these titillizers because I think they sensitize my wife's nipples and make them stand out more firmly on her breasts – the loops make the nipples stay erect and perky looking. The titillizer keeps the nipples from going back under the shirt too. When I hold her body against mine and rub her chest against mine, the nipples are standing out firmly against me. The tiny loops keep the nipples erect and firm. I can feel them better against my chest, and her nipples are guaranteed to get the maximum feel of my chest. Anything that lets the tip of the nipple poke through seems to make it more sensitive, even stuff like loose, crocheted ponchos and shawls that have holes big enough to let the nipple poke out will work. I think it is because, normally, any pressure on the bare breast is distributed over the whole surface, and it all moves somewhat together. When it is just the tip of the nipple being touched, the feeling is more concentrated. When I touch, kiss, wet and blow on, rub, or tease her on just the tips of her nipples, it seems to get to her more intensely. I guess you could even say I can drive her wild that way. (This is another marriage tip on improving your foreplay, guys. Try it.) I don't ever use any of the commonly available nipple clamps because my wife's nipples are very sensitive, and we don't like painful sex games at all. For those who like this sort of thing, there are plenty of such clamps available.

I used this nipple-hole-and-titillizer trick on a bright-yellow shirt and used a marker to draw it as a big happy face. The nipples were centered in the black dots I drew as the pupils in the big happy face eyes. The curve of the chain matched the curve of the face smile. It sure made me smile a big happy face to play with her in the shirt and with her sensitive nipples.

Since having the nipples poking out is already very indecent, there is another way to help keep the nipples in place in the shirt's holes. Cut both sides of the shirt from the center of the bottom of the sleeve seam straight down to almost the bottom hem. Then cut the center between the breasts from just below the neck seam almost to the hem. Then have the wife try it on, and mark the nipple holes to be cut. When the shirt is put back on and the nipples have a little rubber cement around them to lightly fasten the shirt in place, there will be separate panels on each side, and these will be free to move with the breast that it is glued to. The panel will not pull off the breast. It will move with it. A matching vertical cut down the center of the back can also be added.

One teenage-size shirt I picked up had "It's All About ME" and the purple rabbit character that goes with that slogan and is popular with the kids today. As an example of what you can do with any idea from a slogan, here is an example of what I did with this one shirt. I cut it shorter so that it came right up under her bust in the front and used a marker to write stuff all over it. Under "It's All About ME," I wrote, "Because I am the best. Try me and see why" Other notes posted all over were, "I'd love to make like a bunny with you!" "Try me! You'll like it!" "Zero to WOW in 1.3 seconds," "Always Ready," "Get me Started, and I Come Nonstop," "Takes a Screwing and Keeps On Coming," and "Push + Go" centered over one nipple with "Twin Starter Switches" on the other nipple. At the center of the front bottom edge, I put an arrow pointing straight down toward her pussy and wrote, "WOW Zone." On the backside along the bottom edge, I added, "Works Great From Either Side." A nice idea on another shirt was a takeoff on the Nike slogan – I wrote "Just DO ME! Then flip me over" on both the front and back of a brief, shortened tee shirt.

Sex can be a lot of fun if you do it right. The use of sexy slogans is almost limitless. There are too many to list here all the ones I already have thought of. Go to my free **DressForSEXcess.com** website and look under "More Slogan Ideas to Decorate Tee Shirts" to find more ideas from me or from other website visitors who have posted stuff there. Post your own new ideas too.

For putting slogans on anything, you can use markers, which are available in many colors, or you can buy fabric paint at any craft store. Iron-on letters are also available in craft stores in various sizes.

Plain tee shirts let you come up with any theme you like. Draw any picture and slogans for Valentine's Day, a birthday, or any holiday. I look for good green colors and then use them over several days as part of St. Patrick's Day themes. Add slogans like, "Do You Feel Lucky Today?" "Are You a Fucking Irishman? Well, Go Ahead and Get busy! Start Fucking!" and, "My name is Lucky – You Can Be Lucky Too." Orange shirts make for good pumpkin themes for Halloween. This is another one that just seems to beg for the double-O boob-cutout look – draw big pumpkin-style triangle eyes around the boob cutouts, and then make the rest of a pumpkin face. Raunchy slogans are optional. There are plenty of red, white, and blue shirts or with US flag emblems for raunchy "Made in America... Daily!" themes of any sort and for the 4th of July.

You can also probably find color combos to match any other national or team colors to have sexy fun on any holiday. One of my favorite days to celebrate is March 2nd – Texas Independence Day. It is a great day to play, cowboy and cowgirl style – that is what my cover model looks like she is looking forward to. Have a happy Cinco de Mayo every May 5th, even if you aren't Latino and can't speak any Spanish. Red, white, and some maple leaf shapes are all you need to celebrate Canada Day, July 1st. A British Guy Fawkes Day on November 5th or a French Bastille Day any July 14th could both be the excuse needed for a sexy celebration. You can even dress up in green leaves and celebrate Arbor Day, but the date varies by state, if accuracy matters. There are many various religious holidays to celebrate too – don't let the fact that they are not your religion stop you from having fun with them. I think God created sex, so I am sure God would approve of any excuse for a husband and wife to enjoy sex. Any colors will work to celebrate a Dogpatch Sadie Hawkins Day some November 13th – try to modify an outfit that would make Al Capp, Li'l Abner, and Daisy Mae all blush.

There is another very simple modification that can be done on any tee shirt to just add a little peek-a-boo look that can be worn out in public all by itself or can be added to any raunchy modifications that I have already described. Cut out the shoulders on any tee shirt. You can easily cut out the top half of the shoulders on any sort of tee shirt to show a little more skin. This can be the only modification of a shirt to wear in public or a way to expose just a little more skin on any already indecently modified shirt. If a shirt has longer sleeves, you can also just cut holes down the sleeves too for more peek-a-boo skin. This may really appeal to a wife who has a little tattoo right on a shoulder – permanent, henna, or just a decal in the right spot. Any cutout to show a tattoo would work if the wife wants to display the tattoo and is daring enough to wear the cutout item.

To show off a shoulder tattoo or for a nice "off-the-shoulder" look, just modify a tee shirt by cutting off from the middle top of one shoulder diagonally across to under the sleeve on the other side. Eliminate the entire original collar and the other shoulder of the shirt. You can shorten it any way, in addition to cutting off the shoulder. I have done this with a cut from just below the breast level on the leftover shoulder side at the same slope as the top cut, and the shirt ends up with a totally diagonal look – short on the full-shoulder side, long on the shoulder-less side, and the same height across the width of the shirt. As an alternative, cut the bottom from just about 2 inches below where the low-side shoulder was cut, and cut diagonally in the opposite direction from the top cut, and you'll have a shirt that is only about 2 inches tall at the underarm on one side and long on the full-shoulder side.

Your birthday and your spouse's birthday are certainly worth a celebration too. If you have kids, use either their actual birthday or, better yet, figure back about nine months to the date of their conception, and then celebrate with a re-enactment of the event – visit the same locations, have a similar date, or if you are not sure, just make up something in order to have the fun of doing it again. If you don't remember how or exactly when or where the conception occurred, you have my permission to make something up, as long as it is good and you screw bareback for a true re-enactment of getting pregnant. When you are in the middle of screwing during the re-enactment, remember to concentrate on thinking that this time it is going to create a new baby. For going ALL the way together, there is nothing more complete than the husband planting his seed deep inside his wife.

I wonder if siblings who share the same birthday will someday result from this suggestion. I want to put in a disclaimer at this time that this book is written purely for entertainment purposes, and that I accept NO responsibility for unintended consequences that occur from actually using any ideas in this book. Maybe some couples who already have same-birth date children have already tried this trick on purpose, rather than just by coincidence. At least it makes remembering birthdays easier, and you can have just one party for two or more kids this way to be more efficient. As a matter of fact, when I think about it, I have two sons whose birthdays are only 3 days apart in early May. In my case, maybe there is something very seductive and very fertile about those hot summer nights in the beginning of August. I don't remember the specifics from that many years ago, but there were plenty of wonderful lovemaking sessions every day back then.

In another direction, just as a marriage tip, don't forget that most people's skin makes a nice blank canvas to use for any art and/or slogans. You can write or draw on your spouse's body alone or in conjunction with modified clothing. As I start to write down ideas to give you, I realize that each one I write down gives me ideas for two or three more to add – there is a limitless list of suggestions to have fun with if you are adventurous and imaginative.

Again, I have more script suggestions for offbeat holidays to celebrate in role-playing scenarios listed on my free **DressForSEXcess.com** website. Just look under "More Holiday Costume & Celebration Ideas" to find more ideas from me or from other website visitors who have posted stuff there. Post your own new ideas too.

One trick for modifying a top that is really hardly a top is not even about a modifying a top – it is about modifying candy. Find two pieces of hard candy at least one inch in diameter and preferably fairly flat; try a lollipop top. Drill a 3/8-inch hole in the center of each piece of candy – this is a guy kind of idea to do. Then use the two pieces of candy as nipple pasties. I tried Life Savers, but the holes are too small. Soft candy might do, but you'll have to figure out how to make the hole or shape it into a small ring. Put the candy in your mouth to wet it, and see if it will then stick on the bare breast and around the nipple as it dries. The wife must lie down on her back and let it dry when you do this. Any guy can figure out what to do with her as you both wait for the candy to dry in place. (Rubber cement is plan B). When it is dry, you can do whatever you want for fun and end up having the fun of licking the candy off and sucking on the breast until the candy is all gone. This is another situation where just the tip of the nipple sticks out of the hard candy.

If each of you knows a foreign language that the other one doesn't know – try making up native costumes from the country of the languages, and meet and make love without using any common language – set a penalty of some sort to be paid if one of you uses your common language. Of course, I suggest modifying the real native costumes to be more blatantly sexually obscene; perhaps just omit some normal parts of the outfit.

If only one of you speaks a language that the other one doesn't, it also sets up a scenario where you each speak your own language and one of you has to make believe that you can't understand each other. Or the one who knows only the common language can only speak gibberish. You could even play this where you both have to speak gibberish – for example, perhaps both use Indian costumes and be from different tribes and both use make-believe Indian gibberish or sign language. Or for another new language adventure, anyone can put on a blindfold and make love in Braille – strictly by touch. You can forget the blindfold if you can totally black out your bedroom and both do it without being able to see one time. Just throw a towel or shirt over anything like a clock that adds any glow to the pitch darkness.

In addition to the obvious round double-O boob cuts you can make, there are many other cuts that you can make in any tee shirt or other top. Some are very revealing of specific feminine charms, or they can be just tease cuts to promote interest. Many souvenir and tee shirt shops at vacation locations have many tees that have been cut with rows of small slits. Usually they are patterns of parallel slits in rows to give a peek-a-boo look in areas that don't reveal very much underneath but skin. Look at these shirts the next time you are around such beach and summer souvenir places. A cheap thrift shop sale tee shirt can be done in very similar fashion very easily, and in much more interesting or revealing spots. Just remember that any row of slits that do go over the breast area will stretch so that the slits are pushed open and the breast pops out and it becomes the open-breast look.

A tight tee shirt that fits snugly around the bust is best for a few, wide, horizontal, foot-long slits across the upper chest and maybe some more under the bust. The snug pull across the chest is needed to keep the bust area stretched and in place across the bust. The other cut spots just let the skin peek through above and below the bust. Another look is a row of 3-inch slits up and down right in the center-chest area from above to below the bust line. This is going to expose areas of the center chest between the breasts but not the nipple area. Slits down the entire sides can show a lot of peek-a-boo skin and make sliding the guy's hands into the shirt very easy. The vertical slits look like peek-a-boo holes on a loose shirt, but on a tight shirt, the 3-inch vertical slit will stretch open to become a 3-inch round hole.

Shortening any top gives a nice appeal with a look that can tease; how much it teases depends on how short you cut it. This can be shortening just a little to give a teasing look of a midriff peek on up to a cut that even leaves the bottom of the breasts showing and that only covers the nipple area (unless she raises her arms). The best idea is to experiment with the various lengths for fun. You should also use a tape measure to measure the distance from the shoulder top seam down to the hem edge of various tops and make notes of what that distance is for where that length is on your wife. A typical short blouse runs about 19 to 21 inches from the shoulder to the hem. I usually shorten to about 16 to 17 inches to still cover the breasts but still leave a nice bare midriff. Then you can know where to cut for the look and length you want. Of course, it might save some errors by having her try an item on and mark it before cutting.

Your wife may have one of the very popular belly button rings, or the husband just likes the bare belly button look, like I do. In this case, one thing that works well is a cut in the front that exposes the belly button. A scalloped cut in the front that shortens any top and comes up in the middle can look good. I have shortened the middle of a top to about 14 inches for a different look. A simple center vertical cut up a good ways from the hem of even a longer top will also show off nice glimpses of the naval area.

One nice way to make anything a peek-a-boo look on a loose-fitting tee or sweat shirt is just long vertical cuts. Four cuts can make a nice swishy peek-a-boo look. Try a cut from the underarm seam down to near the hem on each side, a center-front cut from a point midway from above the bust line near the neckline and straight down to near the hemline again, and the same cut in center back. This creates four hanging panels still joined at the top and the hem and a view of the center chest, center back, and center of the sides. The breasts are covered by the panel of fabric on each side, but the movement of the fabric may give a guy a glimpse of a breast every once in a while – the possibility will keep him looking at the girl for sure. It gives nice access for his hands any time he wants too. I call this a "hug cut" because my wife loves to be hugged and, in this cut, I love to hug her. I brush the front-side panels aside as we start to embrace, and I can press her bare breasts against my chest. My hands can then go in the side cuts to run up and down her bare back under the shirt. We both love it and get to enjoy the feelings we like.

There is a practical issue to point out for the cool weather. Some of the items I describe, like the cut sweatshirt above, are better ideas for cool weather or a cool house. The sweatshirt arms are still there, and the vertical cuts may let in a little draft, but it still is warmer than some tiny top barely covering anything. Add things like warm boots to outfits in a cool house. A little cool air may perk up a girl's nipples nicely, but goose bumps all over are not sexy to me. I want my wife to look sexy, but I plan my outfits to also keep her comfortable. I try to keep her total exposure down to one area in cool weather. For example, the above sweatshirt and high warm boots keep her warm enough that she doesn't mind the tiniest miniskirt and bare thighs. Even if my wife wears warm sweat pants or jeans to stay warmer, she wears something like a sweatshirt with a drafty hug cut around the house to perk up my interest. The briefest, barely covering outfits are for warmer weather. Of course, I have a plan B too – there is an electric space heater I can use to quickly warm up just the room we are in any time she is chilly without heating up the whole house.

My apologies to any football or baseball fans that might be offended by the following, but common sports shirts can be fun. I have an NY Yankee shirt, and I found my wife a Boston Red Sox shirt. (This would not work well if she were really a Red Sox fan.) You can imagine the role-playing fun of a fight between us. Threats of how "*The Yankees are going to fuck the hell out of Boston every time!!*" can be a lot of fun to carry out for real.

A Rams football tee shirt on a girl, for example, could encourage role-playing script lines like, "*So girl, you like the Rams, do you? Well, baby, how do you like this RAM?*" "*I'll give you all the ramming you can take! Right where it will do you some good!*" "*How does this ramming feel, sweetie?*" "*Ram! Ream! Whatever! I am going to give you the ramming of your life, girl!*" I'll leave it up to you, the reader, to use your own imagination to visualize the acting part of these scenario scripts. One nice part is that you can write your own scripts and make the scenario as long as you like. You don't even have to be a fan of the team on the shirt. It is probably better if you are not a team fan because then you won't mind shortening, modifying, or even ripping the shirts off each other and ruining good shirts that you really care about for your team. However, your own team's shirts are probably the most available sports shirts in your local thrift shops, so maybe you can get some extras to cut up in fun ways.

For more script suggestions for sports team role-playing scenarios, go to my free **DressForSEXcess.com** website and look under "More Sports Team Scenario Ideas" to find more ideas from me or from other website visitors who have posted stuff there. Post your own new ideas too.

A scenario like I just suggested could be expanded to be a part of a larger, more typical role-playing scenario like most fantasy books suggest. For example, if your wife goes alone to a sports bar in the one shirt, you come in separately in the other team's shirt – maybe a same-town rivalry, like an NY Jets-Giants football confrontation. You get to pick her up at the bar.

Personally, I don't usually go to bars, and neither does my wife, not even with friends. I never in my life looked for a girl to pickup at a bar. This lengthy bar pickup scenario does not feel normal or comfortable to us, so it does not appeal to us. Neither one of us have every gone into a bar just to get an alcoholic drink – we just like a glass of wine or a beer with dinner. However, so many professional relationship books mention this particular bar pickup role-playing that I thought I could show how the sports tee shirts can fit into it – what you like determines what you can try.

Rather than a long, involved pickup scenario, I prefer to get right down to the sex part of a role-playing session. It is more like picking up the scenario after the pickup at the bar is complete, as we walk into her place or my place and want to get right to it. This cuts out the whole bar scene part. We like to get right to the screwing around with very little seduction needed – my wife has me permanently seduced and under her wonderful spell. However, you can run your own fantasy as involved and detailed as you like – but you're not likely to end up having any more fun than we do.

CHAPTER 9
More Bottom Modifications

HERE ARE MANY OTHER WAYS that I modify pants, shorts, and skirts too. The simple idea I have in most cases is to modify an item to show more skin. I have to decide what area I want to see more of. Less outfit means more girl exposed – this is the same simple approach used by Victoria's Secret and Frederick's of Hollywood. The more of your wife that they let you see, the higher the price on their outfits. The outfit is just to decorate the girl's body.

There are three ways to expose more skin from existing clothes: cut off the top to lower the waistline, cut off the bottom to raise the hemline, or cut out parts in the middle to expose what would normally be covered. Any one or combination of these three you can think of will be worth trying.

Cutting off the top:

Jeans, various other pants, shorts, or skirts that have a waist fitted to the hip area can usually have the waistband or parts or the top cut off to make a low-rise look if you want to see more belly button or the lower belly area. I think most guys are like me and like to see a very low-rise look hanging very low on the hips. I love that hourglass look to a girl's body, where her waist is narrower and then broadens out to where a *"broad should be broad."* I like to see a bare belly button midriff and a couple more inches below the belly button – I love seeing that feminine lower belly area. A girl doesn't need to worry about having a flat, tight, toned tummy. Guys like skin, and they like curves too. Even an ample woman is usually still very attractive to her husband. Some stretch marks and flab from having babies do not detract from the bare-belly look. Most husbands also realize that they don't still look the same as when they were in high school or when they first got married. (This book is not aimed at the young or newlywed couples – it is for the older married couples who don't look like they did 20 years ago, like my wife and I.) This area is the softest large area on a woman's body, and I like to see it, and better yet, to feel it on my wife.

For example, if I come up behind my wife and hug her from the rear, I don't usually just grab for the boobs to hold her while I kiss her neck. If the outfit permits me, I prefer to slide my hands around her waist and down onto her lower belly and hug her butt to my hips as I press her soft warm lower belly area with my hands. She is so soft and warm there. I like to think about the very center of her femininity right there inside where I am feeling – right where I love to be – deep up inside her belly.

This is the area that makes her a true woman. The one place I like to be more than any other place in the whole world is right up inside this soft belly area of my wife. When we are joined together that way, it is the most heavenly, most wonderful feeling in the world. It makes me think of The Holy Bible's promise, "The two shall become one flesh." I love to see it and think how much I will soon enjoy getting up inside her there. I'll bet most guys think much the same way when they see this area emphasized on their wife. Totally naked shows it off but doesn't make a guy focus on that area and think about that entrance hidden just below, under her clothes, that is waiting for just him to discover it again.

The easiest item to lower from the top is a wrap skirt. Just move the buttons, and cut some new buttonholes. It is easy for even a guy to sew on buttons – my mom taught me how at about age 5 or 6. A simple slit with a knife makes a good enough buttonhole for use in playing with an item in sex games a few times. Even safety pins will do if you can't do the buttons and hole routine. For our purposes, the wrap does not have to still overlap to maintain modesty the way the skirt was originally designed. I have used little girls' skirts that barely covered my wife's hips – they leave a glimpse of bare skin where they hardly meet. Once you have the waistband adjusted, you can adjust the length by cutting the bottom.

One of the most popular and usually expensive costume items always found in many sex catalogs and found a lot on eBay is some version of the little innocent schoolgirl outfit – usually a plaid miniskirt, skimpy top, and maybe knee socks. I find that I can buy as good a looking outfit on a sale day at most thrift shops for less than the eBay shipping charges. There always seem to be plenty of plaid wrap skirts that can be adjusted at the waist and shortened at the hem to be the key part of such an outfit and to create the little innocent schoolgirl look. I have even used a little girls' plaid skirt that had a waistband several inches less than my wife's. I cut up both side seams to make two panels and strung them on a narrow belt like a loincloth. White knee socks and a small white top gave the effect of a young schoolgirl's plaid skirt outfit that is very popular as a sexy costume – mine cost about $2, versus probably $25 for the commercial version, and I thought mine looked better, with a little more hip exposed on the sides.

The biggest problem in lowering the top edge of most outfits is a zipper. Button flies or openings are easier to cut lower. Just cut off the top buttons or re-sew on a button lower and cut a new buttonhole after you have cut off the top. Maybe replace it all with some simple to sew on hook-and-eye combinations or maybe Velcro, which can be sewed or glued on – even a safety pin will work for a one-time use – have a fun sex session, and then toss the outfit.

You can cut a zipper, but it is hard to cut off the top end of a thick zipper. If you do, then you need to either sew a loop of thread around the top of the sides of the remaining zipper to keep it from coming up too far or use a few drops of some strong glue on each side of the zipper at the top to block the slide from going up too far.

Some items, like jeans, have the yoke in the back, which I have previously mentioned making into a peek-a-boo cutout, and you can just use the bottom of this yoke edge as the top edge by cutting off the top down to the bottom of the yoke. The item must be able to stay in place on the hips with the top cutoff, so this only works without additional work if the item fits the hips snugly, since you will also have cut off any belt loops.

On some items, you need to do something to fasten the item up. A few small vertical slits every few inches just below the top edge can let you put either a drawstring or belt in to do this. One thing that works to shorten a loose item several more inches and give it a top hem for a drawstring or belt is to turn the edge over either inside the desired waistband level, or even outside. Fix this permanently in place or use some safety pins to do this. I learned how to sew a straight line on my wife's sewing machine, and I can take a cut edge, flip it over on itself, and run a fairly straight line all the way around the piece to make it like a hem to insert a string tie belt.

To make a string tie belt to put into any hem, I buy shoelaces. They come in many colors to match items, but usually a black or white shoelace will do for almost any color outfit. To insert them, I have a wire coat hanger cut into a long length and curved into a hoop shape. I use the spiral end that joined the ends together at the neck of the coat hanger to overlap and wrap the end of the shoelace into the wire. I then tape it in place with some electrical tape, feed the other end of the coat hanger through the hem, and then pull the shoelace through the hem as I pull the coat hanger out the other opening. Sometimes this coat hanger is also needed on items made with drawstrings, like some shorts or swim trunks, which I buy and which have had the drawstring pulled out or partway in so you cannot use them anymore. This can be the simple reason some people have gotten rid of an otherwise perfectly good item. That coat hanger is a good tool that I keep handy.

One point for making any short, simple, plain skirt is to use any plain tee shirt. Just turn it upside down, put a string into the hem, and cut it to the length you want. I like to use children's tee shirts for this – they are the cheapest item for sale in most thrift shops, and they are smaller. I just use a tape measure to be sure that the shirt will stretch easily enough to fit my wife's hips. From the hem to the bottom of the sleeve on a kids' shirt is usually very short, but I cut from that seam to form the side of the skirt and then cut a longer way up, as far as the collar, in the center front and back to make a skirt with a short side and longer center panel. If the kids' shirt is snug enough to stay in place on my wife's hips, I often do not need any string tie in the hem to hold it in place. If it does get all out of place when we start having sex, who cares? It only has to make her look sexy and vulnerable long enough to get down to the serious loving. It is only decoration to make her attractive and is not supposed to get in the way of our lovemaking.

Common white tee shirts are good to then put any sort of sexy slogan on. I like something like "Fuck me hard, then flip me over" put on both front and back. You can only read it when the skirt is properly in place, but it is seductive and very explicit. When the skirt is all bunched up around her hips while you follow the instructions, you can no longer read it – it will be up to the husband to remember what it said about flipping her over and doing it again, but you guys really should try to follow the instructions that your wife gives you in cases like this.

As a tip that has nothing to do with shortening directly but does deal with using the rest of the material left over from shortening, making a skirt by flipping a tee shirt over, mentioned in the previous few paragraphs, leaves the rest of the tee shirt as scrap. There is a particular look that I like on a girl. It may not be the same with most guys, but it appeals to me personally. You guys can let your wives know if you like this; you gals can try it and then ask your husband if they like it. What I like is a fabric or leather choker – not a necklace but a wide choker. The book's epilogue talks about attending a Broadway NYC performance of the play *Cabaret* and how all the girls playing the nightclub dancers wore black chokers as part of their tiny, sexy costumes. I like that look on a girl's neck; it is sexy looking to me.

The scrap parts from cutting out the tee shirt skirt leave the collar untouched. I like to cut out the crew neck style tee shirt collar and use it for a choker. This is particularly good when it is a turtleneck collar. Sometimes I use a little more than the collar. I cut out just the collar on the sides and back, but I cut from each side down a few inches in the front to make a little triangle about 2 to 3 inches long that hangs down from the collar. I like the look of that extra flap. It has the same effect as a bandana folded in half and tied around the neck like a cowboy might wear (I like that look too), but this sort of choker is much smaller than a bandana.

In addition, in the interest of honesty and a little tip to the wives to help them both emphasize their strong points and minimize their flaws, I will point out that sooner or later everyone's skin gets a little older and forms wrinkles. On an older woman's lower neck, the area right below it is a spot that particularly gets these wrinkles first. This shows up long before the rest of a person's skin shows the wrinkles of age. Any younger guy or gal can look at any older woman they see in the store and see what I mean – all too many of us only have to look in the mirror to see what I am talking about. I have always liked the look of the choker, but now I notice that wearing this little bit of fabric also covers up all the neck wrinkles. For you wives who can see the wrinkles in the mirror, you may want to try these chokers frequently, even if your man says that they don't affect him very much one way or the other. It will hide your wrinkles, and it also gives you a way to make more coordinated outfits. If you make any sort of outfit cut from a colored tee shirt, also make the choker out of the collar area. In a skirt cut from a tee shirt, both your skirt and choker are the same color and material and go nicely together.

But don't think that I am done with that tee shirt skirt scrap – I like to use every bit of what I have to work with. I don't understand everything that turns me on, but there is one more thing that can use that little leftover scrap. I like both wrist and ankle cuffs too. Having my wife's wrists, ankles, and neck all with cuffs and a choker is a turn-on for me. I have purchased dozens of sets of hair scrunchies in all colors and fabrics. I particularly like the bold-colored velvet ones – bright red, royal blue, deep purple, and also pure white and black. I get enough of each color to have four of each. I have my wife wear one on each wrist and ankle, and sometimes I call this a complete outfit – just the four scrunchies and nothing else for just some bare-naked sex, with just the scrunchies to decorate her beautiful body. A matching choker of some sort makes the outfit even better – many other dollar-store hairbands and headbands can be used for a choker too, even if not a perfect match. Almost any piece of fabric can be cut into a choker and fastened with a safety pin. These scrunchies look good with many outfits, particularly if they are color coordinated to part of the outfit.

As for the added use for the leftover scrap, I sometimes use the sleeves too. Particularly if it is a kids' tee shirt, the sleeves are small, and you can just cut them off, and they should easily stretch over a woman's hand and make a nice matching set of cuffs – skirt, choker, and wrist cuffs, all from the same cheap kids' tee shirt in a matching color. I am like many guys, I think, and I like pretty bare feet. Tee shirt sleeves from an adult or a kids' shirt make good ankle cuffs too. In a black or a white tee shirt, it is easy to get a second shirt in the same color to use the second shirt for a second set of cuffs for the ankles and to make a choker with a little different look – for example, maybe leave a little more material on the shirt collar and cut it into a fringe. Use the main part of the shirt to cut out a different style skirt for variety or just to print some other raunchy slogan on it. If you can find a long-sleeve tee shirt, you can make longer, leg-warmer-style leggings rather than just ankle cuffs.

Back to more modifications of a garment: On something like a loose-fitting skirt, this cutting off the top can shorten the skirt as much as you would like, and you don't have to cut the bottom hem at all – it can be the indecent length you want and still have a much more finished look than one of my typical cut fabric edges. A cut bottom edge leaves a ragged edge that will slowly fray, unless you are decent at sewing and can refold and re-hem the cut bottom edge. A few fraying threads don't bother me, and I ignore them as I look for the total effect of the skimpy outfit, and I am looking at the model, not the garment – the garment is just a little decoration to make the model look sexy. My redesigning efforts are not going to be judged by neatness or proper finishing of the clothing – my efforts are only going to be judged by how much fun we have with the resulting sex.

Whereas, on some items, a cut top edge can usually just be folded under on the inside and hidden out of sight for a one-time use to have a neater look with very little effort, there are some items that should almost never be cut to shorten or make cutouts – most loose-knit garments. These can totally unravel very quickly. Sometimes you can tie up the loose end of the yarn but not always. Folding under the edge that you want to shorten is the best way to shorten a knit item.

I tried the following approach to shorten the top edge of a black leather skirt I found very cheap with a broken zipper. It was several sizes too small at the waist but was just my wife's hip size much farther down as the garment flared out. I shortened it at the top to both lower the top and raise the bottom. It was fully lined and had a nice split in the hem that came up about 6 inches and had chrome snaps on the opening. Linings are usually a pain to try and modify on a skirt, and I usually just cut them out. However, on this one, I wanted the bottom edge with the split left intact. I cut the skirt to miniskirt length by cutting off the entire top several inches. The entire zipper and all the tapered top section were removed. I cut through both the leather and lining. Next I cut vertical, one-inch slits in both the leather and lining every 4 or 5 inches around the top. I found a very narrow black belt to fit her hips and wove it through the slits in the top edge. I put the skirt on her upside down and inside out over her chest and then adjusted the belt to fit snugly at the wide point of her hips. Lastly, I pulled the skirt back down from the hem to turn it right side out and right side up, and it was perfectly in place as a micro miniskirt hung from her hips in very sexy black leather. The belt was totally hidden under the slightly thick folded top edge.

I rotated it so that the original hem slit formed an intriguing inverted V up her front over one thigh. The skirt was still fully lined this way. It had a slightly thick look at the waistband, which never showed the belt or anything – it was just folded back over inside the top. It actually looked better than many expensive professionally made outfits. To make anything stay put at the wide point of the hips when you are having vigorous sex means that you have to fasten the belt fairly tight, and it squeezes a roll of flesh out above the waistband. In this case, the folded edge was slightly above the belt as it folded back into the waistband, and the thickness of the belt and doubled-up material filled the indentation caused by the tight belt. Pulled back down, it gave an overall shape that matched her natural hip curve and avoided the roll-over-the-belt look. The belt indentation was hidden underneath the skirt. It did look totally like it was professionally finished and could have been worn out in public by anyone daring enough for something that short. A real leather, fully lined, micro miniskirt from someplace like Frederick's of Hollywood would have cost a small fortune – it cost me $2 for an expensive skirt with a broken zipper at a thrift shop.

For a really unusual look that will work with absolutely anything – try suspenders. I have picked up a few sets of suspenders when I see them at thrift stores or yard sales. I have some nice wide, black sets, a white set, and some bold, bright-colored sets. Be sure the suspenders you get have snap-style toothed grippers on the end (and that they work – I got a set recently and then realized a snap was broken). Formalwear suspenders are made to button in place and are harder to use – they need two buttons on the item at each end to be attached to.

Wide suspenders can be worn with no top at all with the straps centered right over the nipples. The suspender straps don't hide very much and keep slipping off the nipples as the girl moves, but isn't that the fun of using the suspenders as just decoration? You don't really want to seriously hide anything you just like to look at and enjoy. You can try using a matching color string around the center of the bust line – fastened from one strap to the other across the front, around the sides, and to the back straps – to tie all the bands in position and hold them more over the nipples if you want.

If you don't want the look of the strings, try tying the suspender straps in place with clear fishing line instead – it will be nearly invisible. Many camisole and bra straps today use clear, plastic, ½-inch-wide straps trying to look invisible, but I don't know where to get this plastic strap stuff. If the fishing line snaps while you are having fun – so what? That's the breaks! You should be able to laugh and have fun anyhow.

You can also use some string to make two little tiny slipknot loops, like the ends of the commercially available titillizer chains that fasten to the nipples. I have also seen little decorations for nipples in the size and style of earrings, which have this type of slip loop end on them that would also work here. Put on the nipple loops, and you have something to fasten to the suspender straps with some small safety pins to hold the straps in place fastened to the knot of the loops.

Another way to use suspenders is to fasten them fairly wide in front so that they come down outside the breasts. Take any sort of scrap material about 18 inches by 6 inches and fasten it across the breasts to the suspenders with safety pins or any way you can, and you have a little breast cover fastened to the suspenders.

I have a Christmas set of suspenders too. I picked up a huge Christmas stocking during a 75% off, after-the-holidays clearance sale – it's about 5 feet long. The next season I made my wife a nice, barely there, red, holiday outfit with a bra and micro miniskirt to put on and then put her in the big stocking. I used small, child-size holiday suspenders to hold the stocking up on her up to just under her arms. She had to hop around like she was in a sack race to move – but the big stocking came off pretty quickly so I could get to play with my Christmas gift easily.

Cutting off the bottom:
This is much easier to do. Almost anything can be cut off at the bottom. Just cut to get the look you want.

For cutting the bottom of anything for a skirt, there are many options. You can cut straight across. You can cut vertical cuts up a few inches every quarter inch to make a fringe look. You can cut a scalloped edge. You can cut it very unevenly (for an animal print, like tiger-striped material, this makes it look like a real caveman-style animal-skin outfit). You can cut it very short on one side and angled diagonally to very long on the other side, or you can cut it as short as mid-hip length on both sides and leave a longer triangular flap to hang down front and back like a loincloth, or anything in between that you like or in combinations of these ideas. You can make cuts on both a top and bottom that look very similar, like both with fringe or both with scalloped edges, to use as a set or an outfit.

On some shorts, I just leave a 2-inch wide crotch seam and cut up to just below the pockets on the back and to just under the pocket at the side seam on the front. If you want, you can cut out the entire rear pocket area to make a rear like a Brazilian bikini back – not much more than a thong up to the rear yoke detailing.

I have made the cut too severe sometimes, and when the item is tight, my wife has told me it is uncomfortable to her because it cuts right up into her crotch and pussy area. One remedy for that is to make it a totally open crotch – cut out the center seam entirely for several inches and leave just two narrow crotch strips. These will fit on each side of her pussy and not cut up into the center of it, and this doesn't bother her as much. This may solve the problem on some items. I want her to get hot and bothered for me but not bothered by something feeling uncomfortable.

Dukes of Hazard-style Daisy Dukes always look nice too. Trim away the top and bottom until there is just a little left, maybe even a lot less than the TV or movie outfit she wore. Then match it to a nice, brief, little top, probably something just tied in a knot in front and a bandana tied around the neck. Maybe wear it with cowboy boots and cowboy hat.

Sweat pants are particularly nice to cut into shorts and can even make a nice very complete outfit. They are so soft and come in many nice colors to give a change from denim. I like pastel blues because they match my wife's eyes. (A marriage tip, guys: always tell your wife that things go well with her eyes, her hair, her nice tan, etc. and that the modifications show off her great legs, breasts, pretty smooth soft skin, etc. – whatever you like about the look.) Sweats also come in nice bright colors – like fire-engine red, which is a hot, sexy color. I like them to look nicely form fitting, not too loose and not too big. That is the only trouble when finding the right ones to cut – sweats tend to be too loose and baggy. I like to find low-rise sweats that are only 8 to 10 inches of rise above the center crossing of the crotch seams. These are often the medium to large children's sizes, but they stretch so well to easily fit her waist and hips. So many old sweats at garage sales and such have stains on the legs or worn knee areas, particularly kids' sizes. This means that they are very cheap and you are just going to cut off the bad spots anyway. It makes a good deal. I have gotten nice, snug, soft, low-rise short shorts from 25-cent kids' sweatpants.

With sweatpants shorts, I usually don't even bother to put in a crotch-cut for having sex. I leave them as just shorts so she can wear them anytime, anywhere. If we want sex, the soft stretchy fabric lets me just push the center crotch to one side and use a leg opening. The fabric may rub on my cock some, but it is so soft I hardly notice it.

If the legs that are cut off are in good shape, there are some things you should try. Cut out the thigh section and use the bottoms of the legs as a set of decorative leggings.

There are two ways to put on leggings. 1) Put them on her legs inside out and upside down up onto her thighs. Then use a proper size rubber band and put over the legging just above or below the knee, depending on what length you want. Pull the cuff back down to turn the legging right side out and right side up again. This gives an even, folded edge as the top of the leggings. 2) Put them on her legs right side out just a little higher than you want them. Then put a rubber band on just below the top and fold the top back down over the rubber band to form a flap down over the edge of the legging to hide the rubber band. The second way lets you have a fringed top or a shaped flap as the legging top. Either way, you have a very nice coordinated set of shorts and lower leggings and plenty of nice bare thighs – it makes the legs look so sexy with the emphasis on just the bare thighs.

See illustrations 9-1 and 9-2 that show how to put on leggings both ways, using a rubber band to hold them in place.

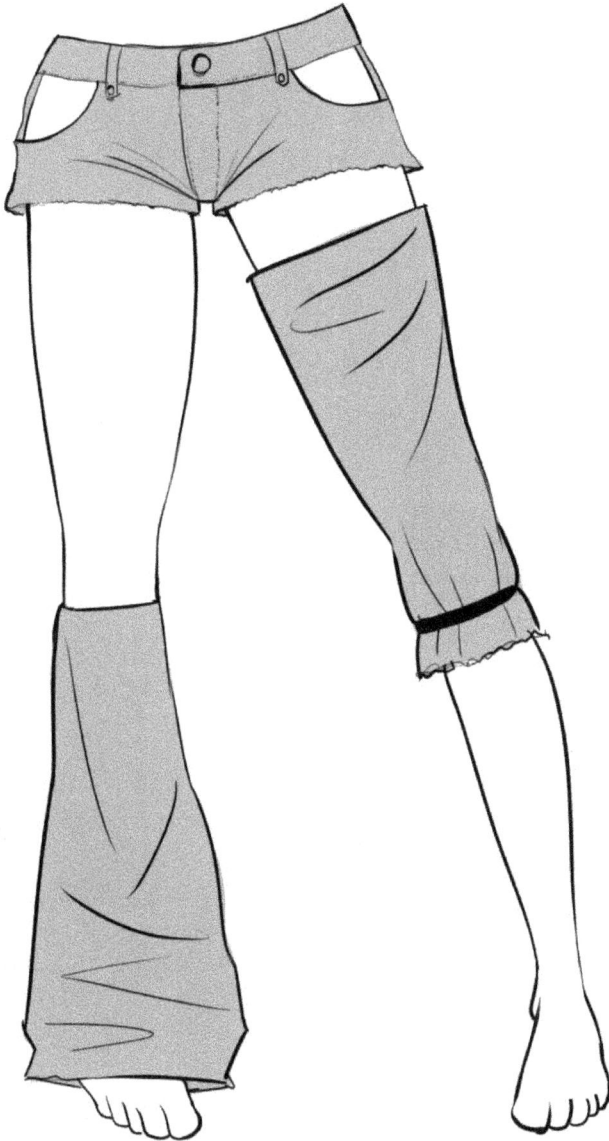

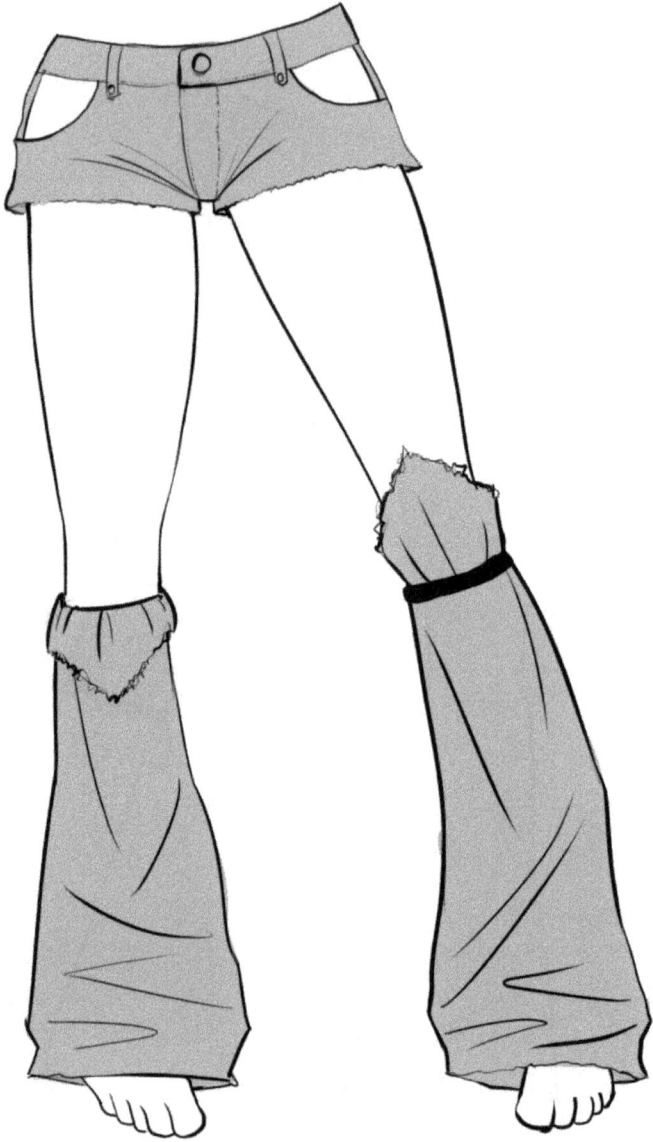

I love a girl with her arms and body fully covered and either boots or leggings on that leave everything covered except her bare thighs all the way from above her knees up to her short shorts or a miniskirt. I don't mind a covered torso and arms, as long as the clothes are loose or stretchy to let me easily slide my hands underneath. This is a good way to enjoy a sexy look with easy access and still let my wife wear something a little warmer in cool weather. She does not mind if her thighs are bare so long as the rest of her is warm. I am a leg man, and the bare thighs are what seem like the most desirable look. I love to mind grope a little, and my imagination always makes me think what it would feel like to caress that bare thigh area and slowly work my way up. I get to do this on my pretty wife quite often – I love it!

When my wife has that bare-thigh look, I like to do a lot more than just mind grope. I love to throw her down in the middle of our bed and lay down along-side her. I cradle her in one arm and begin to make out with her like crazy. I hold her warm body close to me and start to kiss just like we used to do before we were married and before we went any farther than just making out. We 'Suck Face' with serious passion, just like we used to. However, now I get to do a lot more than I used to be permitted to do. With my free hand I roam all over her very desirable body. While kissing I can reach down to her knees with my free hand, and I love to stroke those bare legs while we make out.

I can use my hand, or even my forearm, in between her legs to stroke from her knees all the way up her thighs. To keep her guessing, sometimes I stroke almost up until I touch her pussy and stop, and then I go back to start again at the knees and slowly work back up. Sometimes I barely brush her sex area with my hand or arm, and sometimes I press as hard as I can up against the soft pussy area before I go back to stroke her thighs again. Often I let my fingers play with that soft pussy a few seconds before I stroke her thighs again.

Sometimes I will stroke the outside of her leg and go all the way up to her butt. I like a playful squeeze or a few light pats there before I stroke her again. I may switch that free hand to caressing some other part or her body for a minute, like her breasts and sensitive nipples, but I soon move back to stroking those nice legs again – always stroking up toward the Promised land. A few minutes of that kind of foreplay will drive us both wild with desire. Now you know one of the reasons why I like that bare-thigh look so much.

I think that an outfit that just emphasizes the bare thighs is extremely sexy. The girl is still so available to screw, with the very short stretchy or crotch-cut shorts on or a miniskirt and she looks so good. The idea is so easy to do that you should give it a try just to see how you both feel about the look. There are all sorts of tall boots of every color to create this same look, but boots are more expensive. Of course that bare-thigh look can be done with knee socks too. A girl's sports uniform, like they wear in soccer, basketball, field hockey, and such, can create that bare-thigh look and set up a role-playing seduction game too. Sports shirts with player's numbers and school or pro team names are always cheap in many thrift stores. These can be cut up to be briefer or more revealing too, and they complete the sports look. You can even add the knee protectors. Another tip to give any shorts or a miniskirt the bare-leg look to just emphasize the thighs is to buy some tall, furry leg warmers. I have several sets in different colors – black, white, and animal prints.

I particularly like it with leggings rather than boots because I think bare feet make a girl look sexier. Bare feet add a little bit more of a partially naked look since girls usually have shoes on. I think the barefoot look makes a girl a little more vulnerable and exposed.

The leggings for the bare-thigh look, combined with other bare areas and brief outfits, also look very nice. Alternating covered areas with exposed areas emphasizes the exposure of the bare areas – bare feet, thighs, midriff, shoulders, upper arms (with wrist cuffs), hands, and head (above a choker). Every covered area seems to invite exploration of the covered charms.

See illustration 9-3. This shows a coordinated denim outfit cut from one pair of bell bottom jeans – cutoff, peek-a-boo modified, crotch-cut short shorts, leggings, wrist cuffs, and a denim collar. The one-shoulder blouse is just cut from a plain white tee shirt. She has everything that I like – bare feet, bare thighs, a large bare midriff, bare upper arms and some shoulder, some peek-a-boo skin peeking through, and full easy accessibility to all of her feminine charms. An outfit like in this illustration is exactly what makes me want to throw my wife down on the bed and start to make out with her while I stroke her thighs and ravish her (as described in chapter 17).

If you are cutting up sweats to make the leggings, many sweats have a color line down the outside, and it ties the look of the shorts and leggings together so well. Exact matching colors also tie the shorts and leggings together as a nice set. Any part that you cut off in the thigh area can also be used to make a matching set of wrist cuffs and/or armbands too, using rubber bands to hold them in place. And if you cut a circular ring piece out of the thigh area, it should easily stretch enough to go over her head and make a matching decorative collar to complete an outfit. Or it can be made into a snug choker with a paperclip or safety pin to fasten it snugly in the back. Snug chokers are very sexy looking – particularly if the choker is part of a matching set in some way.

I really like to cut skirts short too. One thing to look for is skirts with layers. I have done dozens of skirts that have all had different layered looks. Some are real layers of fabric, and when I first see one, I always think what it would look like with some bottom or underneath layers just removed. For example, an 18-inch girls' miniskirt with three layers of ruffles can be cut down to a 12-inch micro miniskirt of two layers that won't really hide everything underneath – it looks totally finished, as if it were made that way by Victoria's Secret, and it only takes about a minute to modify it. Doing this provides a very nice short skirt, but there are still finished top and bottom edges, and even if you examine it closely, it is hard to tell the skirt was not originally made that way.

On one nice, white, gauze-type, full-layered skirt that was fairly long, with four layers, I cut out the inner skirt liner entirely. That inner liner made a little sheer shirt for a nice see-through effect in a separate outfit. Next I cut off the bottom layer and ended up with a nice very full and sassy-looking miniskirt. I took the bottom layer I cut off and put an elastic strip (from any sewing or craft store) through little slits in the top edge and tied it around her chest over her bust line. I had a matching top that barely hid anything. It was just a full 6-inch ruffle tied just above the breasts to hang down over them, but she looked very frilly and feminine in the matching top and bottom. It was as sexily attractive as any factory-made lingerie.

Some layered skirts have many layers, and you may want to cut off more than one layer. Another type of layered skirt is a lace over-skirt, which is just a decorative layer of a lace skirt on top of a solid skirt underneath. These are ideal to just trim off everything you can of the bottom layer and turn the top layer of lace into a nice see-through skirt. See-through lace is often what lingerie makers use, and I have made some just as well for only a couple of dollars.

Another denim skirt had a factory-frayed edge finish top and bottom and was made out of several large pieces sewn together in a random pattern, and the edge of each piece had that same frayed-edge look. I cut off the bottom pieces, just leaving the factory-frayed edge on the pieces I left. It was a nice look with an uneven hemline that was very high at some spots and a little longer in others. It just takes imagination when looking for stuff to think about what can be taken off.

Michelangelo said he just removed the extra pieces from a block of stone to reveal what he saw as the statue trapped inside the block. I can look at a factory-made item and see just how I can remove some of it to leave an item that will be more revealing and sexy on my wife. My skill is not really to be compared to his in any way, but I do use the same way of looking at the clothing I find when I am shopping. Often I have seen a picture of something I'd like to try and my mind is looking for an item I can make it out of. Sometimes, first I see an item and an idea just pops into my head. The trick for you guys is to always think about your wife and always think about what is sexy about her. You gals just need to think, "*What can I do to that item that would show off my charms to my husband in an intriguing way?*"

One trick I like to use in making short skirts that both look lower on my wife than they were designed for and are also raised at the hem, without having to modify both top and bottom edges, is to find a skirt a few sizes too large. I even shop the large-size racks for this stuff in stores that organize clothes. By getting a size where the waist measurement of an item is about my wife's hip size or even a few inches larger, I don't have to fool with cutting the zipper and other problems of shortening it from the top – I only have to cut the bottom edge to shorten it as much as I want. A belt will hold it in place if needed, and I can make it as short as I want by just trimming the bottom edge.

Don't forget about the possibility of cutting off unequal amounts for an asymmetrical look. For example, a long denim skirt that fits just right low on the hips can be trimmed to be high on the sides and longer in front and back for a very sexy look. Start by marking the side seams to hip height, maybe just eight to ten inches below the top edge, then marking the center front and back to about a sixteen-inch miniskirt length. Cut from the short-side marks to the long, center marks, and you have a skirt with a triangular look front and back. For sex, that triangular flap just flips up and instantly can be out of the way, front or back.

One thing about larger sizes is that a skirt always gets larger at the hips, so if I have her wear the original waist at the hips, it always gets larger from there down – be sure this will still give you a nice look on your wife from that skirt – try to visualize it as cut short as you are deciding to buy it. There are usually darts and such in this section of a garment that affect the way it will look.

One unusual look from a large skirt that I tried, which looked right because of the original cut of what I had started with, was one where the original waist fit right on my wife's widest part of the hips, and I cut it to only about 7 or 8 inches long in the front. It barely covered anything from the front view. But I curved the cut down on the sides and low across the back so that it was just at the top of her knees in the back. Her bare thighs were seen from the front up against the inside of the back of the skirt. The dress was black, and she wore knee-high black boots with it – those fair thighs looked great against the black background. She wore crotch-cut, black, satin panties that I could just get a glimpse of from the front as she moved. She had on a very formal-looking, ivory, satin, long-sleeve blouse, shortened to just under the bust in front and longer to her normal waist in back.

From the rear of that outfit, it gave a small peak of bare lower back right where her back started to flare out to her hips and just the back of her knees. In the shiny, black, tall boots and skirt, combined with a long-sleeve satin blouse, it looked very formal from the back, with just a glimpse of skin. From the front, it gave an almost-fully-bare-torso look – bottom of the bust to mid-hips, and then those bare thighs. She was very demure from the back but very hot and bare from the front. It seemed very dressy with the black skirt; the high, shiny, black boots; and the satin, white blouse, but extremely sexy with all of her charms easily available.

Cutting out parts of the middle:
Some of the jeans modifications described in earlier chapters, like pocket cutouts, have already been mentioned and are good for exposing some bare skin in the middle of an outfit. These all apply to shorts, skirts with similar pockets, and anything else similar.

Any item that fits smoothly on the figure can have cutouts made to give it peek-a-boo appeal. Just remember that it may sag in some undesirable way once there is a cut in it. You may need to use a backing material, like felt or something, to stiffen the material when you make a cutout. These can be attached with sewing or sometimes glued or ironed on. For just revealing slits, try to do the slits considering the effect of possible strain on any fabric that may pull it open or how the remaining fabric will hang from gravity.

I found a wide, black, leather decorative belt with shamrock cutouts in it. I found a pair of denim shorts that were plain, with no detailing or pockets, just belt loops that the belt would fit and the zipper. I ironed on some adhesive felt backing inside the shorts first and then made matching big shamrock cutouts in the shorts on each side, front and back. I had bare skin peeking through the shamrocks in front on each side of her abdomen and each cheek of her butt to match the belt cutouts.

I am a big micro miniskirt fan to the point that my wife's major complaint when she wears one of my modified short skirts around the house is that she has nothing to sit down on. A chair seat can feel cold when you sit down on it with bare skin. My viewpoint is that I get to see 100% of her great legs and even get glimpses of the main attraction. Then when I bend her over in any fashion to have sex, the skirt is short enough that it never gets in the way – it is not there! On most skirts I cut, the fabric will never reach from her waistband to the center area between her legs. However, with some skirts, I want a different look. Pleats tend to lend themselves more to the longer, swishy, peek-a-boo look with the pleats exposing just glimpses of bare leg.

One of my favorite looks for my wife is a pleated short skirt, like a white tennis skirt or a cheerleader's skirt, with the pleats cut up to the hip line. I have made these in several styles and several colors to match various tops and provide variety. There are plenty of long, pleated skirts available to modify. First, get the skirt that has the right waist and hip measurements and shorten it to the miniskirt length you want – I like mid-thigh length or lower for thin, swishy pleats. Then cut the pleats to expose some of the middle area above the hem for the desired effect.

There are two ways to cut pleats that I have tried. Most cheerleader skirts have a box pleat. Often this has a contrasting color, and box pleats are usually fairly large. Visualize just cutting out the entire contrasting color on a cheerleader skirt for any skirt with a box pleat. On the inner part of the pleat just cut up the crease in the pleat all the way to the top of the pleat on both sides of the inner pleat panel. Then cut across the top to remove the inner pleat surface entirely. This gives a look of panels of fabric with a peek of skin between the panels. Some box-pleated skirts have just four pleats – two in the front at about the center of the thighs and two in the back the same positions. This type also looks good with the highest possible cuts up in front and back of the pleats. The cuts expose the center of each thigh, front and back. Then the front and back center panels look much like a loincloth with panels over her main charms. These panels are ideal to just be flipped out of the way when needed.

The second way to cut that I use is for simple pressed pleats. These pressed pleats give a fabric a zigzag look – like a series of endlessly connected Z's. The pleats can hang loose from the waistband or they are often sewn down flat to the hip level. On these skirts, the pleats are usually smaller and closer together.

On the first such skirt with narrow pleats that I modified, I cut every single pleat, and it ended up looking like a skirt of strings hanging down, rather than the look I wanted. I wanted the pleated look with peek-a-boo glimpses between the panels.

This brings up one point I need to make about things that don't turn out right. If an idea doesn't work, so what! It doesn't mean anything is a failure. It was just an attempt at something better that didn't work out in every way – a learning experience. Take no more than 30 seconds to get over it, and get back on track to what your real goal was. Remember, the goal was making love – SEX'! Your plan B can always be the same for everything you try to modify – remove the costume that didn't work, and get back to what can always work right – good old-fashioned bare-naked sex. Or just go ahead and use the outfit even if the look isn't exactly what you wanted. Better yet, always have another outfit ready if something does not work with the first outfit. Sometimes I just make a mistake cutting, and it just won't work; I just throw it out and consider a couple of dollars lost, but long term, I get a lot of results in lovemaking for my efforts.

There is another marriage tip hidden in the previous paragraph of dealing with failure. Failure is never final. Get over the temporary mental idea that something has failed and make the best of what you do have. It is the old adage, *"Don't cry over spilt milk"* lesson – it definitely applies to all aspects of love.

What I found works best on narrow pleats is to cut up the inner crease of about every third or fourth pleat to make panels 3 or 4 pleat wide. This leaves the look of the pleated skirt, but adds the peek-a-boo effect in the cutouts. I like thin material for this to work best. These panels can have a nice swishy effect on a short skirt, and the pleats are still there to see.

Start cutting the pleats on one side, and as you get most of the way around, stop and count pleats to see where the final cut will end up – if the last panel will be the same, one pleat more, or one pleat less than what you have been cutting, you are OK. If the last panel will end up two pleats off, try to modify your cutting pattern to put the extra pleats into two different panels of pleats or into a larger center panel of pleats.

A last pleat-cutting option can be used to avoid counting the pleats. Just make 4 or 6 total pleat cuts – the first 4 are high cuts up the front and back in the middle of each thigh area – two pleats on the front, two on the back. If you want to add 2 more, it is in the center of each side.

One skirt I cut was a size too large to start with and was a smooth flat fabric from the waist to the center of the hips. The pressed pleats started from a seam at the hips. My wife told me that this type of skirt was probably originally made to go with a matching ladies jacket as a nice woman's suit. I shortened it to mid-thigh, cut the pleats into panels to the hip, and then realized I could do one more thing. Just like cutting slits in a tee shirt or top to show some more skin, I cut vertical slits in the material from the waist to the hip seam to match the cuts in every area of the pleats. I didn't cut the waistband or hip seam, but since this top area was a loose fit, nothing stretched open. I even widened these slits a little to show some hip skin and glimpses of a henna tramp stamp she still had on her lower back.

I like to cut pleats all the way up to the hip line if I can. You can only cut to the top on box pleats or sewn-down pleats, but even if they are not sewn, I only cut up to widest point of the hip. You won't see much of the hip area because the pleat will rarely open to the top when the girl is standing or walking, but it gives the maximum exposure when the pleat does open. Pleats cut this high look good when she sits down too, and I always keep looking to see if I can even get a glimpse of the Promised Land (the pussy). Cutting up higher past the widest part of the hips means that the panels will hang widely apart from the top of the cut, not in the original evenly spread positions.

As a final note about pleats, I will point out how to use them when you get down to the serious business you modified the skirt for – getting screwed. If the wife is horizontal while you are having sex, face up or face down, the center pleats are usually long enough that they can get in the way of the action as they hang down between her legs when she lies down. The natural thing a guy does with any skirt is to take the center pleats that are in the way and flip them up out of the way, but they often keep falling back down and are in the way again in a minute or two. The simplest and quickest thing to do to fix the situation is to just tuck the ends of the center pleats up into the top waistband. I often tuck the pleat panel up the inside of the skirt to the waistband – that way it doesn't just look like it is tucked out of the way, it looks like that panel is missing and cut off to expose the girl's charms. This way, she still has the nice pleated skirt on for decoration, and the rest of the pleats hang over the sides of her body, but the Promised Land is completely uncovered for you to have fun with and not have any distraction from the pleats getting in the way. You can also just flip the center pleats up over the front and tuck them into the waistband the easy way. Either way, just enjoy!

CHAPTER 10
The Streetwalker Look and What the Professionals Say

GUESS WITH MY PREFERENCES for so many totally indecent modifications that I have written about, you would think I only like the trashy streetwalker or call-girl look. Like many of my ideas, I do think that many of these pro hoes go well beyond any Victoria's Secret and Fredericks of Hollywood looks. Well, these types of girls do seem to know what gets a guy's attention – they want to attract business by flaunting their charms. They are businesspeople, and they are in sales. The more attractive they look to the guys looking for commercial sex, the better their chance of making a sale. Capitalism, good marketing, and competition will eventually discover what works best to attract customers in any business. Collectively, these girls seem to have refined centuries of market research down to very specific, results-oriented ways to successfully attract guys. In other words, their approaches work! They attract guys.

Actually, the streetwalkers visible to the public have to keep certain feminine features covered – they can't show the areas a two-piece bikini would cover. Some of my ideas are much more blatantly exhibitionist than the streetwalkers can get away with. Most of my modifications will never be seen in public. I imagine inside a brothel my ideas might be more popular, but this is just speculation on my part – I have never been in a brothel. I have been past several of them, including places like the famous Mustang Ranch in Nevada. They are legal in some of the wide-open, isolated areas, but I never stopped or went in. Usually, I saw lots of cars and 18 wheelers parked at them, so they must have been busy. I could have gone in to look around for "research," but my wife was with me, and it did not seem like a good idea at the time. However, I guess that this book may become required reading in some whorehouses. At least some of these girls can make my unfinished cut edges into finished looks with some better sewing skills than I have.

I think that when a wife decides to wear some of the streetwalker looks, it helps her loosen up her inhibitions and lets her feel like she can enjoy getting into the role. Many books on sexual relationships and sexual problems by the most learned professionals point out frequently how many women have repressed inhibitions about their self-image that are causing them problems. If they can get rid of some of their sexual mental hang-ups, they will enjoy sex a lot more. Acting the role of an uninhibited hooker can reduce any self-conscious inhibitions. This is the same psychology that the professional psychiatrists say reduces some women's inhibitions when a couple uses bondage in their sex play. If the woman is bound or restrained, she is no longer in control and is no longer responsible for what is happening to her, and she is then free to react to and fully enjoy what her lover does. When a wife is playing the role of a hooker, it is not her feelings and desires that she is acting out. It is the hooker's behavior she is copying.

Totally forgetting about acting and looking proper, and instead trying to look brazenly seductive like the streetwalker, is one good way to lose inhibitions. Every wife agreeing to dress for the part should also try totally getting into acting the part and flaunting all her charms at her husband. Think: *"I really need to get his guy to want me or else I won't get any business tonight. Being sure he thinks I am desirable and very good in bed is very important to me – I need a big tip tonight, and I want his repeat business."* Many wives think that they are not really attractive to their husbands anymore. The typical wife thinks her husband is always comparing her to all the sexy pictures that every adult male sees all the time – younger, thinner, bigger-busted, etc. Of course, this aspect of poor self-image is just another hang-up that the professionals analyze and try to solve. Well, every wife ought to try flaunting what they do have and see how well it still works. Guys don't need or expect perfection. Most guys feel like the average timid wife feels in many ways – they just want to feel wanted. Any wife convincing her husband that she really wants HIM will have a happier husband and a stronger marriage. Looking good and being very good in bed ARE very important to her, if she wants to be sure that she gets ALL of his repeat business.

One thing that makes any guy want a particular girl and makes him want to keep coming back for more from that same girl is that such a girl makes him feel special and makes it clear that he turns her on and that she wants more of him. What causes most affairs with a guy is when some girl other than his wife thinks that he is special and makes him feel more like a man. For you wives that want to keep your man, you have to be sure you make him feel that he is super special to you in every way, including the sexual way. For some more valuable advice from the most important book ever written on human behavior, *The Holy Bible*, it always tells a man to love his wife, but it always tells a wife to respect her husband. It does not ever put it the other way around. Take this to heart, and think about how it applies to your relationship. Of course, a wife must work at trying to be very lovable (including in how she looks and seduces him), and the husband must work just as hard at earning the respect that makes him feel more like a real man to his wife. Also, remember the advice I quoted in the Introduction from author Jimmy Evans, in his very Bible-based book *Marriage on the Rock*. It is important that a wife not minimize her husband's sexual needs, but she needs to encourage them.

For the wives that may be feeling that these ideas are not necessary for them to use and who may doubt the validity of my male viewpoint, I suggest that they accept some of the professional opinions by recognized experts, including some women experts. The widely read classic relationship book *The Sensuous Woman* by J (Joan Terry Garrity), subtitled *The first HOW-TO book for the female who yearns to be ALL Woman* has a chapter "Sex – What to Wear," and a section in it "Pleasing the Polygamist." I recommend every wife read her book. Read what this expert says from the female point of view:

"...first I think we ought to see why a woman should learn to be several different people for the man she loves.

"Nearly all men are polygamous by nature. Yet they face the terrible frustration of living in a monogamous society. As much as I hate even to think about it, left to themselves most men would probably never marry. ...."

This is becoming more and more prevalent these days, as shown by statistics on babies born to parents living together and out of wedlock.

"Therefore, it is natural for a man to have a wandering eye and a fertile sexual imagination. He's not betraying you when he looks longingly at that shapely blonde in the drugstore and dreams of devouring her. It's a natural instinct on his part and has nothing to do with the fact that he loves you very much." [See "Mind Groping," chapter 2.]

"Married or not, men are going to continue looking, and a great number will sample other women besides yourself. You may not like it, but you're going to have to live with it.

"It's the women who keep marriage alive and benefit most from it. So get this straight. If she is going to keep her man monogamous, it's the woman's responsibility to give him the sexual variety and adventure at home that he could find easily on his own elsewhere. [Emphasis in the original.]

"I know that's a tall order. You have to fight a woman's most deadly sexual enemy – familiarity – for it breeds boredom in the male.

"To keep him from wandering, your greatest allies are:

1. Imagination.

2. Sensitivity to his moods and desires.

3. The courage to experiment with new sexual techniques, enticing situations and places."

After several pages of case studies, she summarizes with:

"If you learn to keep him off guard and curious about what you will be like next, he'll be too focused on you to stray."

She ends the chapter later with:

"Promise yourself right now to be more inventive in your appearance. I bet you'll learn to enjoy it thoroughly – and he will LOVE it." [Emphasis in the original.]

I believe she is dead right about how ALL men look ALL the time – it is built into a guy's DNA, as I opened with in chapter 2. I also think she may be right about her opinions of *"nearly all men"* applying to the majority of men today, but I definitely don't think the polygamous nature applies to all of us guys. Many men can learn to channel their actual desires and to totally control their actions when they develop the right relationship with one woman. However, it takes both husband and wife working on it to keep that relationship strong and to maintain that self-control over natural male instincts. You girls need to choose your husband carefully to find the right guy and then never stop trying to appeal to his visual attraction.

J agrees with me, *"It is natural for a man to have a wandering eye and a fertile sexual imagination."* I have tried to explain this several different ways. I am sure that J would also agree with my mind-groping observations in chapter 2. J puts her instructions to the wives in the strongest manner with her underlined statement: "It's the woman's responsibility to give him the sexual variety and adventure at home." She calls it the wife's "responsibility" to provide sexual variety.

My questions to every wife reading this are: "*Are you providing some good sexual variety at home? If not some of the ideas I have included in this book, what else are you going to do?*"

What I totally agree with J about is the need for all women to use new techniques to keep her husband's interest focused on her. She puts the responsibility on the wife to be creative. My ideas have been written more from a man's viewpoint in how the husband can promote this same goal. My experience has been as the one who has done the most to encourage my wife to go ahead and use outrageous outfits and even copy hooker looks to be sexy. My wife has tried to learn how I think and what I like. I know that I like variety, and I have wanted to encourage her to try different looks. This book exists because she has been so extremely successful at making me happy. Any wife reading this should not depend on her husband teaching her the way I have done with my wife.

The Holy Bible says, "*To those whom much is given, much is required.*" I have been given a One-In-A-Million marriage. I feel it is my obligation to pass on some of what I have learned about what has helped create this wonderful relationship that has kept our love life in high gear for over fifty years. I think that my wife and I have been living by the advice that J wrote about from long before she wrote it. We are living proof that she has been right on the advice that I have quoted. All three of her numbered points we have totally done for many years. I have always been so focused on my wonderful wife and her seductive ways that the thought of looking somewhere else never crossed my mind. I think that a man's polygamous ways can be eliminated when he has a wife that gives him everything he wants and more, the way my wife does. I don't look anywhere else because I am sure that the grass is much greener in my yard that in anyone else's yard.

Another very respected authority on the same subject is Dr. Willard F. Harley Jr., a clinical psychologist and marriage family therapist with over 25 years of marriage counseling experience. He is the author of *His Needs, Her Needs – Building an Affair-Proof Marriage.* This is another book I recommend to both all the husbands and wives reading this. Below are quotes excerpted from his book.

Dr. Harley first points out a warning that works both ways:

"If any of a spouse's five basic emotional needs goes unmet, that spouse becomes vulnerable to the temptation of an affair."

Note that this can be applied to both husband and wife. The man's five basic needs are quoted farther down. Dr. Harley then goes on to make positive points:

"It feels good to be attractive....

Attractiveness is what you do with what you have....

An attractive woman is made, not born....

Questions for her:

1. Do I take my husband's need for me to be attractive seriously? If not, why not?

2. Does my husband really like the way I look most of the time? Do I?

3. How much care do I take about the way I look? How is my figure? Do I use cosmetics to good advantage? Do I change my hair style from time to time to please my husband by giving him a little variety in the way I look?

"To consider together:

1. Sit down with your collection of photographs – especially those from days when you were dating and from your wedding day. Compare those with the way you look today. Do you need to make some changes? How?

2. Share your answers to the above questions with each other. Be respectful, but be honest."

This is exactly in line with my comments on long hair.

"How to Prevent/Recover from an affair:

Start meeting each others' needs. Try harder, try new ideas, develop interest.

"The "Irresistible" Woman. A wife makes herself irresistible to her husband by learning to meet his five most emotional needs.

1. Sexual Fulfillment. His wife meets this need by becoming a terrific sexual partner....

2. Recreational Companionship... She becomes his favorite recreational companion, and he associates her with his most enjoyable moments of relaxation.

3. Physical Attractiveness. She keeps herself physically fit with diet and exercise, and she wears her hair, makeup, and clothes in a way that he finds attractive and tasteful. He is attracted to her in private and proud of her in public.

4. Domestic Support... She manages the household responsibilities in a way that encourages him to spend time at home enjoying his family.

5. Admiration. She understands him and appreciates him more than anyone else.... She avoids criticizing him. ...."

This # 5 translates to respect your husband. Remember the Biblical teaching to respect your husband – this is the same thing that Dr. Harley has discovered by years of observation and research. Lack of respect is also probably the main cause of marital problems by women who have been brainwashed by the Feminist Movement.

Dr. Harley has so much information in these areas that I could quote many pages of what he has written showing support for putting more fun and more sex into relationships with suggestions like my ideas can do. I recommend that you read his book and check my

DressForSEXcess.com website to get a copy. I'll just list some of the section headings he has divided his material into:

> "*Affection is the cement of a relationship....*
>
> "*When it comes to sex and affection, you can't have one without the other. ...*"

The man wants sex, and the wife wants affection – a wife who will not provide sex will get little affection; a husband who does not give affection usually gets little sex.

> "*Sex begins with Affection....*
>
> "*The typical wife doesn't understand her husband's deep need for sex any more than the typical husband understands his wife's deep need for affection....*
>
> "*The couple that plays together stays together....*
>
> "*Meet your spouse's needs as you would want your spouse to meet yours.*"

This last quote is an application of the Bible's Golden Rule: "*Do unto others as you would have them do unto you.*" But there is one key thing that many people do not consider when applying the Golden Rule. If you are a guy, you should not treat a gal the way you want to be treated – if you are a gal, you do not want to treat a guy like you want to be treated. The Golden Rule should actually be, "*You should treat others the way that they would want to be treated by you, not treating them the way you would want them to treat you. They should treat you the way that you want to be treated by them, not the way that they would want you to treat them.*" This may be a small change, but it is significant. This does not change the Golden Rule at all, but I think it clarifies it in a way that many people do not think about. Many people never bother to look at it this way. This is why I spend so much of this book trying to show wives how men think and why they act as they do, so that the wives will understand their husbands better. Most wives do not really understand their men. Most professionals seem to agree about this, just as those that I have quoted agree. Wives need to try harder to understand and fulfill their husband's needs. I hope that they will find a lot of good ideas on how to attract their husband more.

I think that Dr. Harley's points are so very true! The best way to combine both the affection and the sex is with the fun sex that you can have in a marriage. This means to make it full of laughter and even silliness while still getting around to serious intercourse. It is just having a good time and lots of fun with your best friend and favorite companion. Hopefully some of my ideas will lead to more of this fun sex.

One last quote from Dr. Harley is a section heading, "*Arousal: How It All Starts.*" This is so true – this is what my ideas try to promote. Dr. Harley thinks that it is so important to explain that he has a whole section in his book about it. He goes into why it is important. I too go into Arousal in detail, with practical suggestions and examples of how wives can get their husbands fired up this way. This is what my wife and I use my clothing modifications and other crazy ideas for – arousal. It always works for us – first, a sexy outfit, and we get turned on, and then WOW! It works every time we try it. We have fun with them, and it always leads to us both getting turned on. I doubt that we would have as much sex today or as strong a relationship if one of us had not found something like this to keep things more interesting and such an effective way to turn each other on. I do not have the education degrees of the authorities in the marriage-counseling field, and we have never consulted one for our marriage since our brief required premarital counseling over 50 years ago. However, I think 50+ years of hot love and still enjoying daily sex proves that we have something good going for us that even the best, smartest "experts" do not have. We already cover all the items they teach about and we have always done that. They are right about what they teach and say – we see it has worked so well for us. This book is just to share the ideas that have added to what we have done, and that has been so much fun for us.

Some of my ideas create a lot of strong lust. Some people will think that these lustful feelings are wrong, but I suggest all my readers read the book *Kosher Lust: Love is Not the Answer* by Rabbi Shmuley Boteach. He points out how the strong feelings we share with some of my ideas are the best way to keep a happy marriage and to keep the love fires burning for decades, the way we have done. Rabbi Boteach points out that lust is the secret to a wonderful love life. Love alone will not accomplish the same depth of feelings. I can vouch for the fact that our One-In-A-Million marriage proves that he is right on target. A lot of what we do creates more than simple attraction; it definitely goes far enough to qualify as lust. Since we both read that book, we both laugh about how much we both lust after each other; we both love it.

You may not think that a 70+ year-old girl could ever be very attractive, but my outfits tend to minimize what the years have aged on my wife and emphasize the charms that have held up well over the years. She still has great legs, smooth skin, pretty hair and eyes, and very sensitive areas I have learned to use well. We both think that a big part of why she still looks very good for her age and why we both are still very healthy in our mid 70s (we feel good and we do not take any prescription drugs) is because we do not need any drugs. Our secret is a healthy daily overdose of natural endorphins – the natural result of having great sex. If such a great relationship has lasted this long for us, then I am sure that some of you younger readers can benefit from some of our ideas. I doubt that there will be many readers of this book who have passed the milestones that we have.

All of Dr. Harley ideas are right. The quotes I have picked out are points that show how there is a need for something different in any marriage that is in trouble. **Dull and boring equals trouble**. It also applies to any marriage where the couple wants to avoid trouble ahead of time. If you have nothing else going for you to increase your arousal levels and to add more love, fun, and sex to your marriage from some other source, try my ideas. Girls, go ahead and be your husband's own private hooker and see what develops.

As far as husbands encouraging the wife to play the hooker, I may have had a longer way to go than most guys because my wife was brought up to be VERY conservative (as you can tell from the story about the start of our relationship in chapter 2). I have taken an active role in modifying things and adapting ideas way beyond the Victoria's Secret and Fredericks of Hollywood outfits. My wife has been a very helpful and willing player in my games – it has turned into a true joint effort. This is because it can be lots of mutual fun if you do it right.

I think a good wife can and should be willing to think beyond the traditional sexy lingerie and see what her husband likes, just like J and Dr. Harley write. My book is just to help in giving new ideas and new directions in finding new ways to add more fun in your sex lives. When both husband and wife experiment and share how they feel about some of my various suggestions, this is the best result and the best way to add more fun in a marriage.

There is one thing that I have personally noticed (and that many professional therapists write about) that stops some husbands from trying to help encourage their wives looking sexy. I think many husbands are afraid of other guys noticing if their wife is very sexy and then making passes at her. They are afraid of their wife falling for some stud's pass at her. It comes down to both the husband not being secure in how faithful his wife would be under a serious attempt by some other hot stud to seduce her and not being secure in how manly he is himself in his own mind and in his wife's opinion of him. Therefore, these men don't want their wife to look attractive in public.

I know positively, without a doubt, that there is NO situation where I could not trust my wife. She also knows that there is no girl who could ever tempt me to be unfaithful. We have proven to each other that we could each control both our sexual urges and our behavior for several years even in our very horny teenage and early-20s years. This is when we had the raging hormones of youth, combined with plenty of opportunity, without any formal vows or commitments between us, and we still kept our self-control and did what was right. We have proven to each other that our moral standards and minds have complete control over our biological urges and feelings. Spending almost 5 years winning each other's trust and confidence has been reinforced by 50+ years of growing love. We know that we have one of the world's greatest loves and that true, real love is a lot more than just sex. We both know that no extra marital sex could ever be worth risking the love we have built over 50+ years together. The sex is just part of the fun in our love. We both also know that we have everything we have ever dreamed of just between ourselves. If we do ever think of something new, we don't need anyone new to implement it – we would want to try it with each other.

As a tip to unmarried women that may be reading this, waiting for the commitment of marriage before the sex is the best way to develop a long-term monogamous marriage. I suggest you tell your prospective groom that it is your dream to wait for marriage to have sex and that you want a man who is willing to make your dream come true first. Then you pledge to try to make his dreams of plenty of sex come true for him. In the meantime, tell him that you want to concentrate on becoming best friends in other non-sexual ways – doing things together, getting to know each other better, and learning to have fun in ways that do not need sex. If this works, it will only get better later when you are married and can add lots of sex to the mix.

There is nothing wrong with agreeing with the fact that the trashy call-girl look flaunts a woman's charms to a man. We are not going to limit our fun just because what can attract me to my wife's charms is also used by other women for commercial and immoral seduction. We don't use it in an immoral way, and it is only for our private pleasure – we never expose it to anyone else in any immoral way. No one else needs to know what goes on behind our closed doors; it is just our private little world of sexual fun – LOTS of sexual fun.

Everyone can be a positive lesson to others about something – everyone has a lesson that they can teach, even if totally unintentionally. I think of the minister who taught that even the worst useless bum can be a good example – a good example of what can happen if you waste your talents.

Well, I have seen enough TV shows, movies, videos, advertisements, and pictures of attractive women, movie starlets, call girls, and various sluts to learn about effective flashing of feminine charms that look seductive. I have seen for myself the girls in itsy-bitsy bikinis on most beaches – I have even been on several nude beaches (with my wife). I have even seen the typical teenage girls on the street and in the malls, and many of them look like they are trying to be very seductive and are already copying the hookers. And I have even seen some of the real hookers at work who are visible in many areas in major cities. I just like to look at the positive side of all this feminine seduction. No matter where or how she learned her tricks, I am a willing volunteer to let my wife test or practice her seduction skills anytime, anywhere. I even give her advice and feedback to help her refine her skills and come up with new ideas – she just has to do all the practicing on me.

At the same time, in public, I want my wife to be respected as the very proper, mature, intelligent, responsible, adult woman that she is. For family, friends, church, and business, she dresses conservatively enough to be proper – but she does like being a little perky in her appearance and does not want to look dowdy or old-fashioned. She has great legs and a nice shape, and she is not afraid, in casual situations, of wearing shorts to bare her legs or a top that gives her some bare arms, shoulders, back, or a slight belly button peek look for my interest. When we're away from home in warm weather, she wears halter tops, bare midriff tops, hip rider shorts, and some very sexy looks and lots of bare skin, but nothing trashy in public or past what many other females are wearing in the situation, even if they are a lot younger. The trashy seductive look is reserved just for getting my attention and raising my libido when we are having fun – which is daily if we have the chance. It is also one of the big reasons that we have such a wonderful love and such an active sex life – she is always seductive to me.

My wife is the perfect wife – a real lady by day and a real sexy seductress by night (or any time of day if the situation develops). Any of you wives who may be reading this would have happier husbands if you tried to improve in both ways: be more conservative by day, with other people, and more seductive at night, alone with your husband. I think some of the wonderful attraction of my wife is the range of the difference in her twin roles.

As a tip to those who can take advantage of it, or who need it, we don't wait to make love at night as much as most couples do, or as much as we used to. In our 70s, we have to admit that we do not have the energy we used to have. We are often too tired at bedtime if we wait until then for sex. We are usually able to make love during the day. We set our mutual priorities to use our energy on what is most important to us, and making love is way up on that priority list. This is something for you to consider if being too tired is a common reason to skip having sex.

Sometimes the twin roles do get crossed up in some ways. My wife was a natural blonde in all the pictures of her as a child. Her hair turned light brown at about 12 to 13 years old. When we were first married, it became an occasional fun night out for her to put on a full, long, blonde wig and dress up in a nice cocktail dress for a night out. I teased her about being my mistress – my blonde bimbo in the wig. Later I would tease her about all the fun I had enjoyed on that date with my blonde bimbo mistress, and I teasingly told her what she was missing. She asked if I liked her as a blonde, and I told her it was a natural for her fair complexion and her beautiful blue eyes – she sure was a gorgeous blonde.

She decided she had more fun as a blonde. We found that it was true that blondes have more fun! She decided to dump the wig and go blonde full time. For many years now, she has been blonde all the time. She says she grew up very blonde and feels more comfortable as a blonde. I now tease her about how much more fun I have with her than I did with my brunette first wife. Having a part-time blonde bimbo has really changed our lives – now I have a full-time blonde bimbo. I can now also tease her with all the blonde jokes. But of course, by day she is a very conservative blonde lady.

Seduction, however, is a lot more than just how a girl dresses. My wife can be very seductive to me in a conservative business suit. It is the come-on looks, the warm smile she flashes to me, the slight touch of my hand, brushing against me somehow in an unobtrusive way, and a hundred other small things.

Her attitude is more important than just what she wears or when. With me she is a better wife than any guy can dream of, and her attitude lets me know how much she loves me and wants me. She has had outside sales jobs where she has to cold call businesspeople. Of course, she has met some idiot guys that make suggestive comments and would like to screw anything in a skirt, but she has an attitude that turns them right off. Some of the other women from her office doing the same thing have told her how they have sometimes had trouble with some guys being aggressive. However, my wife has never had any trouble with guys on this job because she has a strictly business attitude and appearance on the job. Attitude is very important in how a woman deals with others and deals with her husband. Many wives do not convey the right cool attitude to men that they meet in public or in business and do not convey the right hot attitude to their husband.

I personally like the soft, natural, smaller-breast look – a Dolly Parton chest turns me off. When I went through school in the late 1950s, almost all girls had the big-breast look – it was because of their big bras, which had more in common with armor plating than today's lingerie. Good girls had solid, padded bras, and it was not proper to see the outline of a nipple through anything. Even swimsuits had a thick, built-in bra. As a boy, my mother even told me once about her own growing up in the 1920s and how girls in her generation used to use Band-Aids over their nipples to prevent them from showing under thin tops. Compare that to girls even using fake nipple enhancers today to get more of the perky nipple look – times really change.

I guess growing up and never seeing many girls with nipples showing and very few real-looking breasts – the way real breasts look, move, and jiggle – made me like it when the feminists started burning their bras in the 1960s. Those '50s bras deserved to be burned. I like the thin-top no-bra look and feel on my wife, and I encouraged her to look that way to entice me. It works well with me! She wears a bra most of the time and always out in public, but at least it is a soft, modern style.

Six months after we started dating, while we were going steady, even though it was over 50 years ago, I still remember vividly the first time I held my wife when she had no bra on. She had been home sick, and I let her know I was outside in the shadows hoping to see her a few minutes one warm spring night. She went out to "walk the dog," and we met in the dark under the trees near her house for a short time. We hugged and kissed, and I instantly felt the difference when I didn't feel that hard bra pressed against me. The difference, even with my shirt and her shirt between us, was electrifying to me. She was soft and feminine pressed up against me. I remember running my hands up and down her back as we hugged, and for the first time, there was no bra strap under her shirt. It felt delightful to just feel the unbroken softness of her skin under her tee shirt as I enjoyed the feel of her shape without the bra strap. I held her harder and closer than usual, and I usually held her very firmly. I never wanted to let her go. Those magical moments hugging in the dark under the trees kept me on a real high for a very long time, and the memory has never died out. It was a few years before I ever had anything like that wonderful feeling again.

I still like that no-bra look and feel. I try to talk her out of her bra quite often, not just to have sex but to just let me enjoy having her around that way – soft and warm to hug, with a little jiggle to watch as she walks around the house, and even maybe the hint of a perky nipple poking out through her thin top. I love it when I see that she has voluntarily left the bra off just to tempt me. That always seems to get my attention, and she knows that it will usually get her more than just visual attention.

It is magical moments like this between two naive, innocent, young lovers, as their love grows very slowly and in little steps along the way, that help create a truly great love story. There is no one else, no ex-anything, no prior relationships or experiences – just starting as innocent novices and learning all about love together. We went very slowly, just one step at a time, where we could savor and appreciate each little step along the way. When I think back about how our love grew, I often hear the line from the old Sinatra song in my mind:

"We're on the road to romance, but let's make all the stops along the way." This is the way to build a truly great love.

CHAPTER 11
Best Sources for Cheap Stuff to Modify

F OR THE ITEMS I CUT UP, I have learned to shop at various thrift shops and similar low-price locations to find cheap items to experiment on. I am not crazy; I have never tried to modify any of my wife's favorite outfits. But some of the ones I have picked up and modified have become her new favorites.

Learn the thrift shops in your area, and shop on sale days. Ask when they have sales – they all do. Some have sales on regular days of the week or of the month or on holidays. Some have an email list for sales too. Pieces can be as little as a dollar or two for an item to cut up and have fun with. One local thrift shop has a big box of stuff for 50 cents each where they put stuff before they get rid of it. To help you find stores in your area, go to www.TheThriftShopper.com. This website covers the whole country and seems to have very complete coverage. Perhaps its biggest drawback is it is slow to remove shops that have gone out of business. The small shops don't always last, and they tend to go out of business often. Please update this website when possible – notify them of new shops, and tell them when a shop has closed. Sometimes things like small church shops are not included. It helps the shops succeed to get them listed.

One local nonprofit shop sells all the children's clothing items at 25 cents each. Many of these easily stretch to look sexy on my wife. This reminds me of the commercial from a TV sitcom of years ago that was played often – I don't remember the name of the show, and I did not watch the show, but I laughed at how appropriate a commercial for the show was to what I had already known. The show had a sexy 20-something bimbo girl and a young girl about age 8 to 10. In the one scene in the commercial, the two girls had on what looked like identical sweaters. The guy in the scene commented on how they both seemed to wear the same size clothes. The young girl's comfortable-size stuff looked stretched to sexy perfection on the bimbo. I think about it every time I pick out some of these girls' items. At those prices, you can afford to experiment.

Garage sales, yard sales, rummage sales, and the like are also good sources if you are looking for bargain-priced items to just have fun with or to cut up and modify. Find where most of these are advertised in your area. Shop early for the best selection; shop late for getting the best deals and to make offers on what is left over. Often the best deals are on stuff that is not pre-marked – you must ask, and then always make a lower counter offer for the piece you are looking at or a lower price per piece if you get several items. If there is a lot you would like, rather than pay attention to marked prices, get a lot all together, and make a big discounted offer on the lot. One dollar a piece for many pieces is normal for wearable items. Carefully look over the items that you pick up before you ask the price or make an offer. Look for stains, dirty spots, rips, holes, torn seams, or missing buttons, and check every zipper to see that it works OK. Some of these faults may be why they are getting rid of these items. Some of these faults may mean that, even at a low price, it is not going to be usable for what you want, but it also gives you a reason to ask for a lower price on the items that you do want.

Some of the best deals I have gotten are by offering to buy a big lot entirely. One sale where there was a big pile of costumes of all types and sizes. Some were complete, and some were just parts. I asked and got a price of $2 each, but I made an offer of $5 for them all and got it for $7 – about 25 to 50 cents apiece. It was late in the day and the costumes had not been selling, and the people just did not want to put them away again after the sale. This is less than the retail price of one of the original costumes – a sexy pirate wench outfit. There were several costumes to use in fun sex play, and the rest went into the costume closet for the grandchildren to play with. At these personal garage sales, the sellers are usually tired from the day's work, and they don't want to have to put all the unsold stuff aback again – they are happy to just get rid of it in many cases by the end of their sale. If they have not sold much of similar items, then by the end of the day, they should realize that they have overpriced the items; mention this thought to them if they don't seem to negotiate much. Personally, we sleep late and make love early on a Saturday when most sales are held, so we go later and get better deals on what has not sold.

One great source is the periodic rummage sales some organizations have, like churches. People donate perfectly good clothes to these sales, and the prices are usually very reasonable during the sale. Since they hate to deal with all the leftovers after the regular sale, many such places have a final bag sale on the last hour or two. This means for $1 to $5 a shopping bag, you can put in as much as the bag will hold. I find that for from 5 to 25 cents apiece for each item, as part of a full bag sale, I can get things to use or cut up. At those prices, who cares if the idea doesn't work out exactly or the fit isn't perfect. For anyone's budget, this is a "use once and then throw it away" price range. We laugh, have fun, and enjoy some great sex for just a few cents an item this way.

Every one of these sales has plenty of usable items, like tee shirts and shorts that you can use to mark up with markers with hand-drawn words or pictures. Just use your imagination, and see the section on marking things up with slogans in another chapter or online. When there is a good bag sale, stock up on tees to use later.

One thing that I always look for everywhere that I shop is belts. These range in price from 25 cents to two dollars most places for anything. Decorative belts can be used to dress up an outfit or used alone on bare skin. Several of my ideas need a drawstring or belt to hold them in place. I like to add a one-dollar belt to the outfit and keep it together rather than have to use one or two belts with everything and have to keep changing them back and forth. The idea is to decorate the female body and not get in the way of using it for what you want

– a pretty belt around the waist is never in the way of the action in the areas I want to pay attention to.

There is one thing that I should point out about some belts and some items of clothing. These are all designed to be comfortable to the girl wearing the item, and hopefully look good, but there is not usually any concern about how the item feels on the outside. For close contact sex, beautiful outfits can be covered in sequins and belts with studs and material and other stuff that can feel very scratchy to the guy when it is against his bare skin during lovemaking. They are usually made to be worn over something, not on bare skin, so they can also be scratchy to the woman if worn on her bare skin. Keep in mind how anything is going to feel when you are rubbing yourself up against the outside of the item. I love the feel of bare, soft, warm, smooth, sensitive, female skin rubbing against my skin, and I have no objection to most clothing – like silky fabrics or cotton or even denim – but anything abrasive, like many sequins, is a distraction from any erotic feelings. Feel the item first for texture and sensation.

You also need to have different lengths of belts. Some belts are for the hips, and some for the waist – one that fits the hips correctly may look too long on the waist. I also like to have different colors of each length to match outfits.

Remember to look for soiled and damaged items – these can be ridiculously reduced for clearance or even put in a pile or bin for 25 or 50 cents to just get rid of. Often at thrift shops, I see a damaged item with things like a broken zipper, missing buttons, or ripped seams that obviously were not noticed when the item was priced or put out for sale. Look for any stains too. I bother to bring it to the shop clerk's attention, and they frequently tell me that it should have not ever have been put up for sale. I offer them a fraction of the original price – say, just one dollar – and they are glad to get it.

Many items are given away to thrift shops or rummage sales because they have a bad spot or some mark that the original owner didn't bother to try to get out or couldn't get out. If you are looking for an item to cut up for a fun, one-time sex session – you can have a little more flexibility and can ignore a slight stain. An item stained enough that you would not wear it out normally may still be fine to use just for sex play. If you like the item design as is or want to use the area with the stain, then it is worth trying plan A – trying a good stain remover to get the stain out – the previous owner may not have even tried this. If this fails, plan B is making the best of it by cutting it up for some other idea that cuts off the bad spot.

I always look for any stains, tears, or other damage and where it is. It is often in an area that I could easily cut out to make the item into something I would like from the rest of it. I recently saw a girl's Hawaiian tee shirt with a chocolate stain right in the middle of the chest. I got it for a quarter, cut out an oval in the palm trees in the center of the chest that eliminated the stain, and had a big peek-a-boo hole showing right between my wife's breasts. Then, for effect, I cut rows of narrow slits in the short sleeves and in a row down below her breasts on each side of the printed area. I also shortened it to be a midriff barer by cutting off most of the area below the printing. It was a real nice look when she put it on – and the stain was gone.

Another time I saw a Texas souvenir shirt with a big uneven stain lower in the center of the front. I cut out almost all the stain with a big scalloped cut from midriff length on the front sides and up to almost between the breasts in the center. Then I cut ¼-inch wide cuts to make a one-inch fringe in that remaining bottom edge. The rest of the stain was not noticeable in the narrow ¼-inch-wide fringe cuts. I added some raunchy slogans with some markers on that one. I remember using, "Texas Girls Like Things BIG! Let Me See How BIG It Is?" and then I crossed out the word "See" and wrote in the word "Feel."

Frequently, just shortening an item will remove any bad spot. One other thing is to ignore the bad spot and take advantage of damage to make a real banged up look. On one blouse, I cut rips and tears and put more stains with some black markers and some to look like a little blood in red. One rip had a breast hanging out part way. I matched this top with a worn-out pair of jeans that had some rips and tears, and I added a lot more, plus a crotch-cut. We set the scenario as her just staggering home from an all-night Animal House fraternity party.

She told me she had been half fucked to death and that she had the time of her life. I then kept asking, *"Did they do this?" "How about this?" "How many times did they do this?"* as I was feeling her up and screwing her thoroughly. She volunteered, *"One guy threw me down on the bed, got on top of me, lubed my breasts, held them together with his hands, and kept rubbing his cock between my breasts a lot to get his cock hard again before he fucked me a second time. Oh, he was so hard to satisfy!"*

I get the ideas from looking at the items and imagining what they can be used for. Sometimes if you plan to modify an item, you can turn it into two items. I just bought a long pullover crocheted white dress. Of course, it was fully lined by a white inner dress that was just attached at the top of the inner dress's shoulder straps. The crocheted dress looked very good on my wife – all that bare skin underneath with holes big enough for her pink nipples to poke out. By being careful to just cut the threads attaching the inside dress, I did not damage either item. I have some nice ideas to use the inner dress for as a separate piece – a two-for-one bargain.

Recently, I got a black leather jacket, which had a $45 thrift shop asking price, but I saw it had a big rip under the sleeve – maybe even done by a customer trying it on when it was much too small for them. It was ruined. I offered $1 and got a counter offer of $3. I took it. I had no plans to fix it or use it as a coat, but it had lots of soft, smooth, glove leather, and it would cost $45, or even a lot more, just to buy that much of the nice soft leather skins at a craft store. (You can also try eBay for leather skins). I haven't done it yet, but I'm visualizing a soft, black, leather bikini, another halter top with a fringe edge, and a leather micro skirt using the hem of the coat as the skirt waistband top – with a drawstring put through the factory hem seam to make a wrap skirt out of it. I like the look and feel of soft black glove leather on bare skin. See my website "Tips" section for how to easily make things with this nice leather. It is very easy to work with this kind of soft leather – it can easily be sewn, but it does not have to sewn, just use a leather glue to make professional-looking hems and seams with soft glove leather. Perhaps a brief ironing of the finished seams will also help. Simple craft store rivets can be used to fasten straps to soft pieces.

At many flea markets, you can see leather shops and look at the prices of things like a leather bikini – they are outrageous. They don't even have some of the features that I like, such as a crotch-cut; I'd still have to work on these readymade items to make them as good as I want them. It is so simple to make this kind of sexy stuff from a cheap leather skirt or jacket like I have. Some of those leather shops have some other very sexy items for sale that you can look at for ideas on what you make to look great on your wife. I bought one very long leather skirt for a bargain price at a rummage sale, and I shortened it into a sexy miniskirt, and I have most of the leather left over. It can be repurposed into several sexy leather items.

There are many ways to come up with inexpensive pieces to make into fun sexy outfits if you want stuff to modify. The only limit to the fun you can have is your own imagination.

CHAPTER 12
Shop Like a Man

M Y WIFE SAYS I "SHOP LIKE A MAN," because I use a tape measure rather than just size labels and eyeballing an item. I suggest you do the same if you are a guy looking for stuff to modify for your wife. Even a girl shopping for herself will save a lot of time trying stuff on if she uses the tape measure to help choose or eliminate what she is going to try on. Many used items do not have a readable size, and sizes can vary a lot. Remember too – thrift Shops often do NOT have fitting rooms, and you almost never get to try stuff on at rummage sales or garage sales. Even if someplace has fitting rooms, it takes time to try things on, and sometimes there is a line for the fitting room. For stuff to use to cut up or for private sex sessions, most of the time, I don't care if it is an exact fit anyway.

This means check several dimensions of clothes of your own and of your wife or husband that fit just right. Check the actual measurements of the intended model. Then also check with a tape measure, as well as checking label sizes of her existing clothes. Lay items flat and measure the waist and the measurement up from the crotch for that size. A normal waist on a woman is about 12 inches up from the crotch. A size 9 or 10 would probably be about a 15-inch waist at that point (times two means a 30-inch waist). Low-rise jeans would be 8 or 9 inches up from the crotch and would measure 17 inches (34 inches at that point). The hips would be about 18 inches (36 inches at the widest point). What you need to keep in mind is to consider how high the waist is for the look you want and what her measurement should be at that point, and the crotch is the point you need to measure up from in any shorts or pants items.

Don't forget that, unless there is a zipper or buttons, the item must stretch or open to the maximum hip measurement to allow the item to be put on. On shorts or pants, I always measure the distance from the crotch to the waistband first. This tells me where the waistband will fall – at the natural waist or lower down on the hips, which requires a bigger measurement. Then I like to be sure the waistband is fastened closed, and I hold the tape measure end in my left hand with the waistband left side of an item, hold the rest of the tape measure in my right hand with the right side of the waistband, and stretch the item out with a GENTLE pull. This tells me the width of the waistband with gentle pressure. I decide whether this is going to be a fit or not. If an item is stretched too tight, it does not look as good to see the roll of flesh get squeezed out above the waistband. Lastly, on a stretch waistband, I pull harder and make sure the entire item will stretch enough to go over the hip measurement too. On an item that unzips or opens up to be put on, I just measure the widest point a few inches lower to be sure the hip measurement is large enough, if there is any doubt about size. Check that buttons are there and that zippers work and look for stains or rips in bad spots – problems in these areas could be why the first owner got rid of the item and can affect its usefulness even if you plan to modify some parts of it. If there are problems you find but you can still use the item, use the problem to negotiate a price discount.

I often shop the girls' section, and my tape measure tells me that something that may have a girls' size 7–8 label and would just fit my 7-year-old granddaughter stretches out to just the size I am looking for to fit my wife. This is particularly true for knit fabrics that stretch a lot. I have seen a children's size 6x stretch to fit just fine.

The girls' sizes are shorter if you want to leave some bare middle. You should know the measurement from the shoulder to what you want the hemline of a top to be. I know that 13–14 inches may leave the bottom of my wife's boobs visible, 15–16 inches just barely covers everything, 17–18 inches leaves plenty of belly button showing, and 19–20 inches will just touch the natural waistline and be right about at the belly button. If the girls' sizes stretch out to the bust measurement, they will have a sexy form-fitting look. I do a quick measurement using my hand span to get a quick estimate where the bust line is on a top and then do a measurement at that level to check how hard I have to stretch the item to reach my wife's bust size.

On a girls' top or any small top, there is one more measurement you need to check. I know that I need about 11–12 inches from the underarm seam to the center label area of the neck on an item. If it is not that large with minimum stretching, then it will be very uncomfortable for my wife to wear – too tight under the arms. This can be modified a little if you can cut below the armhole seam to enlarge the armhole down. She is great about putting up with a little discomfort to look good to me for the short term, but I want her to be thinking about how good the sex feels when I am screwing her, not how uncomfortable the top is feeling.

Another helpful measurement to have is how long from shoulder to hem an item needs to be to have the desired look on a long garment. You want to know whether or not an item like a long tee shirt will come down to cover her butt or not.

One more thing I like to know is exactly where her shoulder is in relationship to my own height. That way I can hold a dress up to where her shoulder comes on me and then look at how long the dress is. I check how far off the floor the hem is – I can tell fairly accurately whether a dress is mini, knee-length, calf-length, or floor-length on her. I can estimate how much I need to cut if I want it shortened and how that overall change would look. Another thing is where her natural waist comes on you – so you can hold up pants and know if they are her length or not in the same way.

Using the tape-measure technique saves time and mistakes. I am often looking for an item that will be a snug fit in some spots. This means that I am working at the minimum size limits – it would be easy to guess wrong and end up just a little too small and be a waste of time and money. If I am very close, I can decide whether or not the price of the item is worth the gamble to try it.

Many times, I have had ladies shopping near me who see me using a tape measure and ask to borrow it a moment. They will be checking something like one of their own body measurements and then checking an item. Shopping like a man even seems to appeal to many ladies. Try it; you'll like it.

Get jeans with an old-fashioned button fly rather than a zipper fly for some modifications. If you want to shorten the top of jeans, pants, shorts, or a skirt, it is hard to do if there is a zipper that goes all the way up in the normal way. If the item has old-fashioned buttons, like some Levi's brand jeans have, you can cut off the waistband or any amount you want from the top to turn them into as low a cut as your girl can handle (before they fall off). Just shorten in one-button increments.

The same goes for shortening from the bottom. You can't shorten above the bottom of the zipper. I saw a magazine picture where the model had only the top 2 or 3 inches of the top of some jeans worn low on her hips, with an attached pair of bold-print panties. Of course, I had to try the same idea. I got a few pair of button-fly shorts and jeans for the tests. I tried some with the panties included, and some without. One was a jeans waistband worn as a low hip rider plus a few inches down all the way around. In the back, it was just the top of the rear pocket level, and then I cut out down and around the entire pocket to leave the rear pockets just as flaps on a totally bare ass. In front, the pocket tops were all that was left attached to the waistband. The matching jeans legs were worn as bell-bottom leggings just below the knee. It was an interesting look – the bottom and top of the jeans, with nothing from knee to hip but the flap pockets. It looked ridiculously lewd. This is the type of look that definitely leads to fun sex.

CHAPTER 13
Where to Come Up With More Ideas

Y OUR IMAGINATION IS THE BEST SOURCE of ideas to use for sexy modifications. Often it is the pattern or design of what you find to cut that can help give you the ideas of how to change the garment.

Check out any tourist trap shops at any vacation destination. All the tee shirt shops have hundreds of printed items with sexy, suggestive, or vulgar sayings that you'll laugh at. If it only costs a few cents or a dollar or two to take a thrift-shop or rummage-sale item and put on your own saying or slogan with a marker; it is worth the fun between just the two of you. Examples are things like modified very short shorts with your spouse's name on them, like "Ken's Piece of Ass" printed across the rear, or a tee shirt with "Sex Machine: Free Test Available" printed on it. Do whatever is fun for the two of you and whatever you can do to turn each other on. You can also buy various sizes and colors of iron-on letters to use for your sayings at any craft shop or even Wal-Mart craft departments.

eBay and Internet sales sites are also good sources for slogan and printing ideas. Try entering "sex" or "sexy" or "costume" for the search term.

Search for the word "costume" on eBay, and you'll see all kinds of high-priced, sexy outfits in the pictures. Once in a while, you'll find a nice cheap auction that you can get a good price on, but watch the shipping charges and only consider the total cost. There is a small window on most eBay search pages marked "Sort" that usually starts out as "Best Match" but has other options that you can consider. I like to choose the sort mode of "Price + Shipping: Lowest first." Look at the pictures, and take notes or print out the pictures, and then come up with ways to make a similar item out of cheap items.

I find that even nice commercial costumes can be improved. For example, many women's costumes have an old-fashioned bodice that includes features like a lace-up corset look with a ribbon lacing up the front of the chest area. I have cut out the panel behind the lacing so that behind the lacing is just bare skin between the breasts. It forms a nice peek-a-boo sexy improvement on the original costume. I just don't cut the very top edge of the middle piece out so that the remaining, little top piece holds the two sides together rather than putting the strain of keeping the sides together on the ribbon tie. Perhaps also leave a narrow strap of the original fabric right at the widest point of the breast line; this will keep the top from stretching too much there.

You need to have the imagination to look at something and think about how it would look worn with nothing underneath it – maybe a lining cut out, shortened, peek-a-boo holes cut, or some other raunchy modification. I try to pull out pages from newspapers, magazines, etc. that have pictures of sexy outfits and then try to find an item that I can modify to look much like what I see. I often do the same thing on my computer – find a sexy look and then print it out so I can copy it. Try going to eBay and search for "sexy women's clothes," and scroll through the photos, printing the photo of what you are going to try and copy.

Even when just reading newspapers or magazines, look for racy outfits on girls in any of the pictures, advertisements, or even the cartoons – anywhere at all. I cut out the pictures or make a sketch or take some notes and add all these to a "Costume Idea" file. Doing this helps imprint the idea in my memory, and months later, I may see something for sale that reminds me of an idea I wanted to try. Sometimes I thumb through the pile of pictures in the file and try to come up with new ideas to try. This might give me ideas of something particular to look for when I am shopping.

One sure source of many raunchy outfits is the various men's magazines – *Playboy, Hustler, Maxim,* and others. No, I don't pretend to read these magazines for the stories – I look at the pictures, of course. Even various pornography outlets have costume ideas. The models in all these magazines are not always naked. Often they have on items or pieces of items that are just what I call decoration for the female body. Why not copy these body decorations on your own wife if it appeals to you? Some of these photo series have outfits like barely there denim shorts, short cutoffs, way-too-small ripped shirts that are just barely tied on, and the attractive use of scarves – stuff designed to look very sexy to the average guy. Make notes or do sketches to add these ideas to your idea file. You wives might come up with better ideas of what men like by also checking the outfits in these men's magazines. Any smart guy will prefer his wife doing her best to copy the sexy magazine outfits for his personal use and pleasure than just looking at the pictures. It will not matter that the wife thinks she is not as pretty as the model, as long as she is willing and available and does it with a fun attitude. A willing wife in the bed is worth a thousand models in a magazine.

For example, I saw a picture of a movie star in an elegant long gown where the top was a halter strap with a narrow fabric band down each side of her chest to the waist. There was no back and a neckline down to the belly button. It was one of those gowns where every guy hopes that she moves wrong and one side slides off a breast; they must rubber cement those sides in place or she must have nipple rings to tie the pieces to. Later I saw a thrift shop sale for a one-piece, plain, dark swimsuit that I got and just cut the center down the front, from just below the top edge to below the belly button level. I had to cut away all the bra and liner material, and this just left just the thin outer layer. With a quick crotch-cut in the swimsuit and worn with a similar-colored short skirt (previously shortened to micro length), the look was very similar to the sexy movie starlet's expensive gown for about $2 and a few minute's time – and it was even sexier with the shorter skirt and easier access. When my wife did move wrong, a breast did pop out, but it didn't bother either of us.

I often think about what sex costs many guys – both on a commercial basis or just to keep a wife happy. Then I think about how much fun I get for an hour playing, screwing, and loving for a $2 scissor job. WOW, what a bargain I get when it is compared in that way.

The nipple candy pasties I mentioned in the "More Top Modifications" chapter are because of a photograph I saw in a magazine of a girl with candy pasties on her nipples. When you see something, make some notes and figure out how you can turn this into a sexy costume.

Many items I see are two layers. These can be very sexy gauze-like sheer tops or skirts that have a modesty layer underneath. They can also be things like crocheted-look swimsuits with a nude-colored lining. I automatically look at these and imagine them without the underneath layer. I can carefully cut out the inner layer by cutting along each seam. This ends up with a sheer item to decorate her charms and give an illusion of a feminine covering but leaves everything seductively covered by just a see-through or mesh layer.

Some items have built-in peek-a-boo appeal like eyelet, crocheted, and mesh items obviously designed to be worn over a modesty item to create a layered look. When I see these, again, I think how they will look with just her sweet charms underneath and peeking out at me. I really love the look of her nipples peeking out of the openings in loosely knit or crocheted item. I keep playing with them to keep them perky and firm to keep them poking out.

The next book I plan, **MORE Dress For SEXcess**, will have many more ideas on making up impromptu outfits. This will be about using things like scarves and belts and just making things up. It will also include making sexy outfits from items that were not originally made to be worn as clothes. It will cover more about making unusual outfits for a couple of dollars that match items selling for big bucks in commercial catalogs. I have a lot of ideas to make role-playing costumes, like an Indian warrior and Indian maiden, a jungle princess, a pirate wench, and lots more. You will also find more ideas right now on the free **DressForSEXcess.com** website. God made the possibilities of love and sex so limitless. The ideas are endless.

CHAPTER 14

Ideas on How to Cut

OR ANY CUTTING OF ANY KIND, remember the wise old carpenter's saying, "Measure twice, cut once!" I have made many mistakes in cutting and not gotten the effect I originally wanted. Look at the garment, and carefully plan what you want to do, and then double-check before you cut. This includes checking the inside, what is hidden inside, where the pockets are and will fall after the cuts, and the weave of the fabric. Be sure how many layers you are cutting before you start – I have looked at the top and had caught another layer underneath in the scissors that I didn't want to cut. At least my mistakes are not on expensive items.

There are many ways to make cuts that will look sexy.

For the really short, cutoff look on shorts, start with the cut at the crotch area at the inside leg seam. Leave only about 2 or 3 inches wide of total crotch left, and cut the leg seams about 1 inch or so below the center seam at the crotch. Cut each side the same. You can leave the center seam or cut out the proper spot and length of the center seam for genital access if you prefer the open crotch on this item. Then decide where you want the outside leg seam to be cut. If you want to leave any front pockets, check how low they go. Sometimes the bottom edge of the pockets will hang down below the front of the shorts. You may like that look, or you can always cut off the bottom of the pockets. You can even cut out the entire pocket clear to the waistband if you want the peek-a-boo pocket cutout look above the pocket front and below the waistband. When trying to make matching cuts on both sides of a piece, make the cut first on one side, and then fold the item in half so that the other side seam is right next to the first side to match the cut position – mark and cut the second side's side seam to get the sides even.

Next decide what look you want and cut the back and front of the legs separately. Sometimes you want a short high cut in front and more coverage on the rear, and sometimes you want a high rear cut to show off the bare ass cheeks. This depends on what look you like. At least for just a couple of dollars each, you can get multiple similar items and try different lengths to decide what you like best. Better to cut once on the long side and have to recut to shorten, than to cut too short the first time. After you cut both sides, hold the item up and compare how the two sides look: Do they look even and the same? Are there any areas that are notched and uneven? You might need to trim the longer side to match the shorter side or to trim certain uneven or notched poorly cut sections.

Depending on the look you want to have, use either an item with no rear pockets and leave a center part just a few inches wide a ways up, and then widen to a very-high-on-the-sides look to have the full ass cheeks bare if your wife has a nice tight ass; or use an item with rear pockets, and try to cut a straight line just a half inch or so below and parallel to the outside bottom pocket stitching. This uses the original pocket design pattern to match the cut you make and leaves a mostly denim-covered butt, but with the bare legs on the side, way above the crotch level if you want – it gives a long-legged look.

For cutting small items to go with a belt, there are some tricks you can try. When cutting pants into chaps, if the waist is too small, cut the front up through the waistband to remove the crotch and the entire front fly and zipper area, but leave the front belt loop on each side. If cutting into leggings, you can cut the back too. Depending on how fancy you want to get, either just cut the center seam out entirely, including the center belt loop, and use matching belt slits on each remaining end of the waistband; or leave the belt loop on one side and a slit on the other side. If you want it more balanced, it is easy to sew on another belt loop on the other side. You can salvage a belt loop from some other project or make one from a small scrap of cutout material, or use a piece of cutout seam to make a belt loop. An alternative is to cut out the center back much wider and cut the waistband just inside the next original belt loops. For a full bare-butt set of leggings, cut out the rear clear around to the backside of the side belt loops. Many chaps, even with the waistband left in, look good with the entire rear cut out from the side seam down to the leg and around to the inner pants leg seam.

If you don't like the look of just chaps and everything else bare – bare butt, bare front lower belly, totally uncovered crotch area, etc. – then you can always add some skimpy panties under the chaps. You can use cute or fancy panties or just use plain panties. On plain panties, you can add a raunchy slogan – something like, "Have you got something I can ride, cowboy?" or "How about a WILD RIDE?" You definitely don't want to spoil the look in order to have sex by taking the chaps off in order to take off the panties. Some panties can be easily pushed aside at the crotch to still have sex while wearing them. To make it very easy, just use a pair of panties with a crotch-cut.

Cutting different materials leads to different problems and creates different results. Something like denim cuts fairly easily, and the cut edges look fairly good, and you get a fuzzy, frayed edge fairly quickly. This look goes good with denim. Perhaps cut a little long, and brush to create the fuzzy edge, and then wash the item to make it fray even more, and it will shorten up. Denim can be cut in any direction without worrying about the weave, but for durability and to reduce long-term fraying, cut along the pattern of the weave, not diagonally. Cutting a denim seam is a little hard. There are often 4 layers in the seam – you need strong, sharp scissors and strong hands. To start a cut in the middle of a garment, pick the spot you want to cut the seams, and start to cut there. To start a cut in the middle of a piece of fabric, you can fold a piece of it and make the first cut to make a little opening. This gives you a hole to let you stick in the one side of the scissors, or you can use a sharp knifepoint and cut a small opening hole to get the scissors in. A sharp knife or a box cutter of some sort is often a help to cut through the tough seams on a denim item.

To cut into a hard-to-reach spot like the inside corner of a pocket being modified, it is often easier to use a knife to start at the hard-to-reach corner and cut out from the corner far enough out to use scissors on the cutting line. To cut a piece into the inside corner of two seams that meet without cutting the seams, it is easier to come into the corner with the scissors cutting in toward the corner along both cuts rather than trying to turn the corner with the scissors and cut the second line out from the corner.

When cutting anything, keep the cutoff scraps until you are finished. Then look over the scraps for any ideas on what they can be used for. Using the same fabric cut off a pair of jeans or from a cut to shorten a skirt or some shorts, as examples, you might make a matching choker, wrist or ankle cuffs, a pair of little triangles for a bikini top, or even a set of nipple pasties. I like to match a denim outfit I have cut up with denim accessories of the same color, like to make nipple pasties. This little touch of matching denim goes very well with a real raunchy bottom. However, I make special nipple pasties – I cut out a circle, a star, or a shamrock and a little pasty cover, and then I cut a tiny 3/8-inch hole in the center of each pasty. When I use rubber cement to glue the pasties on, the center hole lets the nipple itself stick out. The cement holds better without the nipple making a bump in the middle (this is important when you are rubbing up against each other a lot), and I think that just that little nipple peeking out is so sexy looking. My version of pasties is not to cover up her female assets; they are to emphasize and enhance the breasts. I also love touching and kissing just that nipple tip. The pasties keep my wife from feeling anything around the nipple; she feels my touch concentrated on just the super sensitive nipple tip. This drives her crazy, and I love to do that – it makes her very passionate. Sometime the larger pieces can make a lot more than just pasties; the fabric is always a perfect match.

As an example, I found a long, soft, denim-colored granny gown that had an elastic scoop neck, puff sleeves, and a loose blousy look over the bust and then was gathered in under the bust and hung down to the floor. It had a drawstring ribbon under the bust that tied in a bow in front and a little ruffle on the floor line hem. The top looked nice but modest, but the loose-to-the-floor look had nothing sexy about it.

My wife was there when I picked it out at a church bag sale and looked confused but just shrugged at my choice. It was one of my easiest scissor jobs. I just cut off the whole floor-length bottom just below the drawstring and ended up with a nice peasant-girl top that was so short that the ribbon under the bust was needed to tighten it up and hold her breasts up inside it.

I shortened the bottom piece from the top cut edge and cut a one-inch-wide strip off the bottom material for a matching choker that looked good with the low scoop neck. There was enough left from the middle area to cut into wrist and ankle cuffs or wraps. The whole shortened bottom was left, and I had her put it on inside out and upside down like a tube, I fastened an elastic belt around her hips and let the top fall down, turning it right side out over the belt, and the floor line hem now was the bottom of a miniskirt hung from her hips. One granny gown into a seven-piece, coordinated, extremely sexy outfit that looked better than most of what Victoria's Secrets sells – for just a few cents as part of a big $2-a-bag sale.

From the raised bottom edge of the top up under her bust to way down low on her hips, she had the cutest bare torso – as much skin in the middle as any bikini would show. The top, miniskirt, choker, and wrist and ankle trim all matched in the soft, denim-colored material. I loved the look of the modest top and all the bare skin. Not a bad look for about a 10-cent investment and only about 5 minutes with the scissors. When my wife put on that outfit, I got enough sex back to be worth several thousand times my cash investment.

My wife frequently compliments me on my imagination. I instantly saw the potential in this granny gown, and my wife was mystified at why I got it. She later agreed that it made a very complete, coordinated, sexy outfit.

One related marriage tip to any reader is that love is a two-way street, and it will not grow stronger if it is not constantly fed. Feed it regularly – with lots of good sex and with what you say and how you act. Remember, your actions shout so loud that your spouse can rarely hear your words.

You guys, always compliment your model on how well she looks in the outfits – let her know how much she turns you on in them, and if she does the cutting or has the ideas, compliment her for doing such a nice job. Tell her you appreciate it, and start to make some suggestions on something you might like. It might be things such as, *"I think you look so great in denim (velvet, lace, etc.) against your soft skin"* or *"I love you in micro miniskirts. You have great legs and such a nice butt the way that you show them off in those little skirts."*

You gals, always compliment your guy for being such a good, imaginative lover and for the way he loves you, if he is the family scissor man. Give him some ideas to try. If you do the cutting, tell him how much you appreciate his reactions. Tell him that you are so amazed at his imagination and creativity. Ask him to help think up ideas to get more of what turns him on. Ask him to point out what he thinks is sexy or to ask him what he likes – velvet, denim, lace, open-cup tops, bare midriffs, chaps, miniskirts, short shorts, crotch-cut panties, etc.

There is one tip that may be useful if you want to cut a very deep neckline down the front of something – as in belly-button-baring low. If you like a deep, deep neckline, keep this in mind: sometimes things won't stay in place for the barely-covering-the-breast look this gives, and you'll need a tie to hold the sides of the front together. As you cut down the front the first time, leave it ½ inch wider on each side than you think you want. If you decide it needs a tie later, you can start at one point a couple inches either above or below where you want the tie. Cut a narrow ½-inch strip to where you want the tie, but don't cut it off, and you'll have a tie strip on each side to tie together in a bow or sew together to make a strap tie. This won't let it come apart off the breasts unless you untie the bow in your foreplay. It also will not be enough to get in the way of slipping your hands under the sides of the front.

If you decide you need a back tie in such a case to hold the thin flimsy front panels in place, the same trick works if you can cut a long enough strip up each side of the back edge. You'll get two longer narrow ties that you can tie in a bow in the back.

Another technique to put a tie in anyplace it is wanted is to use ribbons or shoelaces. Craft stores have enough ribbon colors to match almost anything color-wise. You can buy it by the roll or by the yard. It is not hard to either machine or hand sew the end of a ribbon anywhere on a garment and make a tie end. Where standard shoelace colors will work, they can also be sewed on at one end. Both can be sewed on at both ends if you want a permanent tie. To fasten a tie without any sewing, just cut a small hole at the point that you want the tie fastened, and then just use the little hole to tie in the ribbon or shoelace using the hole

One pain in the neck on many items is a full lining. Most of the time when I cut out a lining entirely I do it by just trimming it off at the edges. Be careful doing this. I have sometimes cut the garment underneath, since I watch the scissors as I cut only on one side. Be aware of both sides of the scissor, and be positive which part you want to cut. There are some exceptions, like the one I already mentioned, where I keep the lining on the leather skirt, but it is harder to work with. You need a belt or something that catches the lining with the garment material, or else you need to sew it together at the cut edges – or you could try gluing it together.

Many linings that I cut out are the inner layers of a lace, mesh, crocheted, or other sheer top, bottom, or dress. Cutting the thin inner lining from a very thin outer shell must be done very carefully. All too often, I have nicked the top layer, and it has a small cut that distracts for the desired look. One more thing I always cut out is the inner layers of bra tops, like swimsuit bikini tops. The typical bikini top may be brief, but it is designed to hide the way perky nipples show, and it has multiple layers – many even have an extra layer to make places to put in bust-enhancing pads. If I just leave the top layer of something like a bikini top, it is usually very thin material – it even may get slightly see-through when wet. I like it because it lets the nipples make the little bumps in the fabric. Attraction is strongest when the male imagination is utilized. I have 50+ years of exploring my wife's body, but it still perks up my imagination to see the outline of her nipples under any top – I like very sheer or very thin fabrics because of this. I even cut out the lining in bikini bottoms because I like the look of a very thin layer clinging to her pubic area and showing the little crack she has – it is a very feminine shape to check out. If I get the chance to give her a quick feel in the bikini bottom, I can also feel much better through just one thin layer.

Once I even took a look at the skirt lining after I had cut it out and realized that it was a nice, shiny, black, satin skirt all by itself. I turned the top edge over to shorten it to the mini length I wanted, sewed it, and then added a drawstring. I used it inside out because the inner side is the finished side on a lining. It looked pretty dressy as a thin, short, black, satin skirt worn with fishnet stockings and high heels.

On some items, the only modification I make is to cut out a lining. Do you want a real sexy bikini for your wife to wear out into your own yard to sunbathe or into your own hot tub or backyard pool? That is, for any places she is in possible public view and needs to look appropriately dressed but only from a distance, not ever close up. Look for a crochet or knit bikini set. I have found several of these in various colors. They always seem to have a nude-colored lining. I carefully cut out the entire nude lining (this is the hardest thing to cut without catching a piece of the crocheted material as you cut – be VERY careful). The finished look is delightful! Real skin looks much sexier peeking through than a nude cloth lining. She can keep a swimsuit cover-up handy to slip on if needed once in a while in a semi-private location.

I love it when my wife's bare skin provides the nude color under a loosely woven, black, tie-on string bikini out in a semi-public setting. The bikini is not as firm holding its shape with the lining cut out – it is very stretchy. This is a nice feature if you want to get into the hot tub and just push the bra top off to the sides and under her breasts – it acts like a push-up shelf bra. The crotch area easily pushes aside too. Just remember there is a time limit to how long you should be in the hot tub according to the temperature, and exercising in it may even shorten that time limit. Make any hot tub sex a quickie, or adjourn to somewhere else before your time limit is up. A private swimming pool allows a much more leisurely sex session if it is private enough or maybe just dark enough out at night.

We travel sometimes and often have a hotel or resort pool or hot tub available. Frequently, these are deserted when we use them. I have suggested that my wife wear one of these unlined bikinis to the pool under a long tee shirt cover-up. She only has to take the cover-up off a moment and then would be in the pool. It would be the same on the way out. In the hot tub pool, up to her neck with the pool all bubbling, it would not be noticeable that it is her and not the original nude lining providing the skin color. She hasn't done it yet; she is worried that someone may come while she is in the pool and she would feel trapped and unable to get out. Even if she faced away from the pool as she climbed out to go get her cover-up, she thinks everyone would notice that she was bare assed under the suit. She is too much of a lady to try it, and I haven't pushed her. Perhaps some readers will try it. Post the event on my website.

I have a section on my free website **DressForSEXcess.com** where any readers can post any embarrassing ("Em-BARE-ASS-ing" or even any "Em-BARE-BOOB-ing" or "Em-BARE- SCREW-ing") stories from readers using my ideas. If you have a good story to share anonymously, please post it there. There should soon be several stories from other readers there for you to read and get a good laugh from too.

Be careful in what you cut with certain fabrics. It may take a few mistakes to learn from experience, but some loose-weave fabrics will just quickly unravel if cut and not hemmed up again. For example, never crotch-cut a crocheted bikini like I just mentioned about removing the lining. Like a hand-knit sweater, it would just endlessly unravel until it was gone and would just become one long piece of yarn again. You can use iron-on tape to seal some such items. It is best to first iron on the seam seal tape above the line you want to cut and then cut.

When cutting tight items that are stretched when worn, a cut parallel to the direction of the stretch will stretch both sides of the cut in the same direction. If a cut is made parallel to the stretch, the two pieces on each side of the cut will form just the narrow slit in between them when they are stretched. A cut in any other direction will pull open and gap wide as the stretch pulls it open and pulls the pieces apart.

What you do depends on the effect you want. For example, on a tight tee shirt across the bust, a horizontal slit will stay a narrow slit when stretched, but it will also sag if it is left loose. A small vertical slit between the breasts will stretch open into almost a circle when it is stretched.

On loose-fitting fabrics, you need to think about the effect of gravity on the slit to decide what the cut will look like when worn. Normally fabric is hung on the body shape and hangs down from where it rests on the shoulders, belt, or wherever. A horizontal cut lets the fabric stop being held in place by the fabric above it, and it can sag down from the cut. The amount of sag is determined by the horizontal stretch of the fabric. A vertical cut usually does not sag open unless there is some sideways pull. On loose-fitting items, a vertical slit will not open up very much except during movement by the wearer. One problem I learned is in making a peek-a-boo cut from the yoke area on the back of jeans, shorts, or a similar skirt, which I described in a previous chapter. I cut out the yoke clear across the back, including the center seam, and the top of the yoke below the cut sagged a lot. I did not like the sag look, which is why I advise never cutting the center seam.

When cutting the bottom edge of something like a tee shirt top that you want to fall at a certain spot, you need to decide if you are going to leave a rough-cut edge or do something else. If you want to cut vertical cuts to give a fringed-edge look, then you need to leave extra material to do the fringe. If you plan to hem the edge to stop any unraveling, you need to leave the extra material so that the finished edge is where you want it and not too short.

One trick I like is to find a very long tee shirt, hopefully one with a nice sexy slogan (or with room where I can put one), and then cut it off to just barely cover the bust area. This can leave me about 8 to 10 inches of the bottom of the tee shirt. I then use the cutoff piece as a micro miniskirt. The typical knit tee shirt cotton material is easily stretchable to go around a girl's butt, even if it does not cover anything. For example, I found a long, green tee shirt that said, "This Is My Lucky Shirt," on the chest. On the short micro miniskirt made by cutting off the bottom, I wrote "This Is Where I Get Lucky." Another long tee shirt said, "Sweet Thing," on the top, and I wrote, "Try A Piece Of This Sweet Ass," on the short piece that she wore as a skirt.

CHAPTER 15

Tips and Tricks

HERE IS ONE TRICK I HAVE USED to remedy the underarm tightness on items I have already bought that she says are uncomfortable or that look so good that I want to make them fit. I cut the underarm seam at the bottom. Cut down the underarm seam as far as necessary to make the measurement large enough to fit right. The underarm area is not what I am looking at to be sexy on my wife. It is a cut that is almost never noticed in that area. This loosens up the fit of the shirt and cuts out the underarm pressure. It also lets me have a way to slide my hands around her through that cut from the front and feel her smooth back, or, from the back, to feel her breasts – a nice bonus for making that cut.

Most of what I cut with the scissors shows that it has been cut up rather than made and professionally finished to look the way it does – so who cares about one or two more cuts to make it more comfortable? The end result is the great fun sex we have. The whole idea behind modifying items to look sexier is to create an illusion or fantasy or mental image that is not necessarily real or perfect. The image in the mind of the beholder is what is important. The modified items are only helpful to create that image. To reach the goal of great sex, the mind can ignore minor things that are not important and fill in minor details that reality leaves out. Maybe a perfectionist would not enjoy some of my imperfectly modified outfits, but a perfectionist will spend much more time than I do to have the same effective sexy looks, and I don't think that they could have any more sexual fun than we do. I know that the hot sex we end up with is very, very real! It is very, very good!

For hot sex, the only mandatory requirement for the modifications is strictly the functionality for sex. For example, one tip for proper function is the basic crotch-cut. On soft sweat pants or a homemade cut in cotton panties where you added this feature, it probably won't matter if the guy's cock touches the fabric as long as the hole provides access. With something like denim, it is another matter. Tough fabrics need the hole to be large enough and in the right position so that it does not rub on the guy at all. It takes the proper position and width to work right. Don't be afraid to do it and try it. You may have to change it, but you can always enlarge a hole fairly easy. It just may need to be enlarged at a very inopportune time, if you don't check it ahead of time. Also note that, on some items, like jeans, what may be right when the wife lies down flat on her back and spreads her legs may still be a little off if she is bent over at the waist in a different position. It doesn't bother me to have to redo something. I think it is fun to try, then modify, and try again. Think: "Try, try, try, and try again!"

However, if you are trying to get the look of her pussy popping out of very tight jeans, like I talked about discovering in chapter 3, then start with a very small cut and have her try the item on. Decide exactly where the vagina will be in the position that you want to have sex in. This is usually doggie style, to bend her over and enjoy the view of that nice ass in the stretched tight jeans as you screw her, just like you like to look at that nice piece of ass so often when she is wearing tight jeans. Have her bend over to check the position of the hole, and then enlarge the cut just enough to let the pussy pop out – allow several fittings to enlarge it in stages if needed. If she pops out just right, the denim will be on the outside of her outer pussy lips, and the man's cock will not touch the denim. The denim will just be pressing the outer pussy lips together and cushioning the cock from the denim. If the wife is trying this on her own, she may need to get her husband to help check this as she checks the cut hole.

Different items have different requirements that you will learn from experience. For example, a pullover knit top can look good even stretched a lot to reach her bust size – but if it is an item with front buttons, it usually must fit with no major stretching, or else the button area will look very poor when stretched. One exception is a vest or cardigan-style item that you would only button below the bust and where you would want to have that busting-out look that emphasizes her cleavage. A straining button can have a nice look in that way – it might even make a guy hope the button pops open to let the "girls" out – if the button won't pop open, then when he wants more, he can unbutton it himself to let the girls out.

There are several modifications that I have used often when an item would seem a little too tight a stretch for her waist or hips. I have made an outfit out of an item with just about a 16-inch original waist (8 inches laid flat). It was a cute pair of little toddlers' jean shorts. I just cut the entire side seams out and ran a belt through the belt loops, and she wore it like denim panties around her hips with nothing but the belt for most of the way around on both sides. I took out most of the crotch seam, and they became cute, denim, crotchless panties about 8 inches wide front and back with just the belt on the sides. With some matching denim pasties for a top, using rubber cement (with little, half-inch nipple holes in them), it was a cute tiny outfit that was just for decoration on her body. It contrasted the bits of tough denim with all her soft smooth bare skin, and yet she was totally available for my pleasure – and hers.

Use a belt to hold just about anything around the waist. I have used almost everything to turn it into a costume using this system. Any string or belt can be used to hold it in place just like a string bikini bottom. If there are no belt loops on the item, a few small vertical slits will make slots to feed a narrow belt through to hold the item on. A string or strap of any kind can also be tied or sewn to the top corners to use to tie it on like a string bikini bottom.

Use the hem of an outfit to add a drawstring if you need it. Sometimes I use this on the bottom edge of a short top. Many girls' size tops are very short, and I often look for these sizes that have a very loose or stretchy material. I use my tape measure and check if it easily stretches wide enough for my wife's bust size. If it is OK width-wise, then I check the height from the top of the shoulder to bottom hem. This has to be enough to come down and cover her breast – or almost that far. If it is stretchy material, it should also stretch enough to be pulled down over her breast. To keep it down to cover her bust and yet expose the maximum-midriff look that I want, I use the drawstring in the hem, and this makes the top more like a bra, and with the drawstring tied snugly, it lifts her breasts and fits smugly underneath her bust.

A small girls' tee shirt can have the underarm seams cut out totally to the bottom, and it becomes nothing but a flat piece of material with a head hole in the middle. Put her head through the hole, and use a drawstring through the hem to tie it down and under her bust line and around the back. Sometimes even the head hole has to be enlarged a little too; I use a notch in the front of the neck hole. If the tee shirt has some cute picture or saying that you want, it makes the small project worth it. I like something like, "Daddy's Girl" or "Heart Breaker," which you can find on children's tops. Almost any toddlers' shirt is about 14–15 inches from the neck to hem and can be used this way with a drawstring to tie it under the bust.

If you like a very bare-back look, cut the entire back off behind the neck hole, and it turns the top into a tiny halter with just a string tie across the bare back. I had one girls' tee shirt that said, "Cheer, Cheer," across the front. I cut the shirt up into almost a bikini top. From behind the neck hole on the sides, I cut down each side to just outside the wording. I then cut out the front right up between the words and removed the front of the neck. Each side under "Cheer" had a little hem left, and I just used a white shoelace to go through these hems and tie it in the back. It was just a strip up each side to cover her breast with the word "Cheer" above the nipple area, and the strip just went around behind her neck – most of it was just the shoelace around her chest. With a cheerleader-type skirt cut indecently short, I thought she looked very vulnerable and very desirable. It was not meant to be clothing anymore. It was just meant to be raunchy, indecent decoration that would not get in the way for what it encouraged me to do with her.

Shoelaces also are very useful to use as various ties. Some tops are so short that they will not stay down over the bust naturally. This is often because I am using a children's size short top. If there is a hemmed bottom edge, I run a shoelace through it and make a tie to pull it in and hold it up under the bust for the most exposed midriff possible.

I use two versions of shoelace ties. I can cut a small slit in the hem in the front center, run the shoelace all the way around, and tie it in a bow in the center front. The alternative is to cut a small slit under each arm in the center of the sides. Then I run a shorter shoelace around the front from one side to the other and a second shoelace around the back the same way, and then I have a bow tie under each arm at the sides. To run the shoelaces, I have made a tool out of an old wire coat hanger, as I previously described in chapter 9.

This same technique is good for making items like a bra to match a denim miniskirt or short shorts. The cuff end hem of a pants leg will make a good triangular mini bra if the cuff is not too worn. Use the bottom of the cuff hem as the bottom of the bra and the remains of the vertical leg side or center section as the middle of the bra, and then cut the triangles up from the cuff. If the leg is long enough you end the top of the triangle about ¾ inches wide at the top and then cut up parallel to the fabric weave as long as possible to form a strap at the top of the triangle. The twin triangles for the bra and the straps on top will form ties to fasten behind the neck. Use the wire coat hanger to feed a shoelace through the cuff hem to make a string tie to fasten around the chest for the bra bottom strap. As an alternative to the normal shoelace, use a leather rawhide shoelace, or if you can cut one or two long strips of denim fabric out of a matching material, you can put this through with the coat hanger to make matching denim strap. If you have to use two straps, tie them together and bury the knot in the center of the cuff or between the triangles. You can cut the two triangles from the material with one of the existing leg seams in the center and leave them attached so that the seam joins the two triangles, or you can also make two separate triangles from the pants cuff if you don't want them fastened together at the center. This may be needed if parts of the cuff are badly worn in the pants – use only the front, undamaged area from each pants leg to make one triangle from each leg. If you can't make a top neck tie strap as one piece from the triangles, you'll have to sew on a shoelace, rawhide lace, or denim straps to the top of the triangles to make the neck ties.

If you want to have a more fitted bra cup rather than just a flat triangle bra piece, cut small triangular pieces out of the bottom seam about one to two inches wide at the bottom and up to a point where you want the nipple to be. Take a minute on a sewing machine or a couple of minutes with a needle and thread, and sew together the sides of that triangular piece you removed, or maybe just glue the edges together with a slight overlap. This will form a shaped cup to fit better. One more idea to try to use on either a flat or a shaped cup is to leave a little 3/8-inch hole for the nipple to poke out. For a flat bra cup, try the top on, and mark the right spot to put the hole. For a fitted cup, the top end of the piece cut out of the bottom should be where the nipple pokes out.

By combining several of these ideas, an old pair of jeans can be cut into a matching set of indecently short shorts with peek-a-boo holes, a crotch-cut, and a matching bra from the same denim. Use a pair of jeans with a larger waist that fits down on your wife's hips. The jeans can even be cut into a micro miniskirt extending just barely below the bottom of the pant's zipper; it will flare out and won't hide any of her charms. The leftover parts can be made into the bra top, wrist and ankle cuffs, and a choker that all match.

One nice pair of old hip-hugger bell-bottom jeans I found I cut into the usual very short shorts and just removed the thigh area. I used rubber bands to put the lower leg pieces back on her from just above the knee. I used the thigh area material to make into a bra, a choker, and wrist cuff pieces that came all the way up to her elbows and matched the legs. I loved the look of those beautiful, completely bare thighs and her cute bare feet peeking out from the bottom of those bell-bottom leggings and her matching bare upper arms. It really emphasized the bare thighs, bare feet, and bare arms, and her nipple tips were just peeking out of the holes in the little bra triangles. Maybe we have been making love for many decades, but that kind of look makes me want to jump her, feeling like some horny teenager who just had a magic genie grant his wish for a Playboy centerfold of his very own.

Often I have used the bottom-edge hem of an item to put in a drawstring and use it as a waistband – I hang the item upside down from the hem to use it as a skirt. A sweatshirt or tee shirt makes a nice drawstring skirt, for example. Some sweatshirts and tee shirts have vertical seams under the arms; some are seamless and have no vertical seams. With the seam, the item looks better with the seam at the side, and if this is a fairly short seam, it means a high-cut side on the skirt automatically. You can usually cut much longer up into the chest and back area of the original sweatshirt or tee shirt to make the new skirt longer in the front and rear. If the underarm vertical seam is long on a large, tall-size shirt, you can make it an even-length skirt all the way around. This lets you create soft micro miniskirts in colors as variable as any tee shirt or sweatshirt available. I find the cheaper kids' sizes are best because they are just slightly smaller than my wife's hips, and a skirt made from these easily stretches just a little to fit nice and snug. An adult size shirt would be very loose on her hips. At most places, the kids' sizes are also cheaper, and they are usually used very little because the kids outgrew them rather than wore them out. If you have to stretch the item out to fit the hips, I often do not even bother with any drawstring or belt – I just let the stretch hold it in place for me to look at. Once we are into the having-sex stage, who cares where the skirt ends up?

Sometimes I want to use an item that has something printed on the front of the tee shirt or sweatshirt that I don't want to keep on the skirt I plan to make. I have used a ragged-edge cut to cut up and down diagonally in a random pattern to cut around the printing I want to cut out and leave one area a lot longer to make an uneven skirt length. This can cover one leg almost to the knee (the original back of the shirt) and leave the other bare to the hip (the original front of the shirt with the printing cut out).

On a long tee shirt, I have made a matching top and bottom outfit. I cut the top into a short crop top, and the bottom is long enough to make into a skirt hung upside down from the hem with a drawstring or just stretched to fit her hips. If the shirt is a larger size, there is one trick to make it a snug fit. Cut up along both sides of a seam or up any point in a seamless item. This turns it into a big flat panel. Use this with a long string in the hem as a wrap skirt. The string belt must be long enough to go around the waist twice and tie. If you want, you can figure out how to put an extra slit in the drawstring hem and re-thread the drawstring through parts of the hem a second time to be sure the waist is even all around and hide the second pass of the drawstring.

Even one more way to make an upside-down skirt from the bottom of a sweatshirt or tee shirt is to just cut two 8- to 15-inch-wide pieces out of it. The pieces can be square cut at the bottom or rounded or even cut into a random-length ragged edge. Then hang the two pieces on a belt or drawstring through the hem, and it will hang like a loincloth front and back. This leaves totally bare sides with just a belt or string across her sides – it has a nice long-legged look.

If I have used a sweatshirt-type item for this, I still like to use other parts of the sweatshirt too. I am a leg man – I like women's legs. Thighs in particular look attractive to me if they are nicely shaped. I love the very short skirts or shorts that bare the entire leg. Tall boots are a turn-on, and it moves the legs' attraction to just the thighs. I also like a nice barefoot look too. This means that a particularly nice combination is a jungle girl or warrior queen style outfit. Some shirts can be cut to form a sheer, skimpy bra, to look like shoulder armor, or to become a very short skirt to just cover the hips, with calf-to-ankle wraps or armor and wrist-to-elbow cuffs. This leaves bare feet, bare thighs, a bare middle, and bare upper arms. This is a frequently used Amazon woman movie costume and a common look for comic female warriors or jungle girl types.

This means using the leftover material from something like a sweatshirt miniskirt to make a lower leg wrap, a forearm wraps, a choker, and maybe a bra or brief top, making a coordinated outfit from one original garment.

For a jungle girl look, remember that real animal skins would have different colors and patterns. It is easy to mix different garment materials and still have a coordinated outfit. Real animal skins would also have uneven, natural sizes and edges. For one outfit, I started with a leopard-print velour blouse. I cut off every finished edge and made a natural-looking and revealing item. I gave it a short, ragged-edge sleeve on one side, a bare shoulder on the other side, and a shortened bottom hemline that revealed a lot of midriff. I paired it with another velour skirt with a slightly different pattern and print color, and I just shortened it up to a barely covering length front and back and even shorter on the sides. I had enough parts left to make leggings for the leg calves and wrists. I added a brown, suede belt with string ties instead of a buckle, which covered the original skirt waistband. I hung some leather scraps made into a knife holder on the belt. She looked like she was ready to film a jungle movie. Best of all, I wrote the movie script. I played Tarzan, and I got the jungle girl in the love scene. She put on a performance worthy of an Oscar (but it would have been an Oscar for the "Porn Academy Awards" if it had been filmed).

Another costume I made years ago was made from some chamois I got at an auto parts place. (Car wash chamois are nice and soft when new, but NEVER wash them or they get stiff and hard. More expensive chamois from a craft store are not treated the same and can be washed, if needed.) This is a little more expensive than most of what I recommend now, but it is a great look and much cheaper than any similar-looking readymade items. I copied an Indian girl look I saw in a Playboy photo shoot – a loincloth look front and back hung on a rawhide lace, a string-tied halter, and pieces on the legs. I found some $1 elastic Indian-design, beaded headbands and used them for bracelets, upper armbands, and a choker. My wife braided her hair in twin pigtails and looked like Pocahontas to me. I prefer a nice blue-eyed, blonde Indian maiden who loves to let me screw her, rather than just mind groping the girl in the Playboy photos.

A tip to use in putting on wrist and leg wraps made out of just flat scrap material of any sort without any sewing or elastic is to buy a bag of #64 rubber bands (3½ x ¼ inch) at any office supply store. This is also the size that the US Postal Service usually uses to bundle small packets of mail for delivery. I find they are good for everything around the house, and they are the right size to fit a wrist, or just above or below the elbows or knees to hold things in place. In chapter 9 I described how to use these and have the illustrations of how to use them.

Another little tip – use an iron or stiffener on the back or inside to keep the fabric flat and stop the rolling up of things like the points of a star cutout made in the middle of a piece of material. For example, the heart on the back of the vest on the cover illustration may need an iron-on stiffener to make the center of the point in the top of the heart stay down. Without the stiffener, the center point could roll up in a curl that would distort the heart shape. I have had to make a circular, O-ring stiffener to iron on the back of some star-shaped breast pasties that I made so that the star points would stay flat on the breast. I left the center area with just the fabric so that the little nipple holes would not be thicker from the stiffener.

To work with soft, thin leather, you need to use rubber cement to fasten things together. This works well on leather anywhere there is not going to be any strain on that point – good for things like hems or to make finished edges. Figure out exactly what you want, and then carefully apply glue to both surfaces and rub it in (most small containers have a brush applicator). Join the surfaces, and then apply pressure for a while. I use various binder clips for small areas, and for a larger area, I lay the glued item on a table and pile some books on it. In areas where there will be stress, particularly on a small area, I use a needle and thread to reinforce the joint just at the area where there will be stress.

In making items like a leather string bikini or anything where you want a cord in a leather item, put the cord in place first, and then fold over the edge to make a hem right over the cord using the rubber cement. At the ends where the cord comes out of the leather, use a few hand stitches through the cord and all leather layers to attach that spot more securely. You can buy leather laces and cord in various colors in many craft stores to use for this. Sometimes you can cut long narrow strips from your leather material and use this for a perfect match.

Anyone can learn to do minor hand sewing with a little practice – even you guys trying to put something sexy together. Many years ago, my brother got a job selling Singer sewing machines – within days, he was doing demos in the store as he made dresses for his wife. I mainly do handwork with needle, thread, and thimble – it works for small jobs (you need that thimble to push a needle through tougher leather or a denim seam). A real man learns to do what it takes – go for it guys. I don't mind doing these things at all – I like the look and what I get as the end result (I always get to put my end into her end as the end result).

To make a triangular, string bra, here are a few tips. I like to use a pre-made hem for the underneath edge or an original garment if possible. Just feed the string or cord through the hem. Once I just made the triangles into a diamond-shaped, almost-square piece twice the size I wanted. I just folded the pieces in half to form a double-thick triangle. Then I hand sewed the top straps in to both layers. For the bottom, I just laid the string in place in the fold, and as it was, tightened under the bust, it just stayed at the bottom of the cup.

The other ways are: Hand sew a hem for the string in the bottom of the cup triangle; attach the straps to the bottom edges of the triangles by sewing; poke or cut a series of holes along the bottom edge; then thread the string tie through the holes. Or cut the triangle from a big enough piece so that you can somehow cut straps at the ends of the triangles and keep it all one piece.

For the top straps, the best way is to attach the straps to the top of the triangle with sewing or to cut the top of the triangle to end in a long strap out of the same fabric that is attached. One alternative is to use a Y-shaped string as the strap – install it upside down with the twin ends tied to the bottom strap at each side of the triangle. You can poke or cut a little hole in the top of the triangle, run the twin Y ends up inside the triangle, and put the single end base of the Y through the hole at the top of the triangle, and it becomes the strap to tie behind the neck. Make the Y by using a short string tied to a longer string at the proper spot.

Some more ways to put on neck straps are to poke two holes (one will work, but two are stronger) in the top of the triangles and use a longer neck strap tie and double it up. Run one end through the holes in the top on each side. Then both the string in between the triangles and the ends go behind the neck, and the two ends get tied – you have a double strap. A way to do it with one single neck string on each side is to poke one hole in the top of the triangle and put the end of a string through the hole and then through a strong reinforcing backer – even a small-holed #6 stainless steel washer will do (a guy's solution for sure). Tie a knot in the end of the string that is too big to pull through the hole in the washer or reinforcer, and the neck strap is attached. Still another is to tie a tiny loop in the end of the neck string and then make a decorative knot out of the fabric at the top of the triangle to tie it to the loop in the string end.

If what you want in a bra cup is more than a flat triangle, then you have to shape the cup – this may be needed with thicker fabric like leather or heavy denim. I mentioned one way, but there is another way: You start with cutting the cup from one to two inches wider at the bottom than for a flat triangle – depending on the cup size you want. You mark a tall, narrow, inverted V from the bottom to the center, nipple area of the triangle, and then you fold the two sides of the V together and fasten temporarily. You can try rubber cement, straight pins, or anything. This should form the triangle into a cup. If the cup size is right, then you need to sew the seam along the two edges of the V – by hand or machine. After it is sewed, you can use scissors to cut the flap left inside the cup. Then the shaped cup can be made into a bra just like any flat triangle.

One fully exposed outfit, just as feminine decoration, is to make a triangular, string bikini in just the outline-only look. I made this out of scrap material from one pair of jeans. This is the "pocket cutout" version of a bikini – only leave the outline of the bikini around bare skin. This means make a triangle top with the drawstring through a hem as the bottom, but only the hem and nothing above it except the sides of the triangle. The triangle sides go up to a top neck strap, but no more than ¾-inch wide on each side of the triangle area – the entire center cup area should be removed. You have just the outline of the edges of a bra but nothing at all covering the breast.

The bottom of the outline-only outfit can be cut from matching denim jeans or shorts. Leave just the waistband across the front and back – cut away the entire fly, front pockets, and butt areas. On the sides, mark off a ¾-inch line from the waistband to the crotch on each side, front and back, and cut away everything else. This leaves just the outline of a bottom. Everything important is left exposed but decorated in a make-believe bikini outline. Maybe just take any bikini outfit – a factory-made one or one you already made and used – and cut away everything but the outline. You can make a role-playing version of having her wearing invisible clothes like the old fairy tale about the "Emperors' New Clothes."

Frederick's of Hollywood and other lingerie makers sell similar outline-only sets made out of lace and ruffled ribbons for prices around $25 for a few ounces of material. A denim one like I just mentioned is free if you have some material left over, or there is just the cost of the shorts or jeans. You also can go to any craft or sewing store and just buy a few yards of ribbon and make your own lace or ruffled ribbon set for a couple of dollars – just tie or sew the ends of the various pieces together.

One real funky modification I tried once is to modify a set of overalls – the real bib front and back type of overalls with the shoulder straps. My wife had a real farm-girl look dressed up in these, barefoot and in pigtails. A little tee shirt, cut to give it a scoop neck and cropped short right under the bust, left a little bare skin peeking through on the open sides of the overalls to complete the innocent little farm-girl look. She was sexy enough to seriously tempt any farm boy or traveling salesman going by, but I got her first.

The modification to make the overalls easy to screw in was simple. These overalls all seem to have three buttons on each side of the hips to close them up at the waist. I cut the back entirely straight across so that one original side button was on the top to hold the top in place, and the other two buttons were on the bottom to hold it up and fastened closed to the front at the waist. The back was separated into two pieces. This cut caused the center back to sag open, so I sewed one large button on in the center of the top section of the back and made a matching simple buttonhole slit to match it on the center of the bottom. This took the sag out of the back, and the overalls looked almost normal. On each side, I cut down several inches along the side seam at the bottom of the original, side, V slit below the original buttons. This change in the side was barely noticeable because the baggy overalls still hung the same loose way, and there was no pull to open up the slit area. (Some Velcro strips could be used for both the back and side cuts to make the changes almost totally unnoticeable if you wanted to make the overalls fit to still wear out in public.) My wife played the young, innocent, coy, seductive farm girl in the overalls.

However, when I undid the new center button in the back and the two bottom side buttons on each side, the entire front and the top of the back stayed in place, but the whole back seat of the pants fell down below her bare butt in the back. She looked normal from the front, but the true nature of the brazen little farm-girl trollop was exposed from the rear – she was totally bare ass from the backside. She was playing the innocent but brazen little farm-girl tramp, and she got everything that she was looking for – I bent her over forward and gave her fully exposed rear end exactly what she wanted right in the modified overalls. All we needed was a bale of hay to bend her over to complete the real farm-girl seduction setting – we were at home, so I used a table.

As I remember the farm-girl overalls and think about what a ball we had as I write about the outfit, I am making a note to add to my to-do wish list – it will be great fun trying the farm-girl overalls again with HAY and in a real BARN somewhere, someday. We frequently travel around the whole USA – can any readers tell me where to rent a barn by the hour or by the day? I will give a nice gift to anyone who gives me a suggestion I actually get to use. The subject on every item on my to-do wish list is always the same – "To DO my wonderful wife again and again" – it is just the setting and outfits that vary on the wish list. It seems strange, but the more I DO the things on my to-do wish list, the longer the wish list grows. If I live to be a hundred, I'll still never live long enough to finish the wish list I already have.

While I am asking for information from my readers, I want some more information many of you may know about to help me build my wish list. There are many hotels and motels that have fantasy rooms or suites, but these are just some mirrors around the bed and a Jacuzzi. I mean that I want something more than just hot tubs and mirrors. I am interested in theme rooms or especially good resorts for couples. I am familiar with some East Coast spots. In King of Prussia, PA, the old Sheraton hotel and conference center, now I think it is the Radisson Hotel Valley Forge, had dozens of great fantasy-themed rooms. We have enjoyed several of these. The Pocono Mountain area in PA has been a honeymoon destination for decades, where the heart-shaped tubs originated, and they now have champagne glass whirlpools and stuff. I think we have hit every one of these – the heart-shaped bathtubs and the small, private, in-room swimming pools, etc. We have enjoyed these spots. However, there have been some bad spots where we have found the theme rooms are a rip-off. Some are cheap, dirty, hot-sheet type places that should rent by the hour. I have read about the great love hotels in Japan, and from the Internet, I have also noticed some spots like Fanta Suite Hotels (FantaSuite.com) in WI and MN and Fantasy Inn (Fantasy-Inn.com), South Lake Tahoe, CA. I don't know these spots personally. I have a spot on my web page, DressForSEXcess.com, for anyone to enter locations for other fantasy-themed rooms anywhere in the world and to enter reviews or comments about these spots. Any good hotel or motel that is set up as a great romance resort worldwide is of interest. Include whether the rooms are really themed –like some that are built to be like a cave or have great accessories and furnishings, or are they just regular rectangular rooms that are painted up with murals on the walls and ceiling and maybe a special bed and called a theme room. I am interested both for personal use and to help advise readers. For everyone who enters a new spot or review in the USA and gives me a US address, I will try to send out a free gift of some sort, unless I get overwhelmed by info. I hope to build a good database of such places that is good and helps people avoid cheesy spots.

CHAPTER 16
Many Wives Want More Lust

ONE DIFFERENCE BETWEEN OUR LOVE LIFE and the love life of most long-term married couples is probably the level of lust in our physical relationship. I have already mentioned Rabbi Boteach's book *Kosher Lust: Love Is Not the Answer*. He feels that gentle, easygoing sex is the reason as many as a third of long-term marriages end up as sexless relationships, and most of the other two thirds end up with very little sex. He believes that real love needs real passion – lustful active passion. He calls lust the glue that holds a relationship together and that keeps the fire in it burning brightly. This is the role lust plays in our wonderful marriage.

If you read our love story in chapter 1 and the example of my feelings when we rode my tandem bike together as teenagers in chapter 2, you will understand that these years of falling deeply and passionately in love over an almost 5-year period built up a tremendous amount of lust in both of our minds. We never had any form of sexual contact in those years of dating, but there was nothing platonic about our relationship. All of my three and a half years in college were a long-distance relationship, but we were together for usually about two weekends a month for most of those last two years. Those weekends always involved hours of making out. There was a lot of passion, even if there was no sex.

I want to point out one very important benefit from a relationship in which the only passion is kissing and making out for hours at a time, and that doesn't include any other sex. We got very good at kissing. You may not think that there is any great value to just making out this way, but then most people have never done it so much and for so long as the most passionate expression of their love. I think that most long-term courtships either are less passionate and do not include such long make-out sessions or else they move on to having sex. There was also something else that developed with the kissing and making out – sweet love talking. Learning to use sweet words of love along with kissing is a valuable long-term skill.

Don't you readers remember how you felt at ages 19 to 20 when your youthful hormones were raging in your bodies? All the surveys today show that most young people at that those ages have already been having sex to satisfy their sexual urges. We were sharing many hours of hugging and kissing, but that only seemed to increase our sexual desires. It did not satisfy those urges the way we have since found that sex does. I doubt that many young couples have ever built up a more lustful relationship than we did. On our honeymoon, we both expressed our mutual lust – there was no holding back in our lovemaking as we both discovered sex together. We both went at the sex that we were now allowed to share with as much vigor as any young couple could ever share. It was a wonderful time to share our love, and I really appreciated the way my new wife liked what we were doing just as much as I did. All those years of making out had primed her for completely enjoying real sex.

I think that I acted in aggressive, adventurous ways to encourage that bad-boy image that attracts girls. On the third night of our honeymoon, I led my very shy bride out onto a beautiful deserted beach on a hot night. We had another lust-filled lovemaking session out in the dunes on a beach towel. This was not what she had been expecting as a new bride. It stretched her expectations of what our married love would be like.

I remember how she was terrified as I led her out through the deep, black woods that night to reach the beach that she had never been to before. But she was willing to accept what frightened her because of her trust in me. I think this experience set the role of my being the alpha male in our married life. It definitely showed me how much she trusted me, even when she was very afraid – this was reinforcing the

Biblical instruction about how a wife should respect her husband. Trust and respect are closely related. The result of that wonderful night on the beach definitely reinforced her feelings that I truly loved her; planting the same Bible-based positive feeling in her mind. She could see that our love life together was going to be more adventurous than most wives imagine. It was starting off like the storyline in a romance novel.

It was obvious that she appreciated my adventurous streak. She looked forward to it a few days later when I suggested another lovemaking session out on a different beach, where we spent the whole night. We made love in the dark and again in the early dawn light.

I don't think that most guys or gals ever start off their sex lives this way. All too often, a girl's first sex experience is just finally giving in to her current boyfriend's sexual advances in the back seat of his car because she is afraid of losing him if she keeps turning him down. Or perhaps her first time was just because she got so drunk at the party after their prom. Maybe she just gave in to her hormones with a guy she really didn't even love because she felt that having sex would make her feel like she was finally a real woman because she was having real sex.

I could give another hundred such examples for how girls first had sex, and I could give the same for how guys had their first sexual experience. They would all show that it was not an overpowering lust – it was just an event that happened. It was often unplanned and lacked the buildup of long-term anticipation. According to surveys, most people who start their sex lives that way will later think that things would have been better if they had waited. I don't think that any man or woman ever later thinks that having their first sexual act on their wedding night, after a long courtship, was too soon for having sex. When this wedding night is the first sex for both of them, it puts sex into its proper place – the wonderful culmination of their years of falling in love. The specialness of the celebrations on their wedding day – making their lifetime commitment to each other in front of God, their family, and their friends and ending in the long-desired, first complete physical union as husband and wife – is as wonderful as a first sex act can be.

Most people do not start off their love at the high level of mutual lust that we did. They are more afraid of how the other person will react and think about them as a lover the first time that they make love. Most people who have had other sexual partners are hesitant about how they will compare to their new partner's previous partners. They are not as free to acknowledge that maybe they will be clumsy and do the wrong things or act stupid. They are too concerned about being smooth lovers and thinking about how their partner will think about them. In our case, we both knew that it was the first time for both of us; neither of us had any expectations about being a polished, experienced lover. We set out knowing that we just wanted each other so much and that we had a lifetime to explore and work things out. We were free to go at our sex life with gusto, and we expressed a lot of the built up mutual lust.

Most unmarried young people realize that when they are having sex, there is no real commitment involved yet. Maybe they think it will lead to marriage – at least many of the girls do it hoping that it will lead to marriage. But there is nothing guaranteed to be permanent in a premarital situation. Certainly, recreational sex and casual hooking up imply no long-term ties. These situations do not create a lot of built-up lust either. Maybe the first few sex acts in these premarital situations are based on lust, but they soon just turn into a way to regularly satisfy their sexual urges.

This is so different from what my wife and I shared. We made the "until death do us part" pledges to each other before we had any sex. We believed that what we were doing was going to be permanent. We had built up a huge lust for each other, and it was expressed in our lovemaking.

We never had a tentative, unsure attitude toward sex. Sometimes it was slow and gentle, but most of the time it has always been fully expressed lust. My wife has always seemed to enjoy it when I tell her that, "*I want to fuck the hell out of you!*" I like to tell her that she is my angel, and that I want to keep her that way – that is why I have to keep fucking the "hell" out of her. I try my best to do just that, and she always likes it, just like an angel would. As another marriage tip that many books say is part of a great relationship, intimately talking dirty is very appropriate to your lover, even if you never use that sort of language in any other situation.

One time I hesitated stroking inside her, and she just smiled and said, "*More!*" I paused even longer and asked her if she was sure that was what she wanted, and she said, "*Yes, more!*" This has become a favorite joke we laugh at during sex. I ask her what her favorite word is. Her answer is, "*More!*" And that is what I try to give her. We have laughed about it often since then. She often says "*More!*" now, and she still means it. This is just one little example of how I am positive of how much she likes our lovemaking. This knowledge makes me always feel so macho by being able to always please and satisfy my wife. With this sort of lust going on between us, there is nothing mild about our usual lovemaking.

I think that this attitude is a main reason that we have such a great marriage and such an active, fun-filled sex life, even after over 50 years. We started off in the right way, in a way that most couples never experience. Our marriage has been over 50 years of mutual lust. The way so many people treat sex so casually – with recreational sex, frequent hook-ups, both having sex and living together before marriage, and lots of sexual partners – all prevent them from starting off the way that we did. They will rarely have a fairy-tale ending of living happily ever after if they don't follow the fairy-tale storyline the way that we did.

I believe that many wives are not fully satisfied with their sex life because they do not share the lust that still drives our love life. This may be why so many marriages deteriorate into a loveless state or divorce; it may be the cause of most affairs. I see this in the marriage statistics and in the many relationship books that I have read. There are two of these books I recommend that target this idea that most wives want a more manly man.

I recommend *The Married Man Sex Life Primer 2011* by Athol Kay, which strongly supports the idea that most women want a more manly man attitude in their husband. The best comment that I have seen to show how this book reinforces the points that I make is some parts of a long book review that I read on Amazon.com about the book. The review says:

> "Wives – You want that giddy feeling you used to have for your hubby? Buy this book for your husbands!
>
> "Coming from a woman's perspective, this book hit RIGHT ON with the problems I was having being attracted to my husband. It actually tells men how to make their wives want them. It's written by a man, for men, and I appreciated that because the author gave examples with his own relationship with his wife on his daily interactions that work to help her **lust** after him. ...."

[Capitalizing emphasis in original, Bold emphasis added by me.]

Note that this review also supports how lust is a positive feeling in the sexual relations in a marriage. This agrees with what I recommended about *Kosher Lust* by Shmuley Boteach. The Amazon review of *Sex Life Primer* continues:

> "Not only does the book talk about why I was feeling less attracted to my very physically fit, tall, extremely athletic, highly intelligent, well-maintained, loving husband, but it gave specific steps for him to take in order to make me go crazy for him again. I had no idea it was as easy as him becoming more of an alpha-male at home with me. I knew I wanted him to be more assertive in the bedroom and generally in our married life together by making more or most of the decisions such as where we're going to eat or what we're going to do this weekend....

> "This book concentrates on telling you the truth and giving you common sense, logical solutions to the problems.... The author isn't condoning any kind of abuse or jerk mentality, he's just stating the facts – that most women want and need to be dominated in their sexual relationships in order to be truly content and turned on sexually."

Another popular book with the same viewpoint that says men should be more of the alpha male in their family is *Just F*ck Me! – What Women Want Men to Know About Taking Control in the Bedroom (A Guide for Couples)* by Eve Kingsley. The Amazon description points out the book's attitude tells men:

> "You're the Man... Act Like One!

> "Look, I know you're not a mind reader, so I'm going to be blunt...

> "The majority of women like to be fucked. And I mean really fucked.

> "Sure, there are some women who want to lie on their backs, look into your eyes, and gently rock back and forth, but most of us want you to channel the power of the Sun through your penis and give us a good, solid pounding. Act like you want it, for God's sake!

> "In this book, I'm going to lay out exactly what the majority of women want and show you exactly how to give it to them. I've got a section just for you and one for your female partner, so you can feel 100% comfortable letting loose on her vagina in the way she's secretly craving.

> "Some of the topics we'll cover...

> "The Alpha Male – It's more than just being an ex-fratboy douchebag, who thinks he's still on the high school football team. I'll clue you in.

"Dirty Talk – Trust me, she wants it. If she didn't, she'd fuck a mime. Speaking of, did you know Marcel Marceau was divorced three times? Enough said.

"The Art of Being Assertive – Sack up and take control! What to do... and what not to do."

I quote these various books both to show you how these other authors have many ideas that agree with exactly what I am writing and to give you sources of additional information on these matters. I do want to point out that I have all the other books I mention in this book posted in a list on my website, www.DressForSuccess.com, and I would like you to go through my website to get them if you are interested in buying any of them. I get a little credit if you go to Amazon from my link. They are the exact same price at Amazon whether you go there directly or go through my website. If you like this book, please support me by going through my website to buy my recommended books.

Anyone reading this before they make the mistakes that most people make, as I mentioned above, should learn from our story and try to avoid the common mistakes. They need to take sex a lot more seriously and realize how valuable their attitude toward sex should be. For the typical long-term married couple that I am targeting this book toward, it is too late to start over again, and I am not sure how to tell you how to reach the relationship we have achieved doing it our way. But knowing that a love like ours can exist even over 50 years into a marriage, and using some of the information in the books I have recommended, will hopefully show you the way to put some of the lust, some of the enthusiasm, into your marriage to spice it up. You should find lots of good ideas in the suggestions that I make in this book to increase the arousal factor in your relationship. This is a major goal of what I am trying to teach with my writing – increase desire, and increase the pure lust that will put more fire back into a stale relationship.

CHAPTER 17
Getting Ravished for Fun

MANY WIVES LIKE to get vigorously ravished every now and then. You guys just talk about her feelings before you try this, and be careful not to confuse "vigorously" with "violently" – one can just be exciting and very thrilling, but the other can be harmful. My goal is all sorts of fun. But remember, it is not fun unless it is fun for both the husband and wife. For variety, I think that we are both fairly typical in that I often like to act like I am overpowered with desire for her and I won't be denied as I pull off her clothes and mine and ravish her my way. She likes the feeling of being desired so much that I can't resist having her completely and immediately. Try it that way some time if you haven't done it, as long as you both agree to it ahead of time.

This chapter is about going farther than my last chapter about having more lust. If you consider the previous chapter as being *Vigorous*, then consider this one about being *More Vigorous*. With the popularity of the book and movie *Fifty Shades of Grey*, the subject of adding bondage, domination, and even sadomasochism to consenting adult relationships has received a lot of attention. I have only read a few random pages of the book, and it did not appeal to me. However, it seems to have appealed to the fantasies of many women. This is what this chapter adds to the previous chapter.

Many romance novels include exactly this sort of dramatic storyline but usually without the whipping that I think *Fifty Shades* goes into. The heroine gets taken sexually by the hero. She is a willing partner to having her stud make her inner wishes and forbidden desires come true at long last. Both of them get overpowered with wild passion. I am not in favor of any violent, unwilling rape fantasy, even if it may be a popular fantasy for many people. An important aspect of having sex to me is that my wife wants me to do it and that she enjoys my lovemaking; there is no benefit to either one of us of role-playing that she does not want sex or to forcing sex on her when she does not want it. But displays of overpowering passion can be a real turn-on for many people. It is a feeling that I often try to convey in lovemaking.

Probably one of the most famous movie examples of what I mean is in the classic *Gone With The Wind*. Rhett Butler sweeps Scarlett O'Hara off her feet and carries her up the grand staircase to their bedroom to show her what a woman needs. When the movie was made in 1939, bedroom scenes like Margret Mitchell portrayed in her book were not included in the movies. However, the following scene, set as the next morning, clearly shows a radiant and beaming Scarlett. She had obviously enjoyed the passionate lovemaking by a real manly man. I have noticed a very similar response in my wife whenever I play such a role with her for fun. I recommend every husband try this every once in a while. You can either keep her guessing and surprise her sometimes about what you are planning to do or set up the role-playing ahead of time.

As a tip to the wives, I have heard Dr. Laura point out how these few scenes from *Gone With The Wind* are prime lessons of how a woman can lose everything by trying to control her man. The next morning, after the night where she was swept off her feet and carried up stairs to be passionately ravished, she was obviously very satisfied and happy. But when she met Rhett Butler again later that morning, she played it like she had not liked it and felt like he had just used her. She was trying to control him and refused to let him think he had satisfied her. This is a perfect way to lose a husband. Rhett then walked out on her.

The whole story would have been different if she had let Rhett know how much he had satisfied her. Rhett would have felt like a real man and stayed to make her happy again and again. He would have felt very macho to know that he had finally pleased her in the most basic and important way that a man can please his woman. Rhett had done his best to follow the Biblical teaching of loving his woman, but Scarlett refused to follow the Biblical teaching of respecting her man. She wanted to both have his love and have control over him – maybe she just valued control more than getting great sex. Instead, she ended up with neither love nor control. This is a mistake that many wives have made – they try to keep control over their husband and find that this is only a way to lose their man. Accepting the love of a good man without trying to control him is a much better way to have a happy marriage.

If the wife tries to control her husband, the way many wives do, she is going against the Biblical instructions to respect her husband. If she does exercise control this way, she very likely will either lose her husband or end up in constant conflict with him in their marriage. The only other alternative result is that she will succeed in being the one in control; she will be the one wearing the pants in the family. This will mean that she will always find that she has a wimp for a husband. She will be unhappy because her husband will be afraid of ever standing up to be a man. She will complain to her family and friends about her husband because, *"He is not the man I married anymore."*

Instinctively, a wife will not be happy with a wimp for a husband, and she will never realize that it is her own fault because of how she controls him. Just imagine what Rhett Butler would have turned into if he had let Scarlett control him. She would have had him come crawling back to her and apologizing for how he had acted. Scarlett probably would have rationed out her sexual favors as a way to keep Rhett under her control She would have had the control, but she would not have again had the very satisfying sex that she had just gotten from him. She would have turned her strong husband into wimp. A real man just will not let a women emasculate him by controlling him the way Scarlett wanted to do to Rhett. A wife will be much happier in the end if she accepts her husband as a manly man and learns to love him for being that man. True marital happiness is increased when both the husband and wife play the natural role they were made for. I do not mean that a wife should be a doormat for a husband who is over-controlling, but she must not be the one always trying to control him.

There is a stage play I have seen *I Love You, You're Perfect, Now Change*. It was the all-too-true situation of a girl finding the perfect guy and getting married. Then after the wedding, she immediately started trying to change him. Great comedy is often just taking common, real-life situations and exaggerating them. There is an old proverb that when a couple marries, the woman hopes the man will change and the man hopes the woman will never change. All too often, the problem is that the husband usually does not change and the wife does change, and they both end up unhappy.

I am extremely lucky and I know it. I have a wife who only changed for the better after we got married and we were able to add sex to our wonderful relationship.

There are many ways that a guy can avoid that dull, everyday routine in his love life and add some of the bad-boy excitement and appeal. Some things can be planned, and some are just spontaneous things when a guy has the right attitude. The ripping off of clothes is a symbol of urgent passion. Starting with the right outfit and preparation can be helpful to making the sex session go the way you like it.

If you want to dress your wife up fancily in some elegant, old "bag sale" dress and then ravish her and rip her clothes off – it costs less for the costume at rummage sale prices than the price of a cup of coffee. Every rummage sale has plenty of dowdy old dresses for this idea. These were elegant clothes that are years out of date and that nobody really wants. They cost pennies and are disposable, one-time-use items just waiting for such a sexy role.

A hint to make it easier to rip her clothes off – do like the movies or theater would and start some cuts through the seams in a few key places. Well-made clothes don't rip very easily. The place to make the cuts is to snip the main seams anywhere that there are multiple layers of fabric sewn together. This way, when you pull vigorously, the stress is only on one layer of fabric with no reinforcement – it should rip more easily. Be sure you snip a small cut at each seam that you will need to rip, or you could start to rip off the dress and get stuck pulling on a seam that just won't tear. Not being able to rip off the dress could be a distraction from a vigorous macho image that you are trying to portray. Cutting most of a seam and leaving just a small part to rip to have the seam open up is another way to make the dress rip off easily.

One nice variation is to have a full-length, long-sleeved outfit that you rip down off her shoulders and breasts to just below her breasts – this will pin her arms to her sides at her elbows. Then rip off her lower skirt up over her legs and hips. If you do it right, she ends up bound with her arms at her sides and completely tied up by all of her clothes around her middle but not around her legs (you want her to be able to spread her legs). Old, worn-out bras are also very cheap, and this can be part of the outfit to be ripped off. An old pair of panties can also be part of the act. The bra and panties can be precut to rip off, or have a pair of scissors handy to snip them off. It is an extremely vulnerable position for her to be in, and it lets the guy have his way with her. The key thing to look for in the outfit is long sleeves that button at the cuff. This way, the sleeves won't pull off over her hands, and everything that pulls down off her shoulders ends up about at her wrists and waist – you may want to tighten and secure the cuffs with safety pins too.

The ripping-off routine can work both ways. Below you will read about how I ripped my own clothes off to strip down for some urgent sex.

My wife and I share hugs so often that they could become very routine – I think that they should be very frequent and very intimate in every good marriage, but I try to vary them in some way. When we are in private, a typical hug between us means I put my hands around her waist and slide them up under her blouse, even if it means I have to untuck it. I am addicted to the way she feels and how sexy it is to run my hands over her bare skin. I start with my hands at the sides of her waist and slide them around her waist on her skin until I wrap them around behind her. I love the feel of running my hands up and down her bare back. I usually then press my left hand right on her left-side lower back and hug her tightly – I learned that this is what she likes best. I love the way she feels – so soft, so smooth, so warm, and such a delightful, very feminine feel to the hourglass shape of her waist and the curves of her back. When I hug that lower back tightly, she usually reacts much like I feel when I realize that something is even better than I expected. She usually gasps and exclaims about how good it feels when I hold her that way. I can tell how much she honestly likes it. With such encouragement from her, added to how much I like to touch her, it should be no surprise to any reader about how much we hug. She often says something like, "*Thanks! I really needed that.*" I'll usually reply about how good she feels or that, "*Oh, I thought that this hug was for me. Did you need one too?*" She'll always answer, "*Yes!*" and I'll give her another squeeze and tell her that, "*This one is for you.*" Or I'll ask her, "*How many do you need?*" which always gets a reply of, "*A lot!*"

By now, I hope every reader has begun to realize how much holding and all physical contact are really an important part of our marriage – holding hands, hugs, etc. Holding should be a central part of any permanent relationship. Do more of it to strengthen any marriage. Holding more frequently, in any way, will probably increase the amount of sex a couple shares.

Often, around the house, she has no bra on to let me enjoy a quick feel and because I tell her how much I like the way she looks that way. I let her know how much I like the natural look – a little jiggle as she moves and the way I can see the outline of her nipples, as well as getting a chance for a few quick feels. (She plays a big part in encouraging our daily lovemaking.) In that case, for a hug, I usually pull up her top and hold her bare breasts against my chest before I wrap my arms around her to run my hands up and down her bare back or squeeze her some more. I have gotten very good at grabbing both her blouse and my tee shirt in one quick move to pull them up together. Then I'll hug her again and linger in a long embrace as we are pressed up against each other – we both enjoy the skin-to-skin feeling in a hug like this. This makes a real sensual hug! If she has a bra on, I'll sometimes fumble around and unhook it first and then lift up the front to get the same bare feeling because I also love the feel of running my hands up and down her bare back with no straps

I think this shows how mutual holding is the start of building real intimacy in our marriage. Holding seems to include heart, body, and soul when it is so complete. We share each other totally. We both give what the other wants, even if it is just an intimate hug at the moment.

I think the way I frequently take advantage of her like this has a tendency to create some of that bad-boy attitude because of the way I take charge and just do it. I just go ahead and do it so that I can feel her better, and she just lets me have my way with her, even if it is just for a long hug. It shows both that I am in control of what we do and that I really like enjoying her charms. Of course, she also likes it, and it tells her that I find her very desirable. Letting your wife know that you still think that she is HOT and very desirable is important to having a sexually happy marriage. When I take charge and do it – she acts the role of a very willing victim of my passes.

Ever since I first met her, she has always been the perfect image of being a good girl. However, her encouragement of my desires gives her a little wanton, bad-girl image to let me know that she wants sex too. Hugs are usually routine for us, but as an example of being spontaneous, something different happened a while ago during the writing of this book. I had been dressed for work in a button-down dress shirt and tie. It was an older shirt, and that morning, as I put it on, I realized it was getting too much of that old "ring around the collar" look that was not washing out. I had also caught it on something during the day and made a small tear in it. When I tore it, I realized that it didn't matter much. I had already decided to throw the old shirt out and not wear it again.

Right after I got home that evening, as we started a normal "welcome home" hug, I pulled up her blouse and held her against my shirt as I started to undo the bra hooks in the back. "*Let me free the girls,*" I told her, "*The girls want to be FREE!*" Then I pulled the loose bra up and held her against my shirt. "*Now the girls are happy. They're free again.*" Then I realized I needed to unbutton my dress shirt rather than just pull it up. I started struggling with getting my buttons undone. Up to this point, everything was perfectly normal for us. In a big hurry, I was fumbling, and as I got the first button open, I remembered that I was going to throw this shirt out anyway as soon as I got it off. Instantly, the thought hit me, and I just gripped the front of the shirt with both hands and yanked hard as I said, *"I want to feel the girls against me again, and I want them NOW! I can't wait!"*

Buttons went flying everywhere as I ripped the front of my shirt open and instantly hugged her against my bare chest. *"The girls are MINE!"* I exclaimed. My wife started laughing so hard that she couldn't stop for a minute or two. I played the event for all it was worth. I continued to hold her tight and even moved around to rub my chest against her bare breasts. I told her I just couldn't wait to hold her close against me, skin to skin. I wanted her so much. She just hugged me back, put her head on my shoulder, and kept laughing. When she stopped laughing long enough to express concern for my shirt, she hoped she could find all the buttons to sew them back on again – she is always that sort of a sweet helpmate. I finally explained that I had earlier decided to get rid of the old shirt. When we stopped hugging, I slipped out of the shirt and tossed it right into a nearby wastebasket. The spontaneous action turned a very nice sort of routine hug into a memorable fun event. It quickly led to some great sex.

Several times since then, when I had on a button-down dress shirt, I have started to do the same thing again, only to pause just as I have my hands gripping the front of my shirt. *"Oh! Wait! I have to keep this shirt. I don't want to make you have to sew the buttons back on,"* I'll say as I stop to unbutton it. *"The girls will have to wait just a second to feel my chest."* It tempers the bad-boy image of demanding her instantly with the concern for not making work for her, and yet it milks a little more excitement from the one-time, memorable event. However, I will find the right time to do a full repeat of ripping open my shirt someday. I am looking for some cheap, old dress shirt right now.

Sometimes now, if I still have on a dress shirt at the stage where I start to unhook her bra, she says *"Oh, good!"* and she'll start to quickly undo my shirt buttons while I work on the bra hooks. She has a very big smile on and acts real eager about it. This is how what we do seems to slowly change and grow from past experiences. It keeps getting better with time – it never gets dull. Ain't love grand!

She knows that I want her so much, and sometimes I act like I am going to have her – MY WAY, immediately. This is exactly how I feel, and she knows it. Sometimes that is exactly what happens – I have her my way. Maybe it is not as manly as Rhett Butler would act, but it is manly enough to keep winning my wife's heart. Most of the time when I share such an intimate hug or make some other pass at her, it is just foreplay for sex later. But occasionally, within a minute or two of my starting to make a pass at her, we are starting serious foreplay with an urgency to move on to intercourse. It creates a feeling of being slightly naughty, somewhat overpowered, and very lustful in my extreme desire for her. It also means that we always have a lot of intimate fun and often enjoy a lot of spontaneous sex.

For any married couples reading this, ask yourselves how long it has been since you suddenly jumped each other and enjoyed a spontaneous session of making passionate love? Can you even remember when the last time was? I challenge any married reader who is really in love to drop this book immediately, grab your spouse, tell them how much you love them, and jump their bones right now. If you are married, you have my approval to spend the next hour enjoying each other with sex and forget the rest of this book for a while.

_____ Go enjoy your break! _____

Back so soon?

When you guys look for cheap outfits, don't forget to get some men's items that you can rip off as a one-time-use prop to use as a surprise with your wife. Even something stained or the wrong size can work for this trick – you should be ripping it off before she notices the size or stain or before the pre-started cuts make it rip easily. Get a small, tight-fit shirt and try to do an Incredible Hulk act, but you don't need to include turning green.

There is another side point about belts that has nothing to do with clothing modifications but does have to do with sex fun on a low budget, and it can be helpful for bondage scenarios if you want this kind of ravishing sex. Most sex item catalogs and websites sell various "Beginner's Bondage Kit" items and other leather collars, wrist and ankle cuffs, and related items – this stuff is quite expensive for the material you get. Shop for various belts, and you have everything you need to make your own bondage gear. For example, a few shiny patent leather belts make a nice, shiny, decorative set of cuffs and a neck collar. All it takes is a few basic tools and craft items. I will go into this in detail in my second book, **MORE Dress for SEXcess**. Always remember that any bondage games are only to be played between willing partners who have full trust in each other and with some preset safely rules that you need to learn first. I assume that most long-term married couples that I am writing for probably fit this description and can follow these guidelines.

A way to make a beginner's kit with minimal material needed is to buy whatever woven leather belts you find until you have several. These are the ones with about 6 or 8 thin leather strips woven into a belt and they have no holes for the buckle pin – the pin on the buckle just goes through the weave straps anywhere, and they are infinitely adjustable. Just use these as wrist or ankle cuffs. Tighten the belt up to a comfortable fit on a wrist or ankle, and buckle it. This takes about 7 to 10 inches of the belt and leaves the rest of the long strap to tie off as a restraint. If a longer strap is needed, any belt of the same width can buckle onto the end and lengthen the strap by one more belt length. A thin piece of rope can be poked through the weave at the end to have something easier to tie it off with if needed. After a little time shopping in many places, I have a set of black belts for this and sets of both gold and white woven belts for color-coordinated sets. We do not do much with real bondage games, but I do like the look of bondage gear on my wife, which makes her sweet body look very vulnerable and keeps all of her charms fully accessible.

An option is to get wide belts with holes or cut patterns along the entire length of the belt. They can be tightened to a short wrist size, and the long end is easy to fasten with all the holes used to adjust to any length. Many dollar stores have cheap versions of these. I also have a set of denim belts with little grommet holes the length of the belts. A combination of short ball bungee cords and safety pins, if needed, help fasten the long belt ends to anything – bed posts, sheets, etc. These tie-off ends do not have to be strong to have the visual and psychological effect of bondage, unless you like to play at strongly fighting the bondage – the bound effect is usually just for looks.

Consensual play bondage like this creates a very macho feeling for most guys playing the in-charge role. The husband feels like he has been given total surrender and trust by his wife. Really, he has committed himself to be in total charge of pleasing his wife. It will only be mutually satisfying if he does a good job of pleasing her.

Any belt can be cut up into various lengths to make wrist cuffs, armbands, ankle cuffs, or neck collars. If you are using the buckle end, just use an awl or some sort of hole punch to make a new hole for the buckle pin to fasten at the desired spot. If you are using a central part of the belt, you just need to put one hole at each end and then fasten the two holes together when it is in position on the wrist, ankle, or neck. A cheap package of very short, small machine screws from Home Depot will do nicely, or a craft store will have rivet-like fasteners that screw together to fasten the two cut ends using just the punched holes.

A common accessory for sex and bondage play is a blindfold. Don't forget to experiment with sensory deprivation by blindfolds, with or without any bondage aspect. I have seen sleep blindfolds in dollar stores. These stores also have various masks for parties and costumes.

Some are fancy, with feathers and decoration, and some are as cheap as several plain ones in a package for a dollar. It is easy to turn any mask into a blindfold. With all the cutting I suggest in outfits, I always have material scraps around. Take some soft, black material, and cut some small pieces, and then use rubber cement on the inside of any mask to glue on the material and block the eye holes. You can use colored fabric if you want to match the color of the mask, or I use light blue to make it look like blue eyes in the mask. Use two layers if the material is thin enough to see through – the second layer needs to be bigger than the first layer to overlap and glue to the back of the mask, not just be glued to the other layer. Of course, scarves will work fine as blindfolds when tied on.

Another overpriced bondage item I have often seen is an over-the-door bondage set. Most dollar stores have some sort of over-the-door hook to hang clothes on. One or two of these is all you need to anchor a pair of belt wrist cuffs or even just ropes.

Part of bondage games can be to tie up the subject dressed in some one-time-use, disposable outfits and have the fun of slowly cutting off the outfit. You can do it in stages to draw the drama out.

Many psychologists have written about how bondage games often appeal to wives who have trouble enjoying sex because of sexual hang-ups about voluntarily having sex. Being restrained and not able to stop what is being done to her mentally frees her up to just let go and stop trying to have any control over what is happening to her. She is free to enjoy the sex with a manly man who is just having his way with her body.

If you play any of these bondage games, I think it is important to reverse the roles sometimes. It may stretch some of your imaginations and bring up some new feelings to have someone who has been the bound subject become the master in control.

For those of you who don't want to bother with homemade bondage gear, the professional stuff is available at my website.

Remember bondage games are only fun if agreed to by both husband and wife.

CHAPTER 18

Suggestions to SEXcessfully Implement Using Modified Clothes

F YOU ARE INTRIGUED by some of the ideas I have shared, but don't know how to bring up the subject or get started with some of the ideas with your spouse, I want to make a few suggestions.

For wives, it may be easier for you to get started because you can get something that fits right more easily, modify it, and just show up wearing it. First, you need to figure out which idea to use. A typical wife who often wears jeans around the house might feel more comfortable to start with denim jeans and a denim vest.

Do the vest pocket cutouts on the denim vest or a denim jacket, and maybe cut out the back too. Then do the full jeans treatment – cut out the front pockets and the rear pockets, crotch seam, and maybe the yoke area. Just remember that if the jeans are tight, you will bulge out the pocket cutouts and places, as well as the crotch seam. To get the best crotch seam cutout to make your pussy pop out the maximum, you need tight jeans – as tight as you can get into is best – but only do the crotch-cut in those jeans. It is probably best to do the full pocket cutout treatment on looser jeans – the crotch-cut will still work for full sex access, but it won't press the pussy out. Then do only the crotch-cut on nice, tight jeans to try and get the popping-pussy look some other time.

If you do the full pocket treatment, maybe use a marker to write your husband's name on your ass in the left pocket cutout and "ASS" in the right pocket cutout. It will take a little twisting and a mirror (don't forget the mirror will reverse the image – write it out on a piece of paper and paperclip it to the waistband as you write to be sure it matches the mirror image of the name on the paper as you write).

Do the crotch-cut, and be positive you have it positioned right and large enough ahead of time. You want to get it right the first time so the sex session flows smoothly. First, put the jeans on and feel to find the right spot, and then mark it with a marker. Take the jeans off, and make a cut down both sides of the center seam about 2 to 3 inches on each side of the mark, and then cut across the seam to remove it. Try the jeans on, and feel around to be sure it is cut in the right spot. If your husband's cock rubs on an edge of the denim fabric, it will not be very good for him without a lot of wasted time to remove the jeans and enlarge the hole. To be positive, use a dildo, and be sure you can feel your skin all around it when it is inserted and when you bend over, and change positions with it inserted. You may have to lengthen the hole one way or cut out a little more on the sides of the hole to widen it to make it fit right.

I find that I want the vagina entrance to be at the center of the crotch-cut. I like the cut to be long enough to totally expose the entire length of the genital area so that I can reach the clit with my hand to play with it. I also find that I like that much length behind the vagina opening to let the crotch-cut open up enough to prevent any major friction from touching the material. This is also about the right amount to create the popping-out-pussy look on tight jeans. It always seems like I have to make the crotch-cut farther back than I first think it needs to be. I recommend that you check the positioning before waiting until you are ready to have sex.

If you can't find the right vest, I am positive that you can find a cheap tee shirt to use. Pick an idea for tee shirts – like a double-O O boob cutout idea, or just shorten it to just barely cover your breasts in front. Sexy come-on slogans are optional but recommended.

If you don't usually wear jeans around the house, then try some other idea. A short micro-miniskirt cut will always get his attention. I read some recent statistics from a survey of over 5,000 married men. Twice as many liked a very short skirt and lots of bare legs than liked the deep cleavage look on a woman's chest. The survey also said that over two thirds of the husbands liked it very much when their wife made the first move to initiate sex sometimes. So go for it, girls – don't be afraid to try some of my ideas to see how your husband responds.

Once you have the new outfit ready, you need to pick a time when you are alone at home and have the time to enjoy a nice fun sex session. While your husband is busy doing something – maybe just watching TV – change into your new outfit and just walk through the room and don't say a thing. Wait for him to notice – if needed, walk back through again, and pause in front of him. If he is oblivious, ask him if he likes your new outfit. When he does notice it, tell him nice things about how you like making love with him and that you decided to try some new ideas to increase his interest. Maybe tell him some magazine articles suggest doing your housework in the nude but you thought that this outfit would be a little more intriguing than just letting it all hang out. Tell him there are some nice modifications he might not even have noticed yet. Ask him to see if he can find them. You shouldn't need any more of a start than this – something will happen, and it will all go with the flow if he is a real red-blooded male.

For any husband who is trying to introduce some of these ideas to his wife and is a little nervous about it, I suggest that you work on the communication between the two of you a little more. The best way would be to show your wife the book and say, "*I just got this book, and it has some interesting ideas. Listen to the first lines of the book.*" Then read the title and the first two short paragraphs of the introduction to her. Show her the cover, and tell her, "*I'd bet that you would be irresistible to me in jeans like these!*"

If you have already picked out an item or two and have it ready, tell her that you have already fixed up an outfit that sounded good to try. If you haven't done something yet, suggest that you both go through the book and each pick out something that sounds like fun and try it later.

If you prefer starting with a prepared outfit to pull on her as a surprise, not mentioning the book, prepare the outfit, and pick a good time to use it. Then to start, try a line like, "*I read something about adding some variety to our sex life. I decided to try some ideas on making some sexy new outfits for you to wear without busting the budget. How about it if you try on the new outfit I fixed up? You'll look very sexy in it."* If you can find a girl's micro miniskirt that will stretch to fit her and a short tee shirt, ask her to model them for you. She will probably say something like, *"These things won't even cover everything!"* Reply with, *"I'm glad that you recognize what I have in mind. That skirt won't get in my way at all."*

I think I may need to throw in a few suggestions for how to get the time to wear some of these sexy items. Couples with kids never seem to find the time for sharing private time. This was always a main obstacle for us when the kids lived at home. The best advice I can give is that, when there is a will, there is a way. Early mornings and evenings after the kids are in bed are the obvious times to use.

When we had the kids at home, we did things like having frequent "Afternoon Delight" love sessions because we worked hard to fit it into our schedules while the kids were in school. This was one of our favorite ways to have the time back in the 1970s when the song "Afternoon Delight" became a hit. We always had a good laugh whenever that song played. I would ask her, *"Listen, they are playing our song. How about now?"* Outside of school hours, visits to grandma; play date swaps with friends; or activities like sports, band, scouts, and similar things can free up at least an hour here or there to get some private time. You have the most trouble with small children who must be watched more often. Try setting them down in front of the TV to watch their favorite movie or maybe a favorite one-hour TV show. Tell them you have to go through your closets to clean out some old clothes – they won't want to get involved with something like that. Just don't forget to lock the bedroom door. But as they get bigger, you can use some of the things I just suggested more often. The bigger the kids, the more they have their own friends to hang out with and their own activities that they want to do, and the less they want to be around mom and dad – I hope this gives you parents with little ones something to look forward to.

One trick we would use to get longer time periods is to get a babysitter to supposedly go see a movie or attend a party with friends. This sounded reasonable to the kids and the babysitters. We would go off somewhere to enjoy ourselves with a whole evening to have fun. This would range from getting a motel room nearby, visiting a nearby parents' house when we knew they were out of town (to save the motel cost and to make love in the bed my wife used for many years as she grew up), to going out for some outdoor fun if the weather was nice or even just taking a drive somewhere we could park and use the car. Sometimes we would start with a nice dinner out or something else we wanted to do together, and sometimes we just went out for the nice long session of lovemaking.

Things are easier for couples without children around the house. By the time you are empty nesters, things will get easier, and the need to try something new and different may be more appropriate for enjoying some of the ideas in this book. As senior citizens, I will point out that we don't usually wait until we are tired at night to make love. We usually do it early in the day.

One essential thing that you just have to be willing to do if you seriously want to have a happy marriage is to put each other at the top of your personal priority lists. And then you need to prove this with action – to follow through on this and somehow make the time to find the personal time to share your love with each other frequently. Even those of you who say you can't find the time because of the kids should realize that the kids will be some of the biggest winners of having parents who have a very happy marriage. The kids will be big losers if you have an unhappy marriage. This is one of the most important marriage tips I have learned – I hope you will take it seriously to heart.

I remember a survey I read where they said that it was more important to kids to be sure that their parents loved each other than that both the parents loved them. The kids felt more secure with the knowledge that their parents were a secure couple rather than being concerned how they felt about them as a kid. Today, broken families, divorces, and kids living without both of their real parents are all too common. All your kids see the problems with these situations in many of the other kids in school. It is very reassuring to them to see that their parents love each other and to know that they won't soon be subject to a broken home.

Whatever you would like to do, the key is action – just DO IT! Do it now, and start having more fun sex – the sooner the better.

CHAPTER 19

Bonus Ideas

HERE ARE SEVERAL SEX IDEAS that I have picked up and want to share with my readers who have made it to this point. There are many things that a lover will pick up over the course of a lifetime of great sex with a wonderful partner.

Many books advise different sex positions. There are a handful of good, typical positions that can be modified into possibly hundreds of variations. Some of these variations are impossible for anyone except a contortionist. Over the years, we have read all the position books and probably done it in every variation we could get our bodies into. Most of the wild ones are not really too enjoyable for us. We are not into doing it in any position that is not fairly comfortable. We have sex to make love and to give each other pleasure and enjoyment. We are not trying to accomplish any goal of athletic achievement – we are trying to have fun and enjoy the pleasure. However, we are willing to try the very unusual positions to see if there is some unexpected feature that we might find – like hitting a different pleasure spot from a different position.

In our younger days, we even did it one rainy night inside an original 1952 MG-TD car with the top up. If you want to try it in a small car, you can't get much smaller. This little two-passenger British sports car is so small that at one mandatory annual state inspection, the inspector who tried to drive it wanted to fail the car because it was too small – his big feet could not operate the pedals in the cramped foot space, and he said it was unsafe. It was designed for pointy, little, English-style shoes, not his big boots. A supervisor at the inspection location agreed with me that it was not their local decision to flunk a standard, unmodified car that was legally approved by the federal DOT and every state. I am six feet tall, and I admit it is tight with two small bucket seats, a shifter, and hand brake between the seats. Somehow we did manage to do it in the car because it was raining and we had no other good options that night – and we were horny. However, like most of the difficult positions in some of the manuals that we have tried, we only did it once in the MG-TD.

In chapter 3 above, I mentioned how we often used picnic tables. Therefore, we do have some experience with creating variety on picnic tables. We have done it in at least a dozen different positions on picnic tables. We always travel with at least an old blanket to lie on any table we use, and we stay dressed when in doubt about assured total privacy. We pack a loose-fitting, medium-length, very soft, denim-looking full skirt for my wife to wear. It is easy to flip out of the way and yet can instantly be flipped down to look normally presentable. I have a very loose-fitting pair of soft cutoff shorts made from a pair of sweat pants that are easy to pull out of the way for sex, pulling my equipment out of the leg hole.

Here are a dozen ideas for sex on a picnic table:
1. With the man standing at the end of the table the woman lies on her back at the end edge of the table and puts her legs on his shoulders. If the table is the right height, it can be a very comfortable height for the man and allows very deep penetration. However, even with a blanket, the picnic table gets very hard on the woman's back within a few minutes. A few years ago, I also started rolling up a two-inch thick, foam pad to add to our traveling fun bag to make my wife more comfortable. The disadvantage of this position, if outside in a possibly public place, is that this is very obviously a sexual position at even first glance by anyone who could surprise us – the legs over the man's shoulders are a giveaway.

2. With the man standing at the end of the table the woman stands in front of him and bends over to lay her torso on the table. The man enters doggie style from behind her. It is not as hard on the woman because she has her soft side down and her arms to help distribute her

weight, and she can last a long time with no discomfort from the hard table. The foam pad still feels nice if you use it. This is just as comfortable for the man and allows penetration just as deep.

The nice part about this position is that the woman is braced firmly against the end of the table with her legs down and she cannot move forward with the man's thrusts. In most any sexual positions, the woman's body moves a little as the man thrusts against her. With no give to let her body move, with the table edge against her thighs, it allows the man to really drive his cock all the way into her as firmly as she can take it.

In a spot where discovery is possible, this is not an obvious position – it is probably the best for this situation. It allows the man to instantly step away and pull his shorts back into a normal position and the woman is already on her feet and she just has to stand up and move as she flips her skirt back down. Whenever there is this possibility of being surprised, I am always dressed in a shirt and wearing very loose sweat-pant-type shorts. The leg hole on the right pair of shorts is plenty large enough to pull the leg of the shorts up out of the way for sex. My wife wears a loose-fitting skirt that can be flipped up out of the way and yet instantly be dropped down to be properly dressed. In cool weather, I have a pair of sweat pants with the front of the crotch cut out that I wear under the shorts. My wife has a pair of sweat pants with the whole crotch cut out and just wears similarly loose shorts over these pants to hide the cutout yet be fully available. This just looks like a casual layered look, and the shorts layer hides the crotch cutouts. Anyone who thinks that they see something sexual going on and takes a second look only sees two fully dressed people dressed in what they think are regular sweat pants and layered shorts – they do not expect that there is sex going on even if they at first see the two people touching together.

3. The man can straddle one bench seat on one side of the table. He sits sideways to the table with one leg on each side of the bench, not facing the table. Then the woman straddles the bench facing him and sits on his lap. The result is just like the frequently described face-to-face position using a common, armless, straight chair. The woman sits

on top of the man with her feet on the ground and controls the depth of penetration and most of the up and down movement. This combination does not work on some picnic tables because sometimes there is not enough clearance between the bench and the tabletop for her legs to clear comfortably.

4. From position 3, the man can lean back and lie on the bench on his back – his feet can stay on the ground, or he can bring them up on the bench behind the woman and lie totally flat on the bench. This puts the woman in total control as she straddles him. The woman can move forward to be over the man's face to receive oral sex if she wants. She can also lean forward and lie on him face to face to kiss and rub her body against his. This could even be considered another position. When the wife is straddling the man like this it is like the well known 'Cowgirl' sex position, only even more than riding him on a bed kneeling around him since her legs are down to the ground on each side of the husband. She can use her full leg muscles to raise and lower herself to impale his cock into her pussy as deep as she can take it. Of course, she can turn around and ride in the 'Reverse Cowgirl' position too. I don't bother to count that as a separate position in my dozen; we rarely ever use the 'Reverse Cowgirl' in any manner because we like to be able to look into each other's eyes when we make love.

5. Another move from position 3, the woman lies on her back on the bench, and the man stands crouching over her and straddling the bench. The woman's legs will end up over the man's shoulders. This puts the man in total control and allows deep penetration.

6. From position 4, the woman can lie on her back on the bench too. This allows very little penetration or movement. Both partners are lying back on the bench this way. It bends the man's cock down farther than most positions, but it also makes the cock press hard against the front of the vagina against where the G-spot is located and can be quite pleasurable for the woman for a short time.

7. This is when the woman lies face up on the bench with her legs together on the bench. The man straddles the bench and is in total control. Because of the closed legs, there is only shallow penetration allowed into the vagina, but the man can do whatever turns them

both on to rub his cock anywhere on her body, and his hands are free to caress anywhere.

There is a common saying, "*Most men start at the bottom*" (usually meant to be referring to the corporate ladder), but thinking sexually. I like to add, "*But some start at the knees!*" It can be very erotic to move from slowly rubbing and stroking between the woman's knees and then working the cock up all the way between her thighs until you are indeed going ALL the way. A little lubrication between her legs from her knees up makes it feel great doing this knee-to-pussy stroking. A cock between bare thighs beats just stroking her thighs in any other way. Rubbing himself on her torso or breasts is also sexy. The woman can use her hands to hold her breasts together firmly while the man strokes between them. Even oral sex is easy as the man straddles her.

8. This is the same as position 7, except the woman lies face down. This position has some of the same freedom of the man to do what he wants while straddling her except from her backside. He can still start at the knees rather than starting at the bottom.

9. For this position, the man sits on the bench with his back to the table; the woman sits down in his lap facing him. Who has the most movement control depends on whether her feet reach the ground or not. There is good face-to-face contact, and both partners have both hands free to hug and play with each other. The man can also let the woman lean back in his lap or rock back and forth as he holds her hands or arms. Another possible variation is for the couple to reverse positions and to sit with the man facing the table and the woman in his lap facing away, but this does not allow the woman on top to move very much with her back against the table – I don't count this as another position. Not every table has the space between the bench and the tabletop to make these positions always comfortable.

10. This is the same as position 9, except the woman sits on the man's lap with her back to him, her legs either straddling his legs or with his legs spread and her legs in between his legs. Usually, her legs can reach the ground if they do not have to also go over the seat, and she can move up and down and side to side very well. She has limited use of her hands – they will probably be on his knees, but the man has full

use of his two hands, and it is a natural reach to go around her and fondle the breasts.

11. There is another variation of the woman being braced against the solid side of the table and unable to give any movement when the man thrusts against her. For this position, the woman kneels on the middle of a bench and leans over the table with her legs spread and her thighs up against the table edge. Depending on the space between the tabletop and bench and the table's height, the man either stands between the bench and table behind her or kneels on the bench between her legs. The same deep penetration and ability to drive himself home firmly into her can happen here. For comfort, a second blanket or pad of some sort is needed here – both the woman's body is on the table, and their knees are on the wooden surfaces. The man can also quickly move from one side of the table to the other if there is a desire for oral sex since her head is going to be on the other side of the tabletop when she is lying across the table.

12. In an outdoor setting, there may be many good places to lay a blanket on the ground and make love, but not all the time. Sometimes the ground is too wet or too rocky. Being cold or wet detracts from the joy of making beautiful love in an idyllic natural setting. The same can be said for trying to enjoy a passionate moment with a sharp rock poking the person on the bottom in the wrong place. Or sometimes there is just a better view a few feet higher than being on the ground. In these cases, the top of the picnic table provides a drier level spot to do anything that you can do on the ground or on any flat surface. Other than the tabletop being harder, you can also do anything you can do on a bed; it has the same possibilities of anything you can do on a hard floor. Cushioning makes it much more comfortable whenever it is available. There are a lot more positions that you could count here, but I just count ones to make the picnic table position list an even dozen.

The positions we use most are 1 and 2, but our other favorite is all the variations of 3, or 11 is good for some situations. Picnic tables vary in size and design. They are not all the same height, which is often the reason we skip 1 and 2. We have never found a picnic table too low because the man can easily adjust by bending his knees or separating his legs to find the best height to enter the woman. However, sometimes they are too high, which is very challenging. If there are many tables around, check several, because they vary in height a few inches, often even from one end of the same table to the other because of the way the ground may rise slightly at one end of the table.

There are some simple tricks to help solve the picnic table height problem. If the table can be moved, try finding some uneven ground where you can stand a couple inches higher or put the table legs into a dip to lower it. I even carry a tiny folding shovel/pick combo tool in our car. I can quickly scrape the dirt to make a slight hole for each table leg to lower the table end. Some tables have four legs, and you just need to make two small indentations to put two legs into. Other tables are pipe construction and you'll need to scrape out a shallow trough to pull the table end into. Of course, sometimes the table can't be moved or it is on a concrete pad. The other trick is to find something to stand on to adjust your height rather than adjusting the table. Something like a tree branch, some rocks, or the car jack out of your car just laid on the ground will do to give you a comfortable height.

There is something I discovered years ago at a picnic table, which I'll pass along. The table end I used was close to a big rock pile. I found that instead of just standing at the end of the table, I could walk my feet up the rock pile as we made love, and I could push forward with my legs. The legs have the strongest muscles in the body, and when a guy has the right bend in his legs, he can exert tremendous pressure. This is how the strongest weight lifters can lift their heaviest loads – using their legs. I found that my wife could really tell the difference when I pushed forward with my legs as we made love. I can hold myself up on my hands on the table and relax my legs to move backwards; I then push with my legs hard against her for the pressure. In position 1, with her legs over my shoulders, I could just push her farther up the tabletop. In position 2, with her braced against the table edge, I could really press up against her, pelvis to pelvis – like WOW!

I always look for a spot to do this when we have a new location. I have also learned to do the same thing in other locations. We have driven many different motor homes. These always have high beds because there is always something under the beds – outside storage compartments, the generator, or something. There is usually only a narrow aisle around the beds on the side. I find that if we are using the same man-standing positions on these higher beds, just like the picnic tables, I can walk my feet up the wall or cabinets across the narrow aisles from the bed. It lets me really push with my pelvis. My wife knows when I do this and tells me I am "climbing the walls!" She can feel the results as I press against her – it seems to make her want to climb the walls herself!

There are two reasons I think that the extra push that I get from my efforts to climb the walls affects my wife so much. First, I think it is because I stretch her that little bit more inside when I push harder than I usually do. Just the added momentum of pounding her a little bit harder drives me in just that extra fraction deeper. Second, it is because I think the extra effort push presses our pelvic areas much harder against each other than any regular sex does. I think my pelvis bones press against my wife's pelvis area very firmly – this is what limits how far I can go against her. This pressure is right where her clitoris is located. That pressure on her clit stimulates it much more than just stroking her up inside. She seems to enjoy it when I also wiggle my hips while I am pressing extra hard against her. I think that this hip wiggle moves my pelvis at the same time it is pressing hard against her clit, so there is even more clit stimulation.

When using outdoor tables, the most important thing I think is just like in the real estate business – location, location, location. Sometimes the location will be as simple as getting one where the moonlight is right. Other times it is so that we can enjoy the view. Avoiding a spot at night where a coming car would put its headlights on you is important. Usually, there is one main direction where anyone would come up on foot or by car – the entrance to the picnic area parking lot, a nearby trail, or similar situation. In this case, the location is important to be far enough away that you are able to be sure you can see anyone approach before they can see you. The end of the table to use and the alignment of the table are important so that you can easily keep an eye out for any car or person approaching. If we can park near the table, I always position the car between our spot on the table and the way another car or walker would approach. This blocks us from anyone's view long enough that we see them way before they can see us. In the daytime, more distance is necessary than at night.

By far the most important thing to consider for daytime use is the need to avoid a busy day. Timing is important. We have used very popular parks where the day before, on a nice fall weekend, we may have had trouble finding an empty table. But the following Monday to Friday, the dozens of picnic tables are all empty and no one is in the park even on a beautiful day.

The last extra bonus tip I will include here is to describe the best sex toy I have found – and it is just a cheap (about $3 or less) homemade item. Believe it or not, it is a swimming pool noodle. It is a 5-foot long, 3- or 4-inch diameter, round, foam pool toy. It has to be the type with a hollow center. I pick them up at any pool place or dollar store or even places like Walgreens or Home Depot in season. No, I don't hit my wife with the noodle or insert it into anything. The foam noodle and about 10 feet of a stout rope is all it takes to make the item. It is a foot brace to use almost anywhere to get more leverage and forward pressure from your legs while you are making love on any bed or table – just as I first did with the rock pile at a picnic table.

Put the rope through the center of the foam noodle. Tie one end to the leg at the bottom of your bed. Then lay the noodle out in a curve at the side of your bed where you want to stand to make love in any standing position – like the 1 or 2 positions on my picnic table list. Make it about 1 to 2 feet out at the center of the side of the bed. Then tie the second end of the rope to the leg of the bed at the other end of the noodle to hold the foot brace in that position.

Every bed usually has some sort of leg or base to use for this, except perhaps a waterbed, or platform bed. In that case, use a longer rope and try to make a big loop entirely around the base and tie the rope ends to each other or use small screw eyes screwed into the wooden bed frame (but not screwed in too deep or you can puncture the water-filled liner of a waterbed).

I have tried this foot brace at motels with a standard-height bed, and it works OK, but I find that it works best on a higher bed, like a motor home bed or an almost-table-height bed. At home, we have a real antique double bed (I like it cozy rather than a queen or king size). It is a very old canopy bed with the knobs on the edges to wrap the ropes around.

Before box springs, old beds used to have ropes tied back and forth, hung from the knobs, to form a base to put the mattress on. This is where the saying "sleep tight" came from – the bed would sway if the ropes were loose – it felt flatter, firmer, and better if the ropes were tight. Therefore, "sleep tight" meant to sleep more comfortably with tight ropes. We don't use the rope suspension; we have a firm, flat, plywood base at that height. With a mattress on top of this base, the bed is higher than a normal modern bed. When touring many historic homes, I have seen that most old beds were much higher than beds today. I don't see what the advantages of the lower beds are – I do know the advantage of a higher bed. In the old days, I think they were smarter and had the beds at a better height for having sex, like our bed.

It is easy to travel by car with a noodle foot brace, and we have used it at motels. However, the bed height is not as good for edge-of-the-bed sex on a low motel bed. We usually put a stack of several pillows under my wife's hips to bring her up to a better height. This works for her in both face-up or face-down positions. You may need to also use this technique at home to get the best height. For home use, I also suggest trying one of the various sizes of Liberator foam sex pillows. These are available at my website.

This foot brace acts like the rock pile at the picnic table or climbing the wall against the motor home cabinets, and I get much more thrust power from my legs. Now I am used to having this all the time. It is always there and just gets kicked under the bed, hidden by the bed skirt, when not in use. Even while having sex, I can pull it out with my foot in a few seconds when wanted. Without it, my bare feet slip on the bedroom carpet when I push the way I like. I found I have one pair of shoes that grip the floor almost as well, but the foot brace is best.

The difference is great. With the foot brace, I find that I can even hold my upper body up over my horizontal wife without using my arms – without the foot brace, I cannot do that because my center of gravity is above my hips. My feet will come off the floor if I try to do the same thing without also pushing out against the foot brace. I'm guessing I have my legs at a 45-degree angle to the floor and bed when I am using the foot brace.

It may take a little adjustment to get the rope tied at the right length. Try different lengths until you find what works best for you. Have it so that you start with your legs fairly well bent because, as you push, you will be pushing your wife farther away from you across the bed, and you still want to have some thrust pressure left. The noodles do not last too long because you are putting so much pressure on one spot with your feet, and the rope cuts into the noodle and comes through the side of the noodle. The rope is the key to having something strong to push against, but just a rope laid on the floor would not work as well. The noodle is to make the foot brace higher and softer. I have found that starting with a plastic tube through the noodle first protects the noodle and makes it last several times longer. A thick rope will make the noodle last longer too, but at a dollar or two each, I don't mind replacing the noodles every so often.

In installing and using the noodle foot brace you have to consider the bed. You don't push the bed frame using the foot brace because the frame is what the brace is tied to. However, you can easily shift the mattress on the bed as you push hard against the wife using the brace. On our bed, the mattress fits very snugly into the four-poster frame and does not move as we push against the side, but on anything like the typical motel bed, we would push the mattress right off the box frame. To push hard, the brace has to be used at the foot of the bed or with the other side of the bed against the wall. This way the mattress cannot move since it is up against the wall or the headboard.

CHAPTER 20

Epilogue

A S A GOOD CONCLUSION to all my tips and ideas, I am going to give you a good marriage tip for a source to come up with more ways to build a much stronger and better marriage. Dr. Laura Schlesinger has written some outstanding books that should be recommended reading for all married couples: *The Proper Care & Feeding of Husbands* and *The Proper Care & Feeding of Marriage*. After reading these, I realized that my wife could have written the important positive parts of them. Dr. Laura has the subject nailed. On the first page of her introduction in the *Husband* book, she has two very concise and very true quotes from guys that summarize the male animal:

> "As a man, I can tell you our needs are simple. We want to be fed, we want our kids mothered, and we want lovin." – Vince

> "Men are only interested in two things: If I'm not horny, make me a sandwich." – John

Dr. Laura has the training and experience to help people deal with the problems that they have created from NOT following the proper treatment of their spouse. She does a great job of doing this. If you have any problems at all, you need to read her ideas. If you don't think that you have any problems, you still need to read it to reinforce what you are doing right. On her radio show, I have heard many callers give live testimony about how these books have helped, and even saved, their marriages. The answer she tries to teach as the way a marriage should be is to be like my marriage is – with a loving, giving wife.

I have heard Dr. Laura say that all the power in the marriage is in the wife's hands. I give all the credit for the success in our marriage to my wife. It says in *The Holy Bible*, Proverbs 31:10, "*A wife of noble character, who can find? She is worth far more than rubies.*" This is true – a good wife is one of the greatest blessings any man can ever have. This is what every wife should strive to become. This is why Dr. Laura has written the book about the care of husbands for the wives to read, because the wives are the ones in control of the marriage. She did not write a corresponding book for husbands because they are not the ones in control of the marriage. The wife should be the driving force for a good marriage with her love – but it is the husband's job to respond by caring for her needs just as freely as she loves him. A husband has to earn his wife's respect.

For those of you who don't care for Dr. Laura, I will point out again the advice *The Holy Bible* gives. A man should love his wife, and a wife should respect her husband. Don't think about these feelings as what your spouse owes you – think about these feelings about what you need to do to earn these feelings from your spouse. You wives need to work hard at being worth loving by your husband. You husbands need to work hard earning the respect of your wife.

After years of having fun with the things I dreamed up, we have a great love life – we share one of the world's greatest love stories. My wife has encouraged me, and we have grown together in learning how to **Dress For SEXcess**. It has been fun doing, learning, and enjoying. I could give hundreds of examples and descriptions of sexy, revealing outfits that my wife has enticed me with over the years. I will just summarize it by saying that she knows that she has what I like, and she likes to use everything she's got to keep me interested in her charms every day. I will give just one more example.

Several years ago I learned how successful our growth together was in having more fun in our love life because of my wife knowing how to dress to properly seduce me. Once we went to see a revival of the musical *Cabaret* when it was staged at the former Studio 54 nightclub in New York City, which had been converted into a theater designed for this show. It was a nice production with intimate nightclub-like seating at tiny tables on the main floor as the orchestra seating, and drinks were served at the tables. I had gotten tickets way ahead and had seats right up front next to the stage.

My wife wanted to look nice for a special night on the town. It was summer, and she wore a black, bare-shoulder dress – what would be called a nice cocktail dress, short and dressy. This was appropriate for the evening out. She made sure I knew that she had on sexy crotch-cut black panties so that all she had to when we got home was bend over and she was ready for making love right in that sexy outfit. The extra touch she added to look even more seductive to me was a black, velvet choker with an elastic strap closure and an antique cameo centered on the front. She knows I like the little choker look. I thought she was a knockout.

I hadn't thought much about the show, and it had been many years since we had seen the original *Cabaret* movie. I was surprised when the show started. All the girls in the cast were supposed to be the working girls in a mid-1930s Berlin nightclub, and they ALL had on black chokers like my wife did. In the whole theater, it was just my wife, next to the stage, and all the cast girls on the stage, who had the same look with lots of bare skin, with a low neckline, and with a black velvet choker. My wife's choker, with the cameo on it, was the prettiest.

Right then and there, I knew that my wife was a professional at seduction, and yet her skills were all just for me. I was a happy camper to know that I had the sexiest girl in the theater sitting there at my table, holding my hand, and looking lovingly into my eyes. I was going to take her home later, and I knew I didn't have to worry whether or not I was going to get lucky that night – I knew I was going to get what I wanted, and luck had nothing to do with it. It was many years of winning her love and earning her trust that meant that the end result that evening was guaranteed – I was going to get thoroughly screwed. She wanted it as much as I did. I have won her over permanently by years of effort and lots of practice in playing, experimenting, and learning about seduction skills.

When we were out that night, she wasn't even wearing anything modified that showed, because we were out in public. But she knew the little things and the looks that I liked from years of playing together with my redesigned creations. I had used many fabric-cutting parts to make matching chokers over the years. She made sure that she wore things as sexy as she could for me when we went out for a night on the town. She responds to my love for her by always working at keeping me seduced again over and over again – and she is an expert at it.

Call me a "meat and potatoes" man in both my food preferences and my sex preferences. With food, I am always eating too much of good home cooking. I have a big appetite for very good basic food. Then I have to diet it off. With sex, I like lots of good clean fun and a lot of screwing around. I have a big appetite for sex too – I don't think there is such a thing as too much sex with a spouse. At least lots of sex is not permanently fattening. My wife did get very fat from it a few times, but it wasn't a permanent condition.

Sex is even a great exercise to burn off calories. When I eat too much dessert or something, I warn my wife that now I need to work off all those extra calories with her. This usually brings a quick "OK!" and a big smile.

We are in love for REAL – we like to enjoy each other in many, many ways, including lots of sexual fun. The costumes are just for our variety and to let us keep making love often, the way we do, and yet they let us still make it a little different and fresh each time. It takes very little role-playing for us – it is more just like setting the scene with the outfits, and then we have the variety and just go for it. However, the costumes can be used in whatever way you want to use them. I am just trying to give you ideas to spice up your sex life in whatever way turns you on, and each of us is a little different in our tastes.

My wife appreciates my efforts to keep things spiced up and encourages me in the variety of my costumes. Even after years of my doing this, sometimes she seems genuinely amazed at some of the ideas I come up with and with what I see in some of the outfits I start with. Of course, what I see inside the clothing every time is my sweet, wonderful wife's desirable body. I just cut the clothing to get a different peek at her in every outfit.

Love and sex are very serious subjects – most people know this. These are two of the most important factors in most people's lives. How much sex they have, who the sex is with, how much love is involved with the sex, and the attitude of the individuals having sex and sharing love are all major factors in how happy their entire lives are. Love and sex are more important to happiness in most people's lives than even money is. Many very poor people manage to be very happy if they have a good spouse and a good love life. The biggest thing in how happy they are in life about these things is their own attitudes about love and sex – it is mental. Often they can choose to be happy, and they can choose to be unhappy about their situations – it is their own choice. The old saying that, "The best things in life are free," is very true.

Love and sex are dynamic factors – they never stand still. They are always growing or fading. Individuals can work at developing more love, and they can work at improving the sex they have, or they can just crawl into their own little shell and have a pity party because they are not satisfied with their love life and/or their sex life, and that lets both of these things fade away even more.

From start to finish in this book, I have tried to teach my readers how to have more fun by being creative in new ways. I want to include a quote by Mary Lou Cook that sums up my ideas, *"Creativity is inventing, experimenting, growing, taking risks, breaking rules, making mistakes, and having fun."*

Perhaps by far the biggest idea I hope some readers will get from **Dress for SEXcess**, the most beneficial marriage tip of all, may be a change in your own mental attitudes about love and sex. Follow the instructions of the quote about being creative. Love and sex are very serious subjects that you need to learn to NOT take too seriously. A good marriage is designed by our Creator to take two imperfect people and let them join into one very complete being. *"The two shall* be one flesh," says *The Holy Bible*. Married lovers complement each other, each in his or her own way. There is something mystical about good married sex when it is FREELY given and shared in love. My story in chapter 1 should have shown you where I am coming from about this. Lovers should rejoice and be thankful for being able to share their love in marriage through God's gift of sex.

True married love, according to most experts, is two people each trying to continually think and act first in the best interests of their spouse rather than in their own best interests. To understand what this means, read "*The Gift of The Magi*," the classic short story by O. Henry. You can Google it and read it online – it is very short and an easy read. The husband and wife each give up one of their personal finest possessions to get a special gift for their spouse.

Have sex to please your partner, as a gift to them, not to just get a quick moment of personal pleasure. Make it mutually fun – do it with laughter and joy. Don't take it too seriously – it is not like a school exam or a challenge that must be met and overcome or else there will be problems. Don't let any unnatural hang-ups get in the way of sharing good sex. Open up to each other more, share ideas more, find time to make love more often. Do it with the decision that you are going to be happy with, and have fun – you will be happier.

If a husband or wife, or both, can change their mental attitudes a little to add more positive thoughts toward each other, then it may be the most important marriage tip they can learn from this book.

I hope that you, the reader, can have as much fun with some of these ideas as we have had. It will be very good for your marriage to add the variety, the fun, the sex, and the LOVE that we have enjoyed using these ideas in our wonderful One-In-A-Million marriage.

I am asking all the readers of my book to please write an honest review of this book and please post it on the page for my book on **Amazon.com** and any other places that you know for readers to post book reviews. At least a few words about it would be appreciated.

Please also post the review on the review page at my book website, **DressForSEXcess.com**

Please also **take the free survey** linked to the **DressForSEXcess.com** review page to register your opinions about what features on a woman a man likes best. The men's version asks guys to rate what visual aspects of a woman's appearance they like best. The woman's version asks the gals to give their opinions of what they think men like best. I think the results of what men like most will be interesting, and I am very interested in what the differences will be from the women's viewpoint.

www.ingramcontent.com/pod-product-compliance
Lightning Source LLC
Chambersburg PA
CBHW070029100426
42740CB00013B/2635